Huma
Mana

The effects … the world. Governmen… ion systems to produce … pressure to perform is … nd the principles of hu… competitive advantage … for organizational im…

Human … ital question of how far … schools and colleges to transcend the paradoxes of the global reform agenda. It analyses the relationship between leadership, the classroom and results, and uses case studies to explore the extent to which performance is enhanced by distributed leadership and constrained by social, political and economic contexts.

The book is divided into three parts:

- examining the current context of human resource management, by critically analysing globalization, human capital theory, and worldwide trends in government legislation, societal values, and teacher culture(s);
- exploring two pairs of contemporary themes in human resource management, by comparing the roles of leaders and followers, on the one hand, and contrasting learning and *greedy* organizations, on the other;
- looking at how the context and the themes impact on particular contemporary practices in human resource management, by analysing the selection and development of professionals, the remodelling of school teams and the management of performance.

The authors carefully blend advocacy with evidence to ensure relevance for both practitioner and academic audiences across the globe. The book would be of particular use to students on masters courses in educational leadership.

Justine Mercer is an Associate Professor at the Institute of Education, University of Warwick, UK.

Bernard Barker was formerly Chair in Educational Leadership and Management and Director of Postgraduate Research Studies at the School of Education, University of Leicester, UK.

Richard Bird is Legal Policy Consultant to the Association of School and College Leaders (ASCL), UK.

Leadership for Learning Series
Series Edited by Les Bell, Mark Brundrett and Clive Dimmock

The study of educational leadership makes little sense unless it is in relation to who the leaders are, how they are leading, what is being led, and with what effect. Based on the premise that learning is at the heart of leadership and that leaders themselves should be learners, the *Leadership for Learning* series explores the connections between educational leadership, policy, curriculum, human resources and accountability. Each book in the series approaches its subject matter through a three-fold structure of process, themes and impact.

Also available:

Education Policy
Les Bell and Howard Stevenson

Leading Learning
Tom O'Donoghue and Simon Clarke

Forthcoming:

Leadership in Education
Clive Dimmock

School Leadership for Quality and Accountability
Mark Brundrett and Christopher Rhodes

Human Resource Management in Education

Contexts, themes and impact

Justine Mercer, Bernard Barker and Richard Bird

LONDON AND NEW YORK

First published 2010
by Routledge
2 Park Square, Milton Park, Abingdon, Oxon OX14 4RN

Simultaneously published in the USA and Canada
by Routledge
270 Madison Avenue, New York, NY 10016

Routledge is an imprint of the Taylor & Francis Group, an informa business

Typeset in Sabon by
Keystroke, Tettenhall, Wolverhampton
Printed and bound in Great Britain by
TJ International Ltd, Padstow, Cornwall

British Library Cataloguing in Publication Data
A catalogue record for this book is available from the British Library

Library of Congress Cataloging-in-Publication Data
Mercer, Justine.
Human resource management in education : contexts, themes, and
impact / Justine Mercer, Bernard Barker, and Richard Bird. – 1st ed.
p. cm. – (Leadership for learning series)
Includes bibliographical references and index.
1. School personnel management. 2. Educational leadership.
I. Barker, Bernard. II. Bird, Richard. III. Title.
LB2831.5.M44 2010
371.2'01–dc22
2009048765

ISBN10: 0–415–41280–3 (hbk)
ISBN10: 0–415–41279–X (pbk)
ISBN10: 0–203–85081–5 (ebk)

ISBN13: 978–0–415–41280–3 (hbk)
ISBN13: 978–0–415–41279–7 (pbk)
ISBN13: 978–0–203–85081–7 (ebk)

To Ann, Chris, Andrew, Elizabeth, Gabriel and Madeline
in appreciation of their tolerance and support

Contents

Illustrations

Figures

Tables

Acknowledgements

We are indebted to a number of people without whom the book would not have been written. First, we would like to thank everyone who participated in the case studies reported in the book. We cannot name them individually, for obvious reasons, but this does not in any way diminish the gratitude we owe to them.

We would also like to thank everyone who commented on earlier drafts of the book. We are especially grateful to Clive Dimmock for providing detailed and insightful feedback at every stage of the writing process, and to Katy Edge for editorial work on the final manuscript. Thanks are also due to Dave Allman for giving us access to his research data and contributing to the writing of Chapter 5.

When the book was commissioned, two of the authors worked for the Centre for Educational Leadership and Management (CELM) at the University of Leicester. Although CELM has since been subsumed within the School of Education, we would still like to thank our ex-CELM colleagues, particularly Ann Briggs and Howard Stevenson. They may not have contributed to the book directly, but they shared their scholarship with us (not to mention the odd bottle of wine), and their influence on our work is pervasive. We would also like to record special thanks to Ann Holland, Bob Johnson and David Kennedy.

Over half the book was written during a period of study leave granted to Justine by the University of Leicester. She is grateful to Janet Ainley, who facilitated this, and to Trevor Kerry, Saeeda Shah, Alison Taysum and Wei Zhang, who covered her absence.

Finally, we are grateful to various publishers who gave permission for us to reproduce previously published material, as follows:

To Taylor & Francis for allowing us to draw upon:

1 The Norcross case-study data (in Chapter 4), previously published in Barker, B. (2009) 'Public service reform in education: why is progress so slow?', *Journal of Educational Administration and History*, 41(1): 57–72.

2 The Felix Holt case-study data (in Chapters 4 and 5), previously published in Barker, B. (2006) 'Rethinking leadership and change: a case

study in leadership succession and its impact on school transformation', *Cambridge Journal of Education*, 36(2): 277–92.

3 The Shire School case-study data (in Chapter 6), previously published in Barker, B. (2007) 'The leadership paradox: can school leaders transform student outcomes?', *School Effectiveness and School Improvement*, 18(1): 21–43.

To Springer Science and Business Media for allowing us to draw upon the Rihab and Al Fanar case-study data (in Chapters 7 and 10), previously published in Mercer, J. (2007) 'Challenging appraisal orthodoxies: teacher evaluation and professional development in the United Arab Emirates', *Journal of Personnel Evaluation in Education*, 18: 273–87.

To the OECD for:
Figure 2.1, Old-age dependency ratio: ratio of the population aged 65 and over to the population aged 20–64, taken from page 9 of OECD (2005) 'Ageing Populations: High Time for Action' (background paper prepared by the OECD Secretariat), from Meeting of G8 Employment and Labour Ministers, London, UK, 10–11 March 2005.

To Taylor & Francis for:
Figure 4.1, Six models of distributed leadership, taken from page 357 of MacBeath, J. (2005) 'Leadership as distributed: a matter of practice', *School Leadership and Management*, 25(4): 349–66.

Figure 4.2, Leadership practice, taken from page 11 of Spillane, J., Halverson, R. and Diamond, J. (2004) 'Towards a theory of leadership practice: a distributed perspective', *Journal of Curriculum Studies*, 36(1): 3–34.

Figure 6.1, Characteristics of schools as learning organizations, taken from page 77 of Leithwood, K., Doris, J. and Steinbach, R. (1998) 'Leadership and other conditions which foster organizational learning in schools', in K. Leithwood and K. Louis (eds) *Organizational Learning in Schools*, Lisse, Netherlands: Swets & Zeitlinger.

To Pearson Publishing for:
Figure 5.1, Development cycles model, adapted from page 52 of Barker, B. (2001) *Leading Improvement*, Cambridge, UK: Pearson Publishing.

To the Department for Children, Schools and Families for:
Table 9.1, Number of full-time equivalent employees (in thousands) in LA-maintained schools, academies and CTCs in England, taken from Department for Children, Schools and Families (2008) 'School Workforce in England (including Local Authority Level Figures)', January 2008 (revised).

Notwithstanding all of the above, any errors in the text remain our own.

Abbreviations

ASCL	Association of School and College Leaders (an education trade union)
ATL	Association of Teachers and Lecturers (an education trade union)
CPD	continuing professional development
DCSF	Department for Children, Schools and Families (formerly the Department for Education and Skills)
DES	Department of Education and Science
DfEE	Department for Education and Employment (formerly the Department of Education and Science)
DfES	Department for Education and Skills (formerly the Department for Education and Employment)
EOC	Equal Opportunities Commission
FE	further education
FSMs	free school meals
GCSE	General Certificate of Secondary Education
GEO	Government Equalities Office
GMS	grant-maintained status
GTC	General Teaching Council for England
GTCS	General Teaching Council for Scotland
HE	higher education
HEI	higher education institution
HLTA	higher-level teaching assistant
HMI	Her Majesty's Inspectorate
HRM	human resource management
HRS	High Reliability Schools
ICT	information and communication technologies
INSET	in-service training
KTU	Korean Teachers and Educational Workers Union
LA	local authority (formerly local education authority, as regards education)
LEA	local education authority
LPSH	Leadership Programme for Serving Heads

LSA	learning support assistant
NAHT	National Association of Head Teachers (an education trade union)
NAS/UWT	an education trade union
NASBM	National Association of School Business Management (formerly the National Bursars Association)
NCEA	National Coalition of Education Activists
NCLSCS	National College for Leadership of Schools and Children's Services (formerly the National College for School Leadership)
NCSL	National College for School Leadership
NHS	National Health Service
NPM	New Public Management
NPQH	National Professional Qualification for Headship
NUT	National Union of Teachers
OECD	Organization for Economic Co-operation and Development
Ofsted	Office for Standards in Education
PA	personal assistant
PGCE	Postgraduate Certificate in Education
PPA	planning, preparation and assessment
PRP	performance-related pay
QTS	qualified teacher status
SATs	Standardized Assessment Tests
SBM	school business manager
SEN	special educational needs
SET	Student Evaluation of Teaching
SLT	senior leadership team (sometimes also referred to as the senior management team)
SMT	senior management team (sometimes also referred to as the senior leadership team)
TA	teaching assistant
TDA	Training and Development Agency (formerly the Teacher Training Agency)
TTA	Teacher Training Agency
UAE	United Arab Emirates
UK	United Kingdom
UNISON	a trade union for support staff
US	United States

Part I

The current context of human resource management

1 Introduction

Globalization, human capital theory and human resource management

Introduction

This book provides an holistic, research-based overview of the core ideas and key debates in human resource management (HRM) within the education sector. It has been written to help practitioners, students and academics develop an appropriate conceptual framework within which to situate their own research and investigations. To this end, rather than simply reviewing the existing literature, it blends advocacy and evidence to offer readers a clearly articulated critical stance. It challenges the normative best-practice paradigm that dominates the field of HRM in education, and in its place develops a consistent alternative perspective that takes full account of recent national and international trends.

The book argues that previous models of HRM are inadequate to address the issues educational leaders currently face. Whereas leaders in the past were able to gain support and satisfy stakeholders simply by treating people well, today's leaders have to go beyond the principles of humane and equitable management practices because of very significant global shifts in economic patterns, government education policies, societal values and teaching cultures. To succeed in the twenty-first century, educational leaders need a thorough understanding of these global shifts and their implications. That in itself is not enough, however. Twenty-first-century educational leaders also need to view these trends and policies through a critical lens, constantly questioning the assumptions being made and interrogating the evidence being offered. Only then will they be able to ameliorate the worst excesses of a market-driven education system obsessed with spurious standards, and realize the full potential of education. The primary purpose of this book is to provide readers with just such a critical lens.

What is HRM?

Before we develop the argument introduced above, it is necessary to define some key concepts and to outline some key historical trends. The term *human resource management* emerged in the late 1980s as an alternative to *personnel management*. It was intended to convey 'a broader, strategic and more dynamic interpretation of the role of effective staff management in organisations' (Middlewood and Lumby 1998: 9). Personnel management was typically the remit of a separate, specialist, expensive and highly bureaucratic unit within the organization. It was predominantly concerned with operational procedures, and too often offered line managers only belated, unrealistic solutions. By contrast, HRM reflected the strategic vision of the organization and was fully integrated into its day-to-day management. In theory, at least, it allowed managers at all levels to provide customized individual responses to issues, to use positive motivation rather than negative control, to be proactive rather than reactive, and to resolve differences through purposeful negotiation without recourse to an external third party (Middlewood and Lumby 1998).

Initially, HRM was thought by some to be just a passing fad – 'a fragile plant' (Storey 1995). However, it caught the zeitgeist, and hundreds of books and articles have since been written on the subject, and a plethora of claims made about HRM's impact (or lack thereof). Because staff salaries generally account for the largest proportion of an organization's overall costs, consuming as much as 80 per cent of a school's budget (Ironside *et al.* 1997), it is not surprising that attention has become focused on how to get the best, and the most, out of employees. Storey, a professor of HRM within the Open University Business School, suggests that 'human resource management is a distinctive approach to employment management that seeks to achieve competitive advantage through the strategic deployment of a highly committed and capable workforce, using an array of cultural, structural and personnel techniques' (1995: 5). Authors within the field of education have shied away from such business-oriented notions as *competitive advantage*, preferring more nebulous terms like *effectiveness*, *success* or *optimal performance*. Thus, for example, Middlewood and Lumby (1998: 5) claim that 'effective human resource management is the key to *the provision of high quality educational experiences*' and that 'educational organizations depend for their *success* on the quality, commitment and performance of people who work there' (italics added).

Substituting 'the provision of high quality educational experiences' for 'competitive advantage' is an important first step in distinguishing HRM in education from HRM in business. However, as we shall see, much greater differentiation is needed if people working within education are to meet the enormous challenges being generated by human capital theory, neo-liberalism, managerialism and performativity.

Four key concepts

The terms *human capital theory*, *neo-liberalism*, *managerialism* and *performativity* are used widely in the literature but rarely explained, perhaps because they are not easy to define, and different authors use them to mean subtly different things. Below we offer a brief and undeniably superficial explanation of each term. Readers are invited to consult the material we cite if they would like a fuller and more nuanced exposition.

Human capital theory

Economists call the resources available to individuals and groups *capital*. Physical capital is produced when raw materials are converted into saleable goods. Human capital is produced when people acquire desired skills and/or knowledge (Bell and Stevenson 2006). Human capital theory assumes that individuals are motivated to increase their human capital by obtaining relevant qualifications and experience, because this will most likely increase their future earnings. It also assumes that national governments are motivated to increase the collective human capital of their citizenry, because this will most likely increase their competitiveness and global reach. Human capital theory, therefore, contends that the primary purpose of education must be to enhance productivity and support economic growth.

Although this theory has exerted a powerful influence over education policy since the 1960s (Demeulemeester and Diebolt 2005), it has several severe limitations (Bell and Stevenson 2006). First, empirical studies suggest that higher spending on education (either by individuals or by nation-states) does not necessarily create greater wealth. In fact, 'human capital returns are decreasing and knowledge produced by education cannot be the engine of self-maintained economic growth' (Monteils 2004: 103).

Second, in a free market, students cannot be compelled to learn what the economy is thought to need. Would-be drama teachers cannot be forced to take physics degrees, just because a country lacks sufficient scientists.

Third, it is hard to predict what knowledge and skills might be needed in 30 or 40 years' time, meaning that today's school-leavers can never be fully prepared for tomorrow's jobs. So, rather than teaching specific skills and knowledge with in-built obsolescence, schools and colleges should be nurturing creativity and a passion for lifelong learning.

Finally, human capital theory ignores the social and moral purposes of education. These might include learning to live ethically and peacefully in a diverse society, and developing a commitment to social justice. For all these reasons, human capital theory is an inadequate driver of education policy, despite being endorsed by politicians and economists the world over.

Neo-liberalism

In essence, neo-liberalism is 'a theory of political economic practices that proposes that human well-being can best be advanced by liberating individual entrepreneurial freedoms and skills within an institutional framework characterized by strong private property rights, free markets and free trade' (Harvey 2007: 2). At its most simplistic, neo-liberalism proclaims that the market is king. It is thus the state's responsibility to create markets in all areas of life, and then intervene as little as possible. Accordingly, public services must be privatized, wherever feasible (as happened with the UK utility companies), or else be subjected to an internal market, or quasi-market (as happened with UK education, health and defence).

Since the 1970s, nearly every country in the world, including China, post-apartheid South Africa and the countries of the former Soviet Union, has embraced 'some version of neo-liberal theory' (Harvey 2007: 3). It is thus the current hegemonic discourse (Harvey 2007), although, in truth, it is not so much a single, neat, comprehensive and static discourse as an evolving and messy amalgamation of multiple discourses (Popkewitz 2000) – hence the need to write 'some version of' in the phrase quoted above. A key outcome of neo-liberalism has been the wholesale reform of the public sector via a generic process and underpinning ideology usually referred to as *managerialism*.

Managerialism

Managerialism has been a feature of the public sector in the US, Canada, the UK, Australia and New Zealand since the 1980s. The economic crisis of the late 1970s prompted countries to curb government spending and to question the value of a bureau-welfare state (Barker 2009). As a result, the New Right, under Ronald Reagan in the US and Margaret Thatcher in the UK, introduced a series of public sector reforms given the label *New Public Management* (NPM). These reforms 'reshaped the relationship between public and private sectors, professionals and managers, and central and local government. Citizens and clients were recast as consumers, and public service organizations were recast in the image of the business world' (Clarke *et al.* 2000: 45). 'The organizational forms, technologies, management practices and values' (Deem 1998: 47) of the private, for-profit business sector were applied to the public sector in an attempt to make it more efficient. According to Clarke and Newman (1997), New Public Management is characterized by:

- a sharp focus on income generation and efficiency to compensate for reduced public spending;
- a preoccupation with quantifiable targets and outcomes rather than intrinsic and more nebulous processes;
- the adoption of new technologies that facilitate more intense monitoring and measurement, thus invading personal life and space with work demands;
- an emphasis on competition between individuals and organizations that leads to spurious choices and increased stress.

Underlying NPM is a particular ideology (Enteman 1993; Pollitt 1993; Trowler 1998; Peters *et al.* 2000; Deem and Brehony 2005) summarized in the claim that the public sector traditionally wasted resources because it lacked the discipline of the market and allowed its employees too much autonomy (Clarke and Newman 1997).

Even when political parties of the New Left succeeded those of the New Right, the reforms introduced under NPM were extended rather than reversed, for two reasons. First, no government was keen to increase public spending; and second, left-wing politicians saw how the reforms initiated by their right-wing opponents to improve efficiency could also reduce welfare dependency and make professional public servants more responsive to their clients' needs (Flynn 1999; Clarke *et al.* 2000). So, when Tony Blair replaced Margaret Thatcher as UK prime minister in 1997, the Labour leader continued to focus on increasing public sector accountability, reducing expenditure, improving efficiency and seeking business solutions to social problems (Clarke *et al.* 2000). However, he combined Thatcher's market managerialism with greater central control, introducing a hybrid, modernizing version of NPM (Barker 2009) sometimes referred to as *new managerialism*. This is different from NPM in three ways.

First, it seeks to produce longer-term effectiveness as well as shorter-term efficiency. Second, it aims not just to reform institutions, but to achieve Labour's wider political agenda in relation to education, social inclusion and welfare. Finally, it focuses less on cut-throat competition and more on collaboration, stakeholder partnerships and engagement with the wider community (Clarke *et al.* 2000).

While supporters of *new managerialism* claim that public sector agencies have been granted greater autonomy, opponents suggest they are being covertly manipulated by a policy context predicated on prescription, inspection and performativity (see below). In other words, 'Direct central regulation is reduced, but the centre determines the rules of the game, the forms and limits of what can be achieved, so that the system/institution is steered by remote control' (Marginson 1997: 65). The threat of a merely 'satisfactiory' inspection report or a 'below average' ranking in the league tables is enough to ensure compliance.

Although the underlying ideology remains the same, managerialism has been enacted differently in different public sectors. The trends in healthcare or policing, for example, are not identical to the trends in education (Clarke and Newman 1997). Moreover, even within education, different sub-sectors (primary, secondary, further education or higher education) have been differently affected (Simkins 2000). For instance, efficiency-related funding cuts have had a much greater impact on UK FE colleges than on UK schools, whereas external inspection has had a much greater impact on schools than on universities.

Performativity

The term *performativity* was first coined in 1984 by Lyotard, who suggested that the postmodern society had become obsessed with efficiency and effectiveness. The *principle of performativity*, according to Lyotard (1984), means minimizing inputs (costs) and maximizing outputs (benefits), so as to deliver optimal value for money. In this way, quality becomes synonymous with cost-effectiveness (Elliott 2001). In a much-quoted critique of the terrors of performativity, Ball (2003: 216) defines it as,

> a technology, a culture and a mode of regulation that employs judgements, comparisons and displays as means of incentive, control, attrition and change – based on rewards and sanctions (both material and symbolic). The performances (of individual subjects or organizations) serve as measures of productivity or output, or displays of 'quality', or 'moments' of promotion or inspection.

People are valued only for what they produce, and anything that cannot be quantitatively measured is of dubious worth. Good practice is embodied by 'a set of pre-defined skills or competencies, with very little or no acknowledgement given of the moral dimensions of teaching' (Codd 2005: 201). Moreover, all schools, regardless of their circumstances and student intake, are expected by government to achieve these generic skills and competencies. Although this culture of performativity has been discussed in relation to schooling in the US (Hursh 2005), Australia (Smyth *et al.* 2000), New Zealand (Codd 2005), Ireland (MacRuairc and Harford 2008), and elsewhere, it is particularly evident in the work of England's Office for Standards in Education (Ofsted) (Ball 2003; Perryman 2006).

Trust in people is low, and the tendency to apportion blame high (Avis 2005). Although all schools (and indeed, all higher and further education institutions) are subject to a degree of performativity, this culture is especially acute in places that *fail* inspection. All the actors within such schools – be they leaders or followers, teachers or learners – become accustomed to monitoring their every move in terms of what Ofsted would expect, and thus behave as though they are under constant surveillance even when they are not (Perryman 2006). Submitting to this kind of panoptic discipline is perceived to be the only way to escape from the spectre of *special measures* (in which the school comes under increased surveillance from Ofsted, and staff may be replaced if Ofsted thinks it necessary).

The impact of neo-liberalism, managerialism and performativity

According to Ball, neo-liberal markets, managerialism and performativity constitute three interrelated policy technologies that are 'permeating and reorienting education systems in diverse social and political locations which have very different histories' (2003: 215). Although endorsed by powerful agents like the World Bank and the OECD, embraced by politicians across the political spectrum, and legitimated by many academic educators, these technologies 'leave no space of [*sic*] an autonomous or collective ethical self' (ibid.: 226). Instead, they generate,

> various forms of oppression and injustice, including the reproduction and exacerbation of entrenched socio-economic inequalities, the subjugation of teachers, a closer alignment of schooling with the values of capitalist society, and a move towards more traditional and socially repressive pedagogies.
>
> (Clarke *et al.* 2000: 22)

In what follows, and in subsequent chapters, we present a range of evidence from our own research and that of our colleagues, which, in our judgement, convincingly supports the claims being made by Ball (2003) and Clarke *et al.* (2000). It is up to our readers, of course, to consider this evidence and then make up their own minds.

The central argument of the book

The imperatives of globalization are evident in education policy around the world. Although they may not mean precisely the same thing by the words they use, governments from the US to China are driving their education systems to produce more skilled, more flexible, more adaptable employees. Whether accountability is defined in relation to the party (in China), the school district (in the US) or Ofsted (in England), the pressure to perform is all-pervasive, with leaders, teachers and students expected to engage in a perpetual struggle to improve themselves, their organizations and their results. Across the world, countries fear that they may be overtaken by the competition, lose market share or find themselves in a sector where value added is low.

Leaders in education are obliged to look for competitive advantage through strategies likely to enhance motivation, build capacity for organizational improvement and produce better value-added performance. Established models of HRM (see, for example, NCSL 2003a, b) envisage them creating a vision, developing well-planned systems and policies, distributing responsibility through individuals and teams, and transforming everyone in the workforce, in order to ensure that the performance of every individual is optimized. Such models assume that the strategies necessary for success transcend time, place and context, leading to enhanced effectiveness anywhere (Sammons *et al.* 1995).

Education policy-makers endorse these assumptions, and drive this agenda forward by constantly passing new legislation and setting new goals, all of them designed to maximize human capital and combat the consequences of poverty and disaffection. They seek both to *raise the bar*, so that student achievement rises every year, and to *narrow the gap*, so that those from poorer backgrounds do as well as those from richer ones. In England, five separate, though interrelated, elements are discernible in this policy mix (Barker 2008: 670):

- Choice and competition between schools (open enrolment, published performance tables and the promotion of faith, specialist and academy status).
- Qualifications and Curriculum Authority (QCA) regulation of the education market through the National Curriculum and prescribed tests and examinations for all stages of primary, secondary and tertiary education.
- Rigorous accountability, enforced through Ofsted inspections, with sanctions for schools that fail to match required performance levels and criteria.
- An emphasis on leadership and human resource management, including training, to increase motivation and organizational effectiveness, implemented specifically through the National College for School Leadership (NCSL) and the Training and Development Agency (TDA).
- An emphasis on research and evidence-based policy. The inspection framework is based on effectiveness research; guidance on leadership and improvement is based on a sustained research programme (e.g. DfES 2001).

Yet raft after raft of government initiatives, not to mention the huge injections of public money, have produced only limited gains in terms of student attainment, with improvements often reaching a plateau, and progress sometimes giving way to regression (Barker 2008). Within the education profession there is considerable resistance to much of the policy mix, while in the corridors of power and the wider community there is considerable disappointment that more has not been achieved.

It is our contention that the gains have indeed been limited – but not, as is often suggested, because teachers are incompetent or have failed to implement the initiatives appropriately. Rather, it is because the reforms themselves are wrong-headed and contradictory. Creating quasi-markets and lauding parental choice wastes precious resources and undermines equal opportunities and social inclusion. Imposing a National Curriculum and standardized tests stifles teacher creativity and learner curiosity, making *personalized learning* an empty slogan. Subjecting all schools throughout the country to the same inspection criteria ignores the overwhelming evidence that context matters and sanctions are a poor long-term motivator.

Excellence and inclusion cannot be complementary policy goals. Somewhere between 75 per cent and 90 per cent of the between-school variation in examination results is produced by factors outside a school's control, most notably the prior attainment and social background of the student intake (Scheerens 1989; Gray *et al.* 1990; Teddlie and Reynolds 2001). So, the most logical way for schools to improve their results is to eschew, as far as possible, those students who are likely not to perform well in examinations – those with special needs, those excluded from other schools, those from disaffected families. When the complex work of schools is reduced to the simplicities of student attainment and Ofsted judgements (invariably presented in the popular press in the form of crude rankings), inclusion is inevitably discouraged. Discounted also is the immense contribution teachers and leaders make to individual emotional well-being and community cohesion, especially in the face of increasing migration, ethnic diversity, religious intolerance and family breakdown.

What is needed in the circumstances is not another repetition of the hollow exhortation to disseminate best practice more widely, as though uniformity were synonymous with quality. Nor is there any need for yet another set of large-scale national initiatives. What is required, instead, is a greater appreciation by policy-makers, politicians, journalists and academics of the extent to which HRM is fundamentally context-dependent. Such an appreciation would naturally lead to more tolerance of diversity and greater scope for creativity. It would also engender a more realistic and therefore less damaging assessment of what HRM can actually achieve, especially in contexts replete with contradictory reforms. HRM can provide a valuable template for developing consistent and coherent organizational structures and procedures. It can also promote a degree of fairness, equity and social justice, though not if its primary preoccupation is maximizing output and productivity. The one thing it cannot do, however, is single-handedly overcome the disadvantages associated with poverty and social deprivation, and it is foolish to deny the importance of these variables.

The scale and scope of the evidence presented

We have taken English state schools as our starting point because neo-liberal tendencies are 'most advanced' in England (Apple 2004: 19), and modernization of governance 'most extreme' (Ozga 2005: 209). The country has experienced over 20 years of large-scale systematic reform, during which time the assumptions of policy-makers and academic researchers have been tested and refined (Barker 2008). It also established a National College for School Leadership (renamed the National College for Leadership of Schools and Children's Services in September 2009). Allegedly, this is 'the most impressive organization of its kind in the world' (Caldwell 2006: 185), and one that other countries would do well to emulate (Levine 2005). Even those less favourably disposed to the NCSL acknowledge its unrivalled size and coverage (Bolam 2004; Bush 2005).

We have also drawn from the literature on other sectors, especially further and higher education, and have widened our scope to include research from Africa, Australia, Canada, China, Germany, Ireland, Italy, South Korea, New Zealand, Scotland, the United Arab Emirates, the US and Wales. At various points, we have incorporated our own research in the form of four case studies, brief details of which are given in Table 1.1.

Table 1.1 Case studies used in the book

Site	*Description*	*Chapters where found*	*Methodology*	*Further details*
Norcross School	English secondary school in a former mining area with high social deprivation and unemployment, with a long-serving head	Chapter 4: 'Leading school and college improvement'	Repeated interviews over a six-year period	Barker (2009)
Felix Holt School	English secondary school in an older industrial part of the Mid Valley near affluent villages and suburbs, with three heads between 1977 and 2003	Chapter 4: 'Leading school and college improvement'; Chapter 5: 'Empowering groups and teams'	Repeated interviews over a six-year period	Barker (2006)
The Shire School	English foundation comprehensive in a rural and generally prosperous community in southern England, with the same 'outstanding' head since 1995	Chapter 6: 'Designing learning organizations'	Seventeen semi-structured interviews, eight classroom observations and documentary analysis in June 2005	Barker (2007)
Rihab University and Al Fanar College	Two higher education institutions in the United Arab Emirates, with an all-female indigenous student body and a predominantly Western-education faculty	Chapter 7: '*Greedy* organizations'; Chapter 10: 'Appraisal and performance'	Thirty-eight semi-structured interviews, participant observation and documentary analysis over a four-year period	Mercer (2007)

We are aware, of course, that the findings of a single case study are not easily generalizable to other contexts (Robson 1993; Drever 1995; Gomm *et al.* 2000; Bassey 2007). Nonetheless, we believe that there are times when the complexity and subtlety of HRM can be illustrated better through the 'thick description' of a case study than the superficial sweep of a survey or the dry exposition of a literature review. Readers are invited to compare their own organizations with those represented in our case studies, and to make their own 'naturalistic generalizations' (Stake 1995) if there is sufficient similarity or 'fit' (Scofield 1993).

Overall structure of the book

The book is divided into three parts. Part I (this chapter and Chapters 2 and 3) examines the current *context* of HRM by critically analysing world-wide trends in education policy, government legislation, societal values and teacher cultures. Part II (Chapters 4–7) explores two pairs of contemporary HRM *themes* by comparing the roles of leaders and followers on the one hand, and contrasting learning and *greedy* organizations on the other. Part III (Chapters 8–10) examines three contemporary HRM *practices*, namely the selection and development of professionals, the remodelling of school teams, and the management of performance.

Chapter 2 explores the interplay between government legislation and societal values. It describes how the development of individual legal rights and social partnerships are altering the traditional role of education trade unions. It argues that neo-liberalism and human capital theory, with their emphasis on competitive individualism, have given rise to national and supra-national legal frameworks that comprehensively protect employees against every form of discrimination, while still failing to prevent various types of exploitation.

Chapter 3 evaluates the evidence that the changes in government policy, legislation and societal values described in Chapter 2 have led to a crisis in teacher confidence. It describes how contradictory reforms have resulted in a rise in formal professionalism but a fall in professional autonomy, a growing public acknowledgement of the importance of education but a growing public disillusionment with teachers, and a nominal promotion of collegiality and distributed leadership alongside an actual increase in the coercive powers of management. It suggests that the profession needs to champion a new form of *democratic professionalism* in order that the moral dimension of teaching can be reclaimed.

Chapter 4 explores the contribution leaders can make to improving institutional performance and the extent to which their efforts are constrained by social, economic and organizational variables. The concepts and implications of leadership style (NCSL 2003b), organizational climate (Litwin and Stringer 1968; McClelland 1987) and culture (Schein 2004) are explored through two contrasting case studies. These are Felix Holt School, where successive and exceptional leaders have raised the GCSE score from 13 per cent to 70 per cent in six years, and Norcross School, where similarly impressive leadership seems to have been less successful in countering the effects of social disadvantage in a former mining area.

Chapter 5 considers how leaders and followers interact in teams and groups. Belbin's (1981) eight team roles, believed necessary for group effectiveness, are reviewed and contrasted with the recommendations of the NCSL (2003b). The notion of an *intelligent* or *learning* organization is explored, as is the role of communication. The involvement of middle managers in redesigning the curriculum and building capacity is examined through the Felix Holt case study.

Chapter 6 investigates a best-case scenario in which everyone connected with an institution is committed to continuous improvement through lifelong learning, making the sum greater than the parts. Potential strategies for achieving this best-case scenario are explored through a case study of The Shire School, where the head was particularly effective in working with her colleagues to design an intelligent school. Senge's (1999) 'five disciplines' are tested and their limitations discussed.

Chapter 7, in contrast, explores a worst-case scenario in which the institution bleeds people dry, and only the fittest survive. The characteristics of so-called *greedy* organizations are described, and then illustrated by way of the Rihab and Al Fanar case studies from the United Arab Emirates. Potential strategies for ameliorating this worst-case scenario are critically analysed and ways to manage stress, burn-out, ill health and poor performance considered.

Chapter 8 investigates the training, recruitment, selection, induction, development and departure of teachers and school leaders. It highlights how performativity and the standards agenda are narrowing the focus of teacher induction and professional development, thereby jeopardizing the potential benefits. It also contends that the shortage in leadership supply is the result of a flawed government agenda that drowns heads in bureaucracy, bombards them with change initiatives, expects miracles from them, and – the final straw – allows governing bodies to dismiss those who fail to deliver the required improvements.

Chapter 9 explores the drivers behind workforce remodelling in English state schools and critiques the argument that highly skilled qualified teachers are being replaced by much cheaper hastily trained teaching assistants. It argues that unless and until the profession articulates exactly what *formal* knowledge teaching requires, it is impossible to make sound judgements about who should be allowed to do what within schools. The chapter ends by suggesting ways to maximize the contribution of support staff.

Chapter 10 examines the early history of appraisal and its subsequent transformation into a sophisticated system of performance management. It considers the inherent tensions between evaluative and developmental appraisal, and between the needs of the individual and the demands of the institution. It argues that the power dynamics that underlie any appraisal system need to be acknowledged and addressed, because the potential for abuse exists at both ends: in certain contexts, underperforming staff may be able to avoid censure indefinitely, short-changing colleagues and students alike, whereas in other contexts Machiavellian leaders may be able to remove subordinates for no other reason than personal spite. This point is illustrated through the Rihab and Al Fanar case studies.

Chapter 11, the final chapter, assesses the balance between HRM best-practice recommendations and the alternative perspectives discussed in the preceding chapters. To what extent does the empirical evidence cited support the belief that effective HRM policies can help schools and colleges transcend the tensions and paradoxes of the global reform agenda? Can sustainable gains in productivity and output be achieved? These arguments and the case-study evidence presented in earlier chapters are drawn together to identify those features of schools and colleges that, in contemporary contexts around the world, seem either to facilitate or to obstruct the emergence and growth of intelligent or learning organizations. Recommendations are made as to how the challenges posed by managerialism might be overcome, the potential for exploitation restrained, and the transformative power of employees tapped.

2 Government legislation and societal values

Introduction

This chapter explores how the managerialism implicit in the *modernization project* (David 2000; Ozga 2002) and enacted through site-based management has been modified by the development of individual rights in society in general and in the workplace in particular. It explores the traditional and emerging roles of education trade unions, their use of new individual legal rights and their engagement with notions of social partnership. (Note: the term *education trade union* will be used to denote a union to which staff working in the education sector can belong. This term is preferred to *teaching trade union* because some unions, such as the UK's Association of Teachers and Lecturers, are open to support staff, and some, such as the UK's Association of School and College Leaders, are open only to school leaders, including school business managers.) It argues that neo-liberalism and human capital theory, with their relentless promotion of competitive individualism, have given rise to national and supra-national legal frameworks (including the European Court of Justice and the European Court of Human Rights) that comprehensively protect employees against every form of discrimination, while still failing to prevent various types of worker exploitation.

Changes in industrial relations at macro, meso and micro levels

As we saw in Chapter 1, the past 30 years have brought profound changes in the world of work, particularly in the public sector. The same neo-liberal trends have been observed in countries with very diverse histories (Beach 2008) and been supported by political parties of every persuasion (Beck 1999; Exworthy and Halford 1999). While the New Right saw managerialism as a way to promote an enterprise culture in the public sector, thereby increasing efficiency and reducing expenditure, the New Left saw it as a way to make public services less paternalistic and more responsive to the needs of users (Flynn 1999).

Public sector industrial relations have been radically altered by four separate but related drivers (Morgan *et al.* 2000). First, there is the need to control public expenditure; second, there is the promotion of market forces (though privatization, contracting out and internal competition); third, there is the restructuring of organizations to facilitate decentralized decision-making; and fourth, there is the increasing importance attached to the management function, and the importation of management practices from the private sector.

In the UK, these drivers have resulted in cuts in staffing; the development of performance indicators stressing economy and efficiency; the introduction of more formalized individual staff appraisal, including performance-related pay (PRP); more devolved budgetary systems; more management training; greater emphasis on short-term, outcomes-based planning; and more rhetoric about responding to the needs of the consumer. These changes have been seen not only in education but also in the National Health Service (NHS) and the Civil Service (Pollitt 1993). Nonetheless, different public services have responded differently, embracing some policies but resisting others (Clarke and Newman 1997). Thus, for example, NHS managers welcomed PRP in a way that school heads did not (Hatcher 1994).

Differences are also discernible within the education sector itself – one of the most notable examples being the use of multi-employer, multi-union national pay bargaining. This strategy has been retained in English and Welsh higher education and in English and Welsh state schools, even though the School Standards and Framework Act 1998 gave individual schools the right to opt out of any national agreement and set their own rates of pay. By contrast, it was abandoned by further education colleges during the 1990s, when a funding crisis more acute than in higher education or state schooling led both sides to see local pay bargaining and revised working conditions as the only way to ensure the survival of individual colleges (Williams 2004).

In English and Welsh schools, the situation is further fragmented by the fact that six separate unions compete for membership, each on a different platform. These range from the National Union of Teachers (NUT), the oldest, largest and most left-wing of the unions, to Voice (formerly the Professional Association of Teachers), which campaigns under the slogan 'Children First' and opposes any form of industrial action, including the withdrawal of goodwill (Ironside and Seifert 1995). As a consequence, different unions can provide conflicting advice, as they did during the 1985–6 industrial dispute (Ball 1988), and take unilateral action, as the NUT did by refusing to sign up to the social partnership that monitors workload and pay (Stevenson 2007a).

There are variations, too, at the institutional level. Industrial relations are affected by an institution's relative position vis-à-vis its market competitors, its 'cultural starting point', and the individual preferences and styles of particular managers (Simkins 2000). They are also influenced by the activism, trade union affiliations and political leanings of both trade union representatives and rank-and-file employees. Thus, while virtually all the teachers in the failing inner-city secondary school studied by Calveley and Healy (2003) were unionized, many had mixed feelings about the militancy of, and media reaction towards, the minority of colleagues who belonged to both the NUT and the Socialist Workers' Party (Calveley and Healy 2003).

The changing role of education trade unionism

British trade unions increased in power from the time of the First World War until 1979, when Margaret Thatcher became prime minister. Thereafter, however, their influence declined (Ironside and Seifert 1995; Ironside *et al.* 1997), partly because of government legislation curtailing their activities, and partly because of a change in the zeitgeist away from the collective towards the individual. There is now a ban on sympathetic action, meaning that members of one union cannot take action in support of colleagues in a different union; all members of a union must be balloted before any action can be taken; employees have the legal right to refuse to take part in industrial action; and employers have the legal right to deduct wages if workers fulfil only part of their contracts.

Traditionally, industrial relations in schools were less extreme than in other sectors (Ironside and Seifert 1995). This was partly because heads and teachers had similar qualifications, performed some of the same work, and shared traditions of collegiality and flexibility (Johnson 1983, cited in Ironside and Seifert 1995). It was also because heads had less power over employees than managers in other spheres (Hellawell 1990) and were subject to greater external regulation (Carter 1997). However, successive government policies since the 1988 Education Reform Act have seriously undermined this traditional solidarity between heads and teachers in three specific ways (Hatcher 1994; Ironside and Seifert 1995; Carter 1997; Calveley and Healy 2003).

First, parental choice and the operation of a quasi-market based on per-capita funding have forced schools to compete against each other or face a reduction in budget and a resulting cut in staffing and/or resources. Second, employment responsibilities have been delegated to schools, meaning that if a school is not under local authority (LA) control (as is the case with voluntary aided schools, foundation schools and academies), staff sign contracts of employment with their particular school's governing body, not with the LA. This has undoubtedly weakened the ability of trade unions to engage in national bargaining and collective agreements, although, as we shall see, the emergence of a social partnership has gone some way towards avoiding the dangerous managerial vacuum predicted by Ironside and Seifert (1995). Finally, the establishment of the National College for School Leadership and the mandatory National Professional Qualification for Headship (which only the NCSL can validate) have encouraged the development of a managerialist class of senior and middle leaders, almost all of whom have undergone similar courses allied to a common NCSL vision.

Since the 1988 Education Reform Act, education trade unions have waged several campaigns against national tests, excessive workload, school closures, new staffing structures and low pay, but the profession's appetite for industrial action has definitely declined. During the 1985–6 dispute, for example, almost every school in the country was affected. By contrast, on 24 April 2008, when the NUT called a one-day national strike against a below-inflation pay offer (the first such strike for 21 years), only about a third of schools (8,000 out of 25,000) were affected (Curtis *et al.* 2008). Although the education trade unions are more resilient than other public sector unions and the private sector (Stevenson 2007b), traditional forms of resistance are no longer effective (Stevenson 2005), and a 'new realism' (Lawn and Whitty 1992; Hatcher 1994; Torres *et al.* 2000) is emerging.

With the exception of the NUT, education unions working within state schools have abandoned national industrial action as a strategy, though they remain committed to 'increasing and improving services to members . . . regaining leadership in the educational debate, regaining professional status, improving [the] public image of teachers, developing a long-term vision on educational reform, and improving relationships with parents' (Torres *et al.* 2000: 12). Consequently, five of the six school-based unions, the exception being the NUT, signed the national agreement on *Raising Standards and Tackling Workload* (DfES 2003a), hereafter referred to as *The National Agreement*. This was the first substantial collective agreement involving employers and trade unions since the 1985–6 industrial dispute (Stevenson 2007a). By signing it, the education unions entered into an unprecedented social partnership with central government and regional employers.

The rise of new unionism and social partnerships: collusion or constructive critique?

Social partnerships involve employers, trade unions and public authorities (the state and/or local or regional authorities) in the development and implementation of economic and social policy (Bangs 2006). They mediate between the state and the individual, being one manifestation of a distinctive *European social model*. This, according to Jacques Delors, president of the European Commission from 1985 to 1995, represents a middle way between communism, with its denial of the individual, and American and Japanese neo-liberalism, with its denial of the community (Grant 1995). The model advocates liberty, solidarity and personal responsibility, while upholding values of 'democracy and individual rights, free collective bargaining, the market economy, equality of opportunity for all and social welfare and solidarity' (1994 EU White Paper on Social Policy, quoted in Eurofound 2008).

Initially, the UK's Conservative Government refused to endorse the European social model, being the only country in the European Commission not to sign the Community Charter of the Fundamental Social Rights of Workers in 1989, and vetoing the inclusion of a Social Chapter in the Treaty of the European Union (Maastricht) in 1992 (O'Connor 2005). However, when Labour came to power five years later, these objections were immediately withdrawn, and an Agreement on Social Policy incorporated into the 1997 Treaty of Amsterdam (ibid.).

Social partnerships operate differently in different countries (Boyd 2002) and indeed, the social partnership involving English and Welsh schooling is more extensive than any other in Europe (Bangs 2006). Although its original remit was to oversee a reduction in teacher workload and to improve the pay and conditions of school support staff, it now debates 'an unlimited number' (ibid.: 204) of education policy areas, including pay and performance management (Stevenson 2007a).

Opinion is very much divided over whether social partnerships, particularly one as wide-ranging as that with English and Welsh schools, undermine democratic pluralism. Advocates highlight the perceived benefits of having a voice in policy development and point to the contractual gains that have been secured, something that traditional high-stakes/low-return collective bargaining might not have achieved (Stevenson 2007a). Sceptics, however, claim that unions have lost their independent voice and now meekly enforce government policy rather than defending their members' interests or safeguarding their professional values (Thompson 2006). This latter view is the stance taken by the NUT, the largest education union and the one of the government's fiercest critics (Stevenson 2007a). The NUT is vehemently opposed to staff without qualified teacher status (QTS) being responsible for teaching whole classes (NUT 2003), something *The National Agreement* allows in order to reduce teacher workload. Accordingly, the NUT refused to sign, and now stands outside the social partnership. Similarly, the National Association of Head Teachers (NAHT) withdrew from the social partnership in 2005, claiming that the government was not providing sufficient resources to implement workforce remodelling, only to rejoin in January 2007 after a vote by its members (Milne 2007).

Although the government's will has generally prevailed within the social partnership, especially with regard to workforce remodelling and PRP, there have been gains for teachers. Significantly, in 2008, when the NAS/UWT union found that many schools were not implementing *The National Agreement*, they refrained from taking industrial action. Instead, the union lobbied for, and received, legal sanctions. These include a provision in the Apprenticeships, Skills, Children and Learning Bill 2008–09 allowing LAs to issue a warning notice to schools that were failing to implement national pay and conditions. This shift away from industrial action towards legal sanction is operating not only at national level but also at LA level and individual teacher level. Unions are taking advantage of the unprecedented codification and expansion of individual rights in the West to protect their members in the courts rather than on the picket line, a trend explored in the next section.

Globalization, mobilization, individualism and legal rights

All aspects of public life have been affected by an increase in legislation, but it strikes with particular force in the area of employment. Employment law has greatly expanded in recent years to prohibit discrimination on grounds of age, gender, race, ethnicity, religion or belief, disability, and sexual orientation. One driver of this expansion is the perceived need for a modern society to mobilize its entire potential workforce and available intelligence in order to meet the pressures of globalization and an ageing population, but issues of fairness and equality have also played a part.

Age discrimination and retirement legislation

The old-age dependency ratio indicates what proportion of a country's population is of retirement age (65 or over) and what proportion is of employment age (between 20 and 64). In 2005, the average old-age dependency ratio for OECD countries was 24 per cent, meaning that there were 24 people aged 65 or over for every 100 people aged 20–64. By 2050, this ratio is expected to more than double to 52 per cent, leading to higher public spending on health, long-term care and pensions (OECD 2007: 42). As Figure 2.1 (taken from OECD 2005: 9) shows, although some countries will be more affected than others, with Japan being the hardest hit, all will have to deal with rising old-age dependency. To meet this challenge, governments

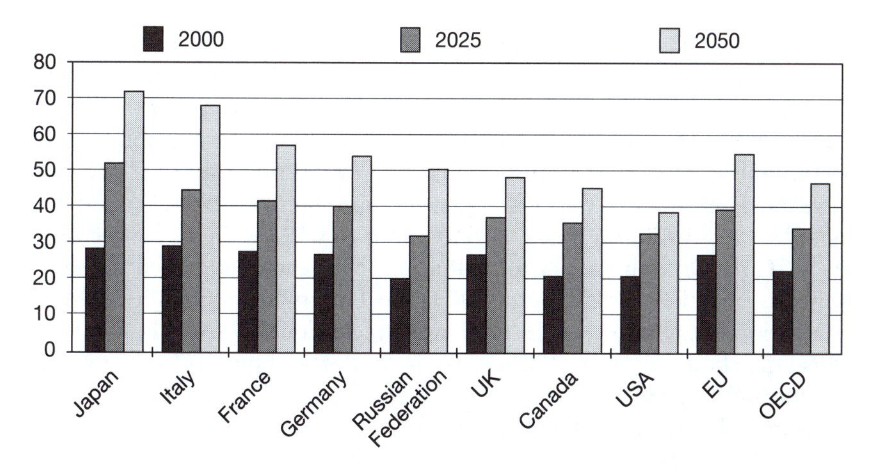

Figure 2.1 Old-age dependency ratio: ratio of the population aged 65 and over to the population aged 20–64

will have to raise statutory retirement ages and/or lower basic retirement benefits.

Employers in the industrialized world have also realized that 100 million baby boomers, born between 1946 and 1964, will retire in the next 20 years, leaving a quantitative talent gap that the next generation simply cannot plug because it is so much smaller in size (Blohowiak 2007). There will be a growing shortage of experienced employees able to step into the shoes of retiring senior leaders, and, as we shall see in Chapter 8, the education sector will not escape this trend (Howson 2003, 2005, 2007, 2008a; Hansford and Ehrich 2006).

However, economic necessity is not the only driver. The legislation is also underpinned by ideals of fairness, and a commitment to civil and human rights. Although it makes financial sense for people to work longer so that they pay more taxes and delay drawing their state pension (Murray 2003), lawmakers seeking to prohibit age discrimination and raise the age of retirement claim they are driven by moral and ethical imperatives, not just money. In general, people of retirement age are fitter and more energetic than in the past, making them better able to cope with the physical and mental demands of work. More importantly, though, work gives a sense of purpose and meaning to life, a benefit that individuals ought not to be denied simply because they have reached a certain age.

Equality legislation

The development of age discrimination legislation has been justified not only in terms of increasing a nation's global competitiveness and reducing its public spending, but also in terms of increasing an individual's social and moral well-being. These same two drivers lie behind similar modern legislation outlawing other forms of discrimination. On 27 April 2009, Harriet Harman, the British Minister for Women and Equality, published the Equality Bill, claiming that it would 'make Britain a more equal place, and help us build a stronger economy and fairer society for the future' (GEO 2009). The aim is to simplify and strengthen the 'complex' anti-discrimination laws that have developed in an ad hoc way over the past 40 years. The Equality Bill will supersede nine previous Acts, namely the Equal Pay Act 1970, the Sex Discrimination Act 1975, the Race Relations Act 1976, the Disability Discrimination Act 1995, the Employment Equality (Religion or Belief) Regulations 2003, the Employment Equality (Sexual Orientation) Regulations 2003, the Employment Equality (Age) Regulations 2006, the Equality Act 2006, Part 2 and the Equality Act (Sexual Orientation) Regulations 2007.

It is intended to strengthen equality law by:

1 introducing a new public sector duty to consider reducing socio-economic inequalities;

2. putting a new Equality Duty on public bodies;
3. using public procurement to improve equality;
4. banning age discrimination outside the workplace;
5. introducing gender pay reports;
6. extending the scope to use positive action;
7. strengthening the powers of employment tribunals;
8. protecting carers from discrimination;
9. offering new mothers stronger protection when breastfeeding;
10. banning discrimination in private clubs; and
11. strengthening protection from discrimination for disabled people.

(GEO 2009)

The new Public Sector Equality Duty set out in the Equality Bill 2009 strengthens previous guidance, requiring public sector authorities to ensure that neither new nor existing policies, programmes or services discriminate against people (even inadvertently) on grounds of 'age, race, disability, sex, pregnancy and maternity, sexual orientation, religion or belief or gender reassignment'.

Although 'the economy', 'productivity' and 'profitability' were mentioned in the accompanying press release, politicians promoting the Bill also spoke of 'fairness', of 'equality', and of individuals fulfilling their potential, building a better life for themselves and their families, and making 'a full contribution to society' (GEO 2009). There was also a strong emphasis on closing the gap between rich and poor, and on overcoming discrimination 'by class'.

The Equality Bill acknowledges that its contents have been informed by policy statements from the European Union, particularly European Parliament Directives on equal pay and equal treatment for employees, irrespective of gender, race or ethnic origin. The Bill has also been influenced by similar statements from the United Nations. It is not therefore surprising that much of it mirrors the jurisprudence of other countries around the world.

Family-friendly legislation

Related to, though not coterminous with, the issue of gender discrimination is a growing perception that social dislocation is increasing as a result of the ever more onerous demands being made by employers in what have been called *greedy* organizations (discussed at length in Chapter 7). Legislators have responded to this by creating opportunities for parents to take time off work in order to be with their families, particularly after the birth or adoption of a child. Although men and women have different views on what constitute family-friendly employment practices (Dermott 2001), statutory maternity, paternity and adoptive leave are now fully established, following the Work and Families Act 2006. In addition, the Employment Act 2002 gives parents of children under 6 (and disabled children under 18) the right to request flexible working in order to facilitate childcare, a right the Work and Families Act 2006 extended to employees caring for adults.

Critics of the British government's record on family-friendly legislation argue that it does not go far enough in supporting family life, in two respects (James 2006): first, statutory maternity and paternity pay are so low that couples feel unable to take their full parental leave entitlement; and second, employers are under no obligation to agree to requests for flexible working. James (2006) also contends that government legislation maintains unjustifiable distinctions by offering more generous provision to employees as compared with contract or agency workers, to mothers as compared with fathers, and to parents of younger children as compared with parents of older children. So, although government legislation has expanded to reflect society's growing recognition of the many forms discrimination can take, and has recently been harmonized to provide a more coherent and consistent legal framework, more still needs to be done.

Case studies: court cases on stress, disability and workplace bullying

As well as being covered by the laws described above, the British education sector has been affected by individual court cases that have set precedents for dealing with, *inter alia*, teacher stress, teacher disability and workplace bulling. The modernization project, with its emphasis on site-based management, has made individual teachers and school leaders responsible for the outcomes of central government policies, even when they have little control over them. By ruling against particular schools and/or their LAs in a number of landmark cases, the English courts have upheld this process of individualization.

For example, although *The National Agreement* represents a nationwide response to the problem of teacher overload, stress is still seen as an issue for individual teachers and their school managers, not just in the UK but also in Australia (Kelly and Colquhoun 2003). As we have seen, education trade unions have resisted the intensification of teachers' work via both traditional industrial action and the modern social partnership. However, neither of these two collective strategies has had as much impact as the individual court case brought by a certain Mr Barber against Somerset County Council (see Knott 2004).

Mr Barber took early retirement at the age of 52 in March 1997, having suffered a mental breakdown in November 1996. He had been working 60–70 hours per week because of staff restructuring at his school, and in May 1996 his doctor signed him off work for three weeks with depression. Although he discussed his concerns in separate meetings with each member of the senior management team (SMT), they took the view that everyone was under pressure and that the financial position of the school would not allow any modification to his workload. In the original court case, the LA, through the school, was deemed to have been negligent, and Mr Barber was awarded compensation. The Court of Appeal overturned the decision, claiming that Mr Barber's employers had not breached their duty of care. The House of Lords disagreed, however, and in April 2004 restored the original verdict of negligence, though reducing the level of compensation. The judges in the House of Lords concluded that 'even a small reduction in his duties, coupled with the feeling that the senior management team was on his side, might, by itself, have made a real difference' (*Barber v. Somerset County Council*, quoted in Knott 2004: 89). This landmark ruling has led to an increase in teachers raising issues of stress with the aid of their unions, and thereby forcing their school management to reduce their demands. Since stress is often caused by pressure exerted by the SMT, the threat of action on stress is clearly a potent one.

Just as Mr Barber's court case changed the way school leaders deal with teacher stress, Ms Meikle's court case against Nottinghamshire County Council forced them to reconsider their obligations towards employees with disabilities. Ms Meikle, a textiles and cookery teacher, became 'sight-disabled' in 1993 and the court found that she had been unlawfully dismissed in 1999 because her school had failed to accommodate her disability. Specifically, the school (1) had not provided large-print documents, particularly of the cover roster; (2) had timetabled her in classrooms that were some distance apart; and (3) had not reduced her teaching load so that she could complete paperwork at school and in daylight (see *Meikle v. Nottinghamshire County Council* 2003).

The case of *Majrowski v. Guys and St Thomas' NHS Trust* (2006) imposed further constraints on management by setting a precedent for staff to claim they are being bullied and harassed by senior managers. Mr Majrowski had been publicly humiliated by his supervisor and given unrealistic targets to fulfil. The judges had no difficulty in finding he had been harassed. The case was of interest to lawyers because it presented a new way to hold employers liable for a criminal act of harassment.

Case study: teaching excluded pupils

In 2003, NAS/UWT defended and won a case in which it had balloted to take strike action to refuse to teach an excluded pupil who had been sent back to school. The case, known as *P. (FC)* [2003] UKHL 8, was highly significant because it potentially allowed the union to force the SMT to withdraw pupils from classes at the will of the staff. A subsequent case, identified as *O. v. The Governing Body of Park View Academy and others* (2007), established that the head could be forced to uphold the wishes of staff even without a staff ballot. All subsequent cases have endorsed this ruling. This is a new combination of legal and industrial action, ensuring teachers within a particular school are not forced to teach excluded pupils against their will.

Case study: indirect discrimination against part-time workers

The European Directives being incorporated into the British Equality Bill prohibit both direct and indirect discrimination, the latter being said to exist 'where an apparently neutral provision, criterion or practice disproportionately disadvantages the members of one sex' (Europa n.d.). A number of cases in the European Court of Justice have established the basic principle that since most part-time workers are women, direct discrimination against part-timers constitutes indirect discrimination against women. Two such cases (concerning pension rights) were brought by UK part-timers, Shirley Preston and Dorothy Fletcher (Eironline n.d.). The Equality and Human Rights Commission (n.d.) cites three similar cases before concluding that 'it is now beyond doubt that a pay practice which results in full-timers being paid more than female part-timers is prima facie discriminatory'. Such an unequivocal statement on equal pay is very welcome, but part-timers also face reduced promotion prospects – not only because it may take them longer to acquire the necessary experience, but also because employers often view managerial positions as requiring a full-time commitment (Moreau *et al.* 2005, 2007). This more subtle form of indirect discrimination against women has yet to be tackled effectively.

The discussion so far indicates something of a paradox. On the one hand, the professional control exercised by teachers has in many respects diminished; they feel at the mercy of external pressures; the influence of their unions has declined; and the will for collective action has decreased. Yet on the other hand, legislation and the courts are clearly limiting the powers of employers, and unions are starting to use the law as a new weapon with which to defend their members. The union legal department has become significantly more important in relation to the establishment of members' rights. Given this paradox, it is hard to predict what will happen to education unions in the future, but the next section explores one possibility.

Social justice unionism

We have seen how, within the education sector, traditional industrial unionism has given way to *reform unionism* in which unions bargain constructively for changes in both government policy and teachers' conditions of service (Stevenson 2007a). Whether reform unionism will be subsumed within *social justice unionism* remains to be seen. In a much-quoted declaration 15 years ago, both major US education unions called for 'a broader conception of the interests of teachers and of teaching . . . a better partnership with the parents and communities . . . a new vision of schooling . . . [and] a new model of unionism' (NCEA 1994). This new model, labelled *social justice unionism*, 'retains the best of traditional unionism, borrows from what has been called "professional unionism," and is informed by a broader concept of our members' self-interests and by a deeper social vision' (ibid.).

Stevenson (2007a: 243) argues that the NUT's refusal to join the social partnership could be seen as social justice unionism, but he also acknowledges that this is 'a high-risk strategy' since the other five school-based unions did not have quite the same qualms. In similar vein, Rottmann (2008: 999) suggests that 'although [Canadian] teachers' unions may be sites for social justice activism, they are not yet social justice organizations' because of 'the ongoing gaps between rhetorical and material commitments to social justice'. In 1999, Beck (1999: 232) predicted that 'unconstrained individual choice and . . . consumer sovereignty' would make it 'progressively more difficult to build political support for positions which stress collective societal responsibilities organized around principles of social justice and progress back towards greater egalitarianism'. This may go some way towards explaining why education unions in the West have so far failed to turn the rhetoric of social justice into reality.

In parts of the developing world, however, education unions have been more active, and in some cases more successful, in promoting social justice. Synott (2007) describes the ten-year battle for legal recognition waged by the Korean Teachers and Educational Workers Union (KTU), which included hunger strikes, mass sackings and a year-long imprisonment of the union president. Synott (ibid.) recounts how the union has not only defended its members' interests but also championed fundamental human rights. So, as well as campaigning against a reduction in teachers' pensions and a flawed system of teacher evaluation, the KTU has also challenged the government over its pathological antagonism towards North Korea, its development of a national database that would have made confidential records freely available, and its treatment of people with disabilities. In this way, the KTU has facilitated the democratic development of education and contributed to the development of national values, something its Western counterparts still aspire to but achieve less and less frequently.

Conclusions and caveats

This chapter has described the government legislation that has been enacted in England and Wales, and looked specifically at the evolution of the social partnership formed by five of the six school-based unions, the Department for Children, Schools and Families and Local Authorities. Although these developments reflect the *European social model* promoted by the European Commission, it would be wrong to assume that the situation is the same throughout Europe. While British education unions have campaigned against many elements of the National Curriculum and boycotted national tests (Hatcher 1994), their French counterparts see similar central regulation as the prerogative of a unifying state. Conversely, while tens of thousands of French teachers marched through Paris in May 2008 to protest against job cuts (BBC 2008a) and pension reforms (BBC 2008b), British teachers took virtually no action against the large-scale workforce remodelling described in Chapter 9, and the far-reaching salary reforms that saw *Teaching and Learning Responsibility* payments replace *Management Allowances*.

Outside Europe, the context is different again. In the US, for example, competitive pressures produce a less protective environment for employees. There, education unions are seen as a cost burden and an example of producer capture, where the interests of those who use the service are of less importance than the interests of those who work providing it (Brimelow 2003). Similarly, in China, although there is a single national union for teachers, it is neither free nor democratic because of 'the lack of civil liberties in the nation as a whole' (Cooper 2000: 256). The situation in the United Arab Emirates is even more extreme. Here, expatriate employees, who make up 80 per cent of the workforce, have no union representation and are forbidden to strike. The system of Emirati sponsorship allows local employers to cancel expatriate work visas at any time for any reason. This means the former employee has just 30 days to find another job, or else they and all their dependants must leave the country. Understandably, this system of sponsorship has a huge impact on all aspects of HRM, and the situation is discussed at length in Chapter 7, '*Greedy* organizations'.

In some parts of the developing world, however, the picture is not so bleak. In South Korea, education unions have proved to be a formidable force in the fight against ideological oppression and rural poverty (Synott 2007). It might therefore be concluded that social justice unionism only gains momentum when the alternatives becomes truly dire for the majority of students, teachers and parents. Beck (1999: 234) writes of,

> the self-interested conspiracy of silence among the relatively affluent majority of voters in many of the world's most advanced economies . . . [which] may operate to set strict limits on the extent to which seriously redistributive or egalitarian policies can hope to command significant electoral support in these societies.

It is tempting to imagine that educationalists stand outside this self-interested conspiracy, not least because social justice is an enduring aspiration for education unions. It has to be acknowledged, however, that concrete actions to turn this aspiration into reality are rare, and genuine successes rarer still. Perhaps the crisis in teacher confidence, explored in the next chapter, can help to explain why this is so.

3 Teacher culture(s) and the crisis of confidence

Introduction

Not surprisingly, the changes in government policy and societal values analysed in the preceding chapter have had a profound effect upon both the teaching profession as a whole and the work of individual teachers. Moreover, technological advances, especially the exponential growth of the Internet and sites such as Wikipedia, have called into question the teacher's previously privileged access to knowledge. In addition, workforce remodelling (as described in Chapter 9) has prompted a reassessment of which aspects of education actually require the expertise of a qualified professional and which might be done by other adults.

As ever, the debate is characterized by contradictory developments. These include:

- an increase in formal professionalism but a decrease in professional autonomy;
- a loosening of control in some areas, such as school finance, but a tightening of control in others, such as curriculum;
- a growing acknowledgement by society and policy-makers of the crucial importance of education but a growing disillusionment with teachers and a corresponding decline in their perceived status and authority;
- a nominal promotion of collegiality and distributed leadership but alongside greater coercive powers for management.

There is a well-established (though not uncontested) narrative that these developments have led to the proletarianization of teachers and the demoralization of the profession. For those who subscribe to this narrative, the resulting crisis in teacher confidence threatens to undermine all attempts at educational improvement.

Defining teacher culture(s) and the teaching profession

Although the word *culture* is used extensively in the literature, different authors define it differently. Hofstede's seminal (1991) survey of 116,000

IBM employees in 72 countries is by far the most widely used (and abused) study of national culture. Here, culture is 'the collective programming of the mind which distinguishes the members of one group or category of people from others' (Hofstede and Hofstede 2005: 4). Specifically within the field of educational leadership, Schein defines culture as,

> the accumulated shared learning of a given group . . . *a pattern of shared basic assumptions that was learned by a group as it solved its problems of external adaptation and internal integration, that has worked well enough to be considered valid and, therefore, to be taught to new members as the correct way to perceive, think and feel in relation to those problems.*
>
> (2004: 17, italics in original)

There are three levels of culture (Schein 2004: 25–37). At the surface level are artefacts. These are the group's visible outputs and may include its physical environment, language, myths, stories, rituals, ceremonies and published values. This level is easy to observe but hard to interpret. The artefacts are derived from the group's espoused beliefs and values, which is the second level of culture. The group's original beliefs and values usually emanate from their leaders, but they endure only for as long as the group is convinced of their worth; they can be supplanted by alternative beliefs and values if the group finds that they do not help with problem-solving. On the other hand, if the group's espoused beliefs and values are repeatedly tested and are found, through first-hand experience, to work reliably in overcoming challenges, they become the group's underlying assumptions. This is the third level of culture, and the most stable. The underlying assumptions of a group define their reality and delineate what can and cannot be thought.

The culture of a group gives meaning to human endeavour and generates shared values, beliefs and assumptions. It helps people make sense of the world, guiding and shaping behaviour. Because culture is shared, it ensures members of a group act consistently. It also provides a sense of identity and a common purpose.

Although national and organizational cultures figure more prominently in the literature, occupational cultures are occasionally mentioned. To quote Schein again:

> If an occupation involves an intense period of education and apprenticeship, there will certainly be a shared learning of attitudes, norms and values that eventually will become taken-for-granted assumptions for the members of those occupations. It is assumed that the beliefs and values learned during this time will remain stable as assumptions even though the person may not be in a group of occupational peers. But reinforcement of those assumptions occurs at professional meetings and continuing education sessions, and by virtue of the fact that the practice

> of the occupation often calls for teamwork among several members of the occupation, who reinforce each other. One reason why so many occupations rely heavily on peer-group evaluation is that this process preserves and protects the culture of the occupation.
>
> (2004: 20–1)

Likewise, for Hargreaves:

> *Cultures of teaching* comprise beliefs, values, habit and assumed ways of doing things amongst communities of teachers who have had to deal with similar demands and constraints over many years. Culture carries the community's historically generated and collectively shared solutions to its new and inexperienced membership.
>
> (1994: 165, italics in original)

The strength of teaching's occupational culture is a moot point. In spite of workforce remodelling, teachers are frequently the only adult in their classroom, making individualism and isolation defining features of the job. Furthermore, managerialism and the rapid pace of change mean that some teachers feel a stronger allegiance to their particular institution than to the teaching profession per se. Of course, context makes a difference. While a mid-career education union representative may be strongly influenced by the culture of the profession, a young, ambitious primary teacher may be more influenced by the culture of their own school, and an established university research fellow more affected by the culture of their specific discipline. For this reason, it is more accurate to write of teacher cultures, in the plural.

The teaching profession is a similar misnomer because professionalism is 'a heterogeneous and ambivalent ideology' (Hatcher 1994: 55). It is 'neither static nor universal, but located in a particular socio-historical context and fashioned to present and mobilize particular interests' (Stevenson *et al.* 2007). Different groups, including union leaders, bureaucrats and academics, use the concept to advance competing agendas (Grace 1987; Sachs 2001). Thus, government policy-makers claim that teachers *as professionals* must accept their proposed reforms, while, at the same time, union representatives claim that teachers *as professionals* must oppose them.

Teaching sits as a relative latecomer among the traditional, or classical, professions of divinity, law and medicine (Hargreaves and Goodson 1996; Gillard 2005). During the eighteenth and nineteenth centuries, teachers in English private schools were thought to be born, not made – and teachers in state-run elementary schools were trained, not educated. Accordingly, neither group were seen as professionals, or aspired to this status. Things began to change in the early twentieth century, when it became clear that the benefits of compulsory schooling would not be realized unless teacher training improved (Gillard 2005). The 1902 Education Act increased the number of teacher training colleges and the concept of a *public sector* began to develop. The professional status of teachers was acknowledged in the 1944 Education Act (Gillard 2005), and for the next three decades they enjoyed a commensurate level of autonomy.

The era of autonomy

Traditional notions of professionalism incorporate expertise/specialized knowledge, altruism/responsibility, and autonomy (Bottery 1996; Furlong 2005). Because the work done by professionals is complex and unpredictable, they need access to a specialized body of knowledge, and the autonomy to be able to apply this knowledge as they see fit. Yet they must exercise this autonomy responsibly, and therefore must first develop appropriate professional values.

Teachers in England have never enjoyed as much autonomy as doctors and lawyers (Whitty 2006), but for most of the twentieth century they were subject to surprisingly few constraints. For example, the preface to the 1918 *Handbook of Suggestions for Consideration of Teachers and Others Concerned in the Work of Public Elementary Schools* states that,

> [t]he only uniformity of practice that the Board of Education desire to see in the teaching of Public Elementary Schools is that each teacher shall think for himself, and work out for himself such methods of teaching as may use his powers to the best advantage and be best suited to the particular needs and conditions of the school. Uniformity in details of practice (except in the mere routine of school management) is not desirable even if it were attainable.
>
> (cited in Lefstein 2005: 333)

Sir John Maud, a British education minister, expressed similar sentiments in 1946 when he declared that 'Freedom is what the teacher needs more than anything else . . . perhaps the most essential freedom of the teacher is to decide what to teach and how to teach it' (cited in Taylor 2008: 235). Likewise, the apocryphal comment allegedly made by George Tomlinson, Maud's successor, that 'Minister [meaning himself] knows nowt [meaning nothing] about curriculum' (cited in Alexander 2000: 549) was a statement of policy, not ignorance.

Indeed, between the First World War and the early 1980s, what UK teachers taught and how they taught it was limited only by the examination boards. There were no formal assessments at primary level, except the 11+ for entry to grammar school, and many secondary school pupils took externally moderated exams that their own teachers set and marked. Individual teachers chose their courses and their materials, being constrained only by logistics, not external fiat.

The contested era of *uninformed professionalism*

While authors agree that UK teachers had greater autonomy prior to the 1980s, they disagree (often quite acrimoniously) over whether or not this was a good thing. Hopkins (2007: 44) contends that in the 'not-so-halycon days' of the 1970s 'a thousand flowers bloomed and the educational life chances of too many of our children wilted' because educational provision was too patchy and piecemeal. Likewise, advocates of the *High Reliability Schools* project (HRS) argue that the kind of autonomy and flexibility prevalent in the 1970s does not make schools effective, whereas importing the 'right first time, every time' systems of the air traffic control tower and the nuclear power station does (Reynolds *et al.* 2006; Stringfield *et al.* 2008). They point to the fact that over a nine-year period the GCSE results of the 12 secondary schools taking part in the HRS project improved considerably, both in real terms and in comparison with other schools. Sceptics point out that these impressive test results were achieved by stifling all creativity and risk-taking on the part of both staff and students.

Another critic of the era of autonomy is Michael Barber, 'the key architect of New Labour's policies' (Whitty 2006: 1). On several occasions, Barber has spoken of four phases of reform, labelling them *uninformed professionalism*, *uninformed prescription*, *informed prescription* and *informed professionalism*. The 1970s were characterized by *uninformed professionalism* because teachers at that time lacked the knowledge, skills and attitudes needed for a modern society. This was followed in the 1980s by a period of *uninformed prescription*, when the Conservative Government brought in the National Curriculum for political rather than educational reasons. The election of New Labour in 1997 heralded the arrival of *informed prescription* and a raft of allegedly evidence-based policies, including the Literacy and Numeracy Strategies and standards-based teacher training. By 2000, teachers had acquired the knowledge, skills and attitudes previously lacking, and could therefore be granted greater autonomy from government prescription. The age of *informed professionalism* had arrived (Barber 2005, cited in Whitty 2006).

Not surprisingly, many people who taught in the 1970s and 1980s take issue with Barber's contention that in this period 'the profession itself was uninformed' and that under Margaret Thatcher the system moved from '*uninformed professional judgement to uninformed prescription*' (Barber 2001: 13–14, his italics, quoted in Alexander 2004: 16). Among them is Alexander, who calls Barber's fourfold division 'as distorted and partisan an account of recent educational history as one is likely to find' (ibid.: 16). Likewise, for Dainton (2005: 161), Barber's terminology is 'not only deeply hurtful, but much more important, historically inaccurate' because teachers in the 1970s and 1980s did engage in high-quality professional debate, both nationally and locally. For example, the national Schools Council produced excellent materials based on rigorous research. The Nuffield Foundation developed science teaching, and the London Institute of Education developed English teaching. The London Association for the Teaching of English held a series of conferences and published a magazine, *Teaching London Kids*, that debated the changing nature of the capital's population and the changing needs of its children. Numerous teacher centres were set up so that colleagues from local schools could meet on neutral ground to share ideas and develop materials (Thornbury 1973). There was 'an abundance of strong, positive energy, a wealth of creativity and a sense that, through our individual and collective endeavours, teachers had a voice, and that we really could make a difference' (Dainton 2005: 162).

Nothing was imposed, of course. Teachers were expected to use their professional judgement to decide what was most valuable for their students at any given point. Inspection, prior to the establishment of Ofsted, was thorough and professional but rare, with Her Majesty's Inspectorate (HMI) working on the basis of advice and guidance, not compulsion or coercion. There were bureaucratic elements in secondary schools (Watson 1969), but individual teachers still had space to exercise their own judgement, because heads respected their professional status and believed schools should be collegial places. A good example of this is the pseudonymous Beachside Comprehensive researched by Ball (1981) in the 1970s. Even though the school did not claim to be democratic, the head nevertheless assumed there would be a vote of all staff on the issue of mixed-ability teaching.

The contested era of *informed professionalism*

Not only has Barber been attacked for labelling the 1970s as the era of *uninformed professionalism*, but he has also been criticized for claiming we are now in an era of *informed professionalism*. Dainton (2005: 163) asks:

> Can we really call 'delivering' someone else's thoughts, ideas, strategies and lesson plans 'informed professionalism'? Is the current emphasis on performing and attaining rather than on learning and achieving something that an 'informed professional' could willingly sign up to?

Likewise, Pring (2001) argues that it is demeaning, not empowering, to make teachers pursue imposed targets and deliver a pre-packaged product. Pedagogy, with all its rich complexity, is being reduced to downloadable *best practice* lesson plans (Alexander 2004). Over 2,000 of these are now available from government websites (Furlong 2005; Whitty 2006), and Stevenson (2007a) quotes a primary head lamenting the fact that, as a result, some teachers can no longer plan lessons for themselves. This is 'impoverished professionalism' (Stevenson 2007a), not *informed professionalism*.

Critiques of Barber also contend that teacher preparation courses are worse, not better, than in the past, because now they focus on practical training rather than transformative education (Furlong *et al.* 2000; Furlong

2005; Whitty 2006). All trainees in England currently spend at least two-thirds of their time in schools (typically 120 out of 180 days), and some school-centred routes allow trainees to avoid having any contact with a higher education institution (HEI). Even university Postgraduate Certificate in Education (PGCE) courses contain little about the history, philosophy, sociology or politics of education. They do not look in detail at child development or the relationship between intelligence and ability. Neither do they consider the factors that affect educational achievement or how the brain handles information (Gillard 2005). Yet such 'academic disciplines' are 'vital' (ATL 2005: 4) because without them, trainees cannot critique the status quo, and alternative possibilities become literally unthinkable (Beck and Young 2005: 193). What trainees get instead, however, are the government's 33 Professional Standards for QTS (TDA 2007). Although these have recently been tweaked to incorporate a greater emphasis on reflexive practice, they still offer only limited scope for critiquing government policies or developing professional values (Whitty 2006).

The debate rests upon what exactly is meant by teacher professionalism, and the definitions offered by politicians (on the one hand) and by those actually working within education (on the other) could hardly be more different. In November 2001, Estelle Morris, the then Secretary of State for Education and Skills, made a speech entitled 'Professionalism and trust: the future of teachers and teaching'. In it, she listed six characteristics of a modern profession, as follows:

1 high standards at key levels of the profession, including entry and leadership, set nationally and regulated by a strong professional body;
2 a body of knowledge about what works best and why, with regular training and development opportunities so that members of the profession are always up to date;
3 efficient organization and management of complementary staff to support best professional practice;
4 effective use of leading-edge technology to support best professional practice;
5 incentives and rewards for excellence, including through pay structures;
6 a relentless focus on what is in the best interests of those who use the service – in education, pupils and parents – backed by clear and effective arrangements for accountability and for measuring performance and outcomes.

(Morris 2001: 19)

Her emphasis on regulation, 'what works', efficiency, effectiveness, rewards, accountability and measurement reflects contemporary government thinking, but academics, teachers and education unions prefer to highlight the profession's moral purpose, commitment and compassion (Bottery 1996; Goodson and Hargreaves 1996; Pring 2001; Sachs 2001, 2003; Ball 2003;

Hargreaves 2003; ATL 2005; Yarker 2005; Thompson 2006). For this group, 'principled professionalism' is underpinned by strong values, beliefs and moral purpose (Hargreaves 2003: 131). It involves discretionary judgement, embracing the moral and social purposes of education, collaborating with colleagues, working authoritatively but openly with the wider community, actively caring for students, being committed to continuous learning, and recognizing and appraising others of the complexity of the teaching task (Goodson and Hargreaves 1996: 20–1). It means being inclusive, working collaboratively, acting ethically and with passion, having fun and 'creating an environment of trust and mutual respect' (Sachs 2003: 149). Given such different definitions, and, by extension, such competing expectations, it is little wonder that many teachers suffer a crisis of confidence that leaves them confused and demoralized.

The crisis of confidence

According to the national General Teaching Council for England (GTC) surveys conducted and analysed by Hargreaves *et al.* (2007), teachers believe their status has steadily declined since 1967, when the Plowden Report was published. Teachers in the 2003 survey were particularly disillusioned, having endured 'discourses of derision' (Ball 1990) since the 1970s. A third said they would leave the profession within five years. Teachers in the 2006 survey were slightly more optimistic, perhaps because of substantial pay increases and the prospect of *workforce remodelling*. Even so, 68 per cent of the 70,000 respondents thought the general public gave them little or no respect, while 55 per cent said the same about the government and 49 per cent said the same about parents. To a large extent, teachers feel 'undertrusted, undervalued and over-regulated by . . . government' (Hargreaves *et al.* 2007: 96). Teachers working in poorly performing schools feel particularly maligned, as do ethnic minority teachers, special educational needs (SEN) teachers, supply teachers and early years teachers.

Interestingly, teachers' pessimism is not shared by the general public or the media. Surveys by MORI in 2003 and 2006 indicate that, although the public sector is thought to be less efficient than the private sector, teachers are trusted and respected almost as much as doctors, and more than professors, judges and priests (MORI/Audit Commission 2003; MORI 2006). Similarly, although most teachers believe they are badly treated in the media, a systematic review of the press reveals that the image of the profession has improved considerably since the early 1990s, with teachers now being generally portrayed in a positive and supportive light (Hargreaves *et al.* 2007).

Notwithstanding the above, many teachers report an increase in stress and emotional turmoil caused, in their minds, by government policies that are inconsistent and rushed at best, and morally suspect at worst (Ball 1994, 2003; Woods *et al.* 1997; Jeffrey and Woods 1998; Barker 1999; Smyth *et al.* 2000; Troman 2000; Troman and Woods 2000; Gunter 2001; Scott *et al.* 2001; Munt 2004; Gillard 2005; Yarker 2005; Thompson 2006). Most teachers believe their jobs have become more demanding over time, and for many, the work expected of them is increasingly at odds with their own ideals.

The intensification of work

More than a decade ago, it was claimed that teaching was becoming more intense and more diverse, because of new assessment and accountability regimes, staff cuts, the fragmentation of families, and the government's drive to make schools more responsive to all their stakeholders – be they parents, employers or the wider community (Hargreaves 1994; Carter 1997; Ironside *et al.* 1997). It was suggested that extended professionalism was 'a rhetorical ruse, a strategy for getting teachers to collaborate willingly in their own exploitation as more and more effort is extracted from them' (Hargreaves 1994: 118).

Longitudinal studies of teachers' hours confirm that they still regularly work in excess of the 48-hour weekly average stipulated by the EU Working Time Directive (EU 2000) and that workforce remodelling has failed to address this issue (MacBeath and Galton 2007; Angle *et al.* 2008). In 1994, primary and secondary teachers in England and Wales worked on average 48.8 and 48.9 hours per week during term-time. By 2008, these figures had increased to 52.2 and 49.9. The figures for heads and deputies were even higher. The long hours should be sufficient cause for concern, but added to this is the fact that many teachers now find their job emotionally draining. They have no control over what they are required to deliver, their performance is 'scrutinized forensically' in relation to imposed targets (Stevenson *et al.* 2007), and their personal and professional values are undermined (Scott *et al.* 2001; Ball 2003; Yarker 2005).

This trend is not confined to the UK. Teachers in Germany feel 'powerless' (OECD 2004: 39), while those in Italy are experiencing a 'crisis of identity, deterioration of self-image' (OECD 2003: 7). Teachers working in Chicago with low-income African American and Latino students talk of 'a moral crisis' (Lipman 2009: 47), while those at an Australian school with a large multi-ethnic student population testify to 'the debilitating effects . . . of the neo-liberal "truth game" called *economic rationalism*' (Munt 2004: 577–8, italics in original).

The lack of control

Countless studies have found that most teachers are motivated primarily by the chance to facilitate student learning and achievement (see, for example, Dinham and Scott 1998; Scott *et al.* 1999, 2001; Zembylas and

Papanastasiou 2006; Addison and Brundrett 2008). Yet the space within which teachers can *make a difference* to their students' lives is being consistently narrowed by government policies. Previously, teaching was a conversation between generations about values, and a struggle to make sense of the physical, social, moral and aesthetic worlds (Pring 2001). It was mediated through art, artefacts, drama, literature, poetry, philosophy, history, science and social practices. The end-point could not be predetermined. With the advent of (new) managerialism, however, teaching has been reduced to finding the most efficient means of achieving targets predetermined by those outside education (ibid.).

Delivery has become the defining metaphor, with energy and predictability being valued more highly than creativity or initiative. Education is like a parcel around which various policies are wrapped (in England, these might be the National Curriculum, the National Strategies, Standardized Assessment Tests and Ofsted inspection). The aim of the wrapping is to ensure that similar parcels get delivered to every student, with their contents intact. The process is deliberately teacher-proof, and the teacher, like the postal worker, cannot and should not add anything to the process. Someone else decides what goes into the parcel and nothing outside the box can be delivered. If we incorporate the worst-case ramifications of workforce remodelling into the analogy, we might, in the future, see a small number of senior postal workers/advanced skills teachers sitting in the central sorting office/staffroom. Their job is to grade the parcels by size and shape so that the packages their junior colleagues/teaching assistants deliver actually fit through each student's letterbox. All the letterboxes and all the parcels are similar in size, and even the staff in the sorting office cannot alter the contents. If the packages contained the building blocks for a worthwhile and fulfilled life, the lack of control might just be bearable. As it is, most teachers view the contents as boring and utilitarian, and a sizeable minority see them as toxic waste.

The clash of values

Ball (2003: 223) has written movingly of the 'structural and individual schizophrenia of values and purposes' experienced by many teachers. They become unsure how to act, and those who decide they must play the accountability game lose their self-respect by having to treat children as outputs, 'mere nuts-and-bolts on some distant production line' (ibid.: 220). People are valued only for their productivity, and teachers concentrate their efforts in areas where they are most likely to add value. Accordingly, those on the C/D borderline get special attention, while those predicted to get As or Bs, and those with SEN, get sidelined (Sikes 2001).

Ball (2003) draws upon UK teachers quoted in the *Guardian* newspaper, an Australian teacher in an independent school quoted by Smyth *et al.* (2000) and several English primary teachers quoted by Jeffrey and Woods

(1998). His conclusions match those of a larger study involving over 3,000 teachers and school leaders in Australia, New Zealand, the UK and the US (Scott *et al.* 2001). Participants in this study were asked to identify what satisfied and dissatisfied them at work. Four system-level issues were identified by teachers and school leaders in all four countries.

First, participants resented being expected to overcome social problems (such as unemployment, poverty and family breakdown), especially as they were not given adequate training or resources. Second, they felt bitter about the erosion of their professionalism and a perceived reduction in their status and autonomy. Third, they decried the increase in paperwork, and the way people who knew nothing about education (education administrators, politicians, the press and school governors) could interfere with their work. Finally, they lamented the breakdown of collegial relationships between school leaders and classroom teachers, and the emergence of staff rivalry, especially in Britain, where heads have more discretion in terms of pay and promotion.

Critics might argue that Scott *et al.* (2001) asked a leading question designed to elicit a comprehensive list of problems. However, their sample size is larger than most and their data remarkably consistent. Over 40 verbatim quotes are included, each attributed to a specific respondent. A selection is given below, and the cumulative effect is compelling:

> Teachers gain little respect . . . I feel more like a slave than an educator.
> (Australian classroom teacher, 27)

> Erosion of professionalism – we are completely emasculated by the National Curriculum/Ofsted targets.
> (UK head of department)

> Classroom teachers are bombarded with paperwork. We spend so much time on useless paperwork that planning, evaluating and teaching time are seriously impacted.
> (US classroom teacher, 49)

> I am very concerned at the increased stress levels being experienced by teachers. I joined this profession 24 years ago and felt I contributed more to children's education because I had time to relate to the children I taught. Now I am under so much pressure to reach standards I have little time to really talk to the pupils. I feel more like a machine as the years go by with little time for reflection.
> (UK classroom teacher, 46)

> Teachers feel like puppets; other people pull our strings. There is little vision left in the teaching profession – it's been weeded out over the last 10 years and is still being weeded out.
> (UK classroom teacher)

> The philosophy and practices of teaching have changed markedly from being collegiate and cooperative to being divisive and competitive. The principal has created a culture of distrust and rivalry between teachers and faculties. Many teachers are now perceiving undermining of their colleagues, plagiarizing programs, stealing resources as a means to get on with their careers.
>
> (Australian classroom teacher, 35)

Parallel developments in further and higher education

The crisis of teacher confidence evident in compulsory schooling is also being played out in further education (FE) and higher education (HE). The concept of professionalism is particularly problematic in FE (Robson 1998) because of the way most people 'slide into' the sector, rather than making it a conscious career choice (Gleeson *et al.* 2009), and because of the large number of staff on part-time and temporary contracts. Even so, current government policies are deprofessionalizing FE lecturers in specific ways. Just as school teachers complain about having to deal with the consequences of greater social disruption (Scott *et al.* 2001), FE lecturers worry about being required to take on hard-to-reach students. Accredited subject specialists fear they may lose their sense of professional identity and status by having to teach generic key skills to vulnerable or marginalized groups. This shift from teaching to welfare creates ethical dilemmas too, because college funding is so closely linked to recruitment, retention and certification (Gleeson *et al.* 2009).

In HE, the funding regime up until recently has been less draconian, but academics in this sector still have concerns about how widening participation is affecting standards, how commercialization is affecting the curriculum and teacher–student relationships, and how the measurement of research outputs (encapsulated in the Research Assessment Exercise) is affecting the balance between teaching and research. Clegg interviewed 13 academics from a range of disciplines at a new (i.e. post-1992) statutory university (i.e. former polytechnic), and found that 'despite all the pressure of performativity, individuals created spaces for the exercise of principled personal autonomy and agency' (2008: 329). The picture in schools of education, however, is more mixed, perhaps because these departments have two distinctive characteristics.

First, initial teacher training courses are subject to considerable government intervention. We have already seen how, in England, the DCSF and TDA are progressively restricting the content, pedagogy and assessment of PGCEs, leaving little room for academic disciplines or the lecturer's own professional judgement. Second, many education staff, particularly in the new (post-1992) universities, joined HE at a time when they were not expected to conduct research or publish in academic (as opposed to professional) journals. In the current climate, however, most university leadership teams expect their education department to play 'the Research Assessment game' (Deem and Lucas 2007: 129) just as competitively as every other department (Sikes 2006; Deem and Lucas 2007). This presents a particular challenge to education lecturers, as almost all of them have already had highly successful teaching careers outside academia. Developing a new research identity may take these people longer than colleagues in other departments who have come straight from a full-time PhD.

Deem and Lucas (2007) conducted 40 semi-structured interviews with academics at three Scottish and two English education departments. Two of the Scottish and one of the English departments were in new (post-1992) universities. Although only one of the five departments had a long history of funded research, a third of the respondents thought of themselves first and foremost as researchers. Just over a third thought of themselves as teachers, and the remaining third offered a combination of research, teaching and administration. Somewhat surprisingly, in four of the five departments the majority of academics said they valued research more highly than teaching.

By contrast, all of the participants in Sikes' (2006) study of a school of education at a different *new* university resented the requirement to be research-active, mostly because they had such high teaching loads:

> There was an overall understanding that everyone shared. This was to the effect that the demands made upon them were conflicting, excessive and were, in large part, the consequences of the push for New University to compete with 'traditional' universities.
>
> (Sikes 2006: 566)

What these two contrasting studies show is that in higher education the crisis of teacher confidence is mediated by the culture of the education department, and the university as a whole. In some places, education lecturers are just as schizophrenic as their colleagues in schools, but in others the tensions seem less acute.

An important caveat

Although the discussion so far has painted a fairly bleak picture of the crisis in teacher confidence, not all the changes wrought by managerialism have caused widespread anxiety or generated universal resistance. Some changes (such as salary increases) have received widespread approval, and some of the government's prescriptions have actually been welcomed. For example, primary teachers unsure how to teach maths have been very grateful for the detailed schemes of work and approaches provided by the National Numeracy Strategy – 'Better a compliant technician than an incompetent professional' (Stronach *et al.* 2002: 124). Similarly, some school management teams like the simplicity of national grades and national standards, as evidenced by one deputy head, who said:

> [We] agreed as a senior management that target-setting would be an excellent vehicle for actually monitoring and tracking pupil progress whilst also addressing professional development needs and use the data that we had collected there to say, 'shall we do this, shall we do that?'
>
> (ibid.: 121)

Likewise, in HE some academics have embraced the new managerial opportunities because they see collegiality as inefficient or are too young to have known anything different (Beck and Young 2005).

Even within the same individual, 'an economy of performance' linked to the audit culture can sit in 'uncertain conflict' alongside various 'ecologies of practice' based on professional dispositions and commitments (Stronach *et al.* 2002: 109). The nurses and teachers Stronach *et al.* studied had split personalities, with each person occupying a plurality of competing roles simultaneously:

> The result seemed to be a constant jockeying of stories, selves and practices as teachers and nurses tried to come to terms with a welter of recent innovations, the pressures of their respective audit cultures, threats to their preferred professional styles, or otherwise accommodated or resisted political attacks and external impositions.
>
> (ibid.: 118–19)

The way forward

Clearly, it is unhelpful merely to bemoan the passing of an alleged golden age. The clock cannot be turned back, and therefore teachers must work together in order to regain their confidence and project a professional image that does them justice. One way of doing this is to reiterate the moral imperative of teaching at every opportunity (Campbell *et al.* 2004; Codd 2005; Yarker 2005). The teacher's job is not just to ensure students score highly on standardized tests. It is also to *make a difference*, by helping learners develop as moral human beings capable of living worthwhile and fulfilled lives. This is especially incumbent upon those who work with children, but it also applies to those working with adults.

Dainton (2005) suggests three other specific strategies. First, all organizations that represent teachers (including unions, subject associations and the GTC) should come together in order to draft a common statement of professionalism. This would counteract the sort of government pronouncements typified by Morris (2001). Second, workforce remodelling needs to be reconsidered because it rests on an impoverished view of what teaching and learning means. Instead, the profession should ensure that all teachers have much more input into what is taught and how. If teachers have more control over their work and are allowed to exercise their individual creativity, the job will be much less exhausting, and workload much less of an issue. Third, teacher education must be reformed so that beginning teachers understand more deeply the moral dimension of their work, and gain the knowledge (of history, sociology, pedagogy, child development, curriculum, and so on) they will need in order to develop the minds and hearts of their learners.

In similar vein, Sachs (2001, 2003) calls for what she terms *democratic professionalism*. Whereas traditional professionalism is exclusionary, democratic professionalism requires teachers to work collaboratively and co-operatively with other education stakeholders, especially excluded groups of students and members of the community, in order to eliminate injustice, exploitation and oppression, not just in their own classrooms but also beyond the school gates. Democratic professionalism is nurtured when teachers and schools constantly encourage:

- the open flow of ideas, regardless of their popularity, that enables people to be as fully informed as possible;
- faith in the individual and collective capacity of people to create possibilities for resolving problems;
- the use of critical reflection and analysis to evaluate ideas, problems and policies;
- concern for the welfare of others and 'the common good';
- concern for the dignity and rights of individuals and minorities;
- an understanding that democracy is not so much an 'ideal' to be pursued as an 'idealized' set of values that we must live and that must guide our life as people;
- the organization of social institutions to promote and extend the democratic way of life.

(Sachs 2001: 157)

At the end of Chapter 2, we concluded that, in much of the West, social justice unionism remains an aspiration rather than a reality. Looking at the list above, it seems that the same must be said of democratic professionalism. Sachs (2001) has told the teaching profession, in no uncertain terms, what is required. Whether it can rise to the challenge remains to be seen. Perhaps the global banking crisis will have weakened the discourse of neo-liberalism sufficiently for alternative ways of thinking to take hold. If so, the teaching profession may well have been handed a golden opportunity to overcome its crisis of confidence and rediscover its true vocation.

Part II

Contemporary themes in human resource management

4 Leading school and college improvement

Great expectations

This chapter explores the contemporary theory and practice of transformational and distributed leadership, and considers how far government agencies are justified in their hopes of greatly improved student outcomes. Two contrasting case studies, illustrating how specific school leaders have introduced and sustained major improvement initiatives, help us reflect on the realism of official expectations. Is the UK government's focus on distributed leadership justified?

As was indicated in Chapter 1, modest conceptions of educational management, based on a broad commitment to moral and philosophical goals and a sound understanding of human nature, have been reframed and absorbed within a new and challenging transformational paradigm. Twenty-first-century leaders are expected to maximize and mobilize human creativity, skill and effort so that levels of achievement rise; differences between institutions are reduced; performance differences between social groups are reduced; and human capital contributes to economic success.

Although reform has stalled in many countries, with mandated initiatives failing to lift stubbornly resistant trends in student performance, there is growing optimism that schools can transform themselves and their communities. Policy-makers are convinced that, with a system-wide approach to leadership, four 'key drivers' (personalized learning, informed professionalism, intelligent accountability and networking) will produce sustainable change (Hopkins 2007). Intensive research has generated detailed evidence about what works in leadership (Leithwood and Riehl 2003), while NCSL programmes suggest that best professional practice can be identified and coded so that average leaders can learn and apply lessons from more able and successful colleagues, thereby improving their own productivity and performance (NCSL 2003b).

Current transformational models have their origin in the US business recession of the 1970s and 1980s. The profitability and survival of large-scale industrial corporations were threatened by overseas competition, especially from Asia, where innovation, relatively low costs and an emphasis on high-quality products were combined in an apparently irresistible formula. A new model of leadership was needed to transform old, smokestack industries into efficient, adaptable enterprises, and to mobilize the untapped human potential of American companies and thereby revitalize US business. Trapped in an unimaginative, declining world of mass production and low profitability, corporations wanted to believe that 'there is no limit to what the average person can accomplish if thoroughly involved' (Peters 1989: 282).

Business experts rejected the command and control systems associated with the industrial era, and reported that successful companies were re-engineering themselves to emphasize shared values and employee participation. Outstanding managers were listening to and rewarding their staff, as well as investing heavily in training so that skills were upgraded to meet constantly changing workplace requirements. Old-style systems of personnel management, with their reliance on bureaucratic structures and specialist advice, no longer seemed adequate. Organizational development theorists assumed that if individuals had some control over how their work was done, they would be more satisfied and perform better. Leadership was to be seen in terms of selecting, leading, motivating and developing employees to enhance their commitment and performance. Extraordinary results were expected from this process of empowerment (Larsen *et al.* 1996).

Educators were quick to diagnose similar problems in their school systems, where industrial-era methods prevailed, and top-down, linear approaches to change were seen to fail:

> The basic organization of schools – age grades, didactic instruction, centrally imposed curricula, hierarchical structuring of personnel, elaborate and artificial codes of behaviour – all reflect a linear, mechanistic and deterministic view of teaching and learning.
>
> (Hopkins 1984: 8)

The vulnerability of Western economies in global markets contributed to a growing pressure for schools to become much more effective in developing skills and attitudes that would improve future productivity. Schools, like the industrial firms they served, were increasingly expected to strengthen their 'capacity to deal with change' (Van Velzen 1987: 11) and to recognize their wider responsibility to society for student outcomes. School improvement research consistently contented that commitment and results would improve when students and staff were directly engaged in organizing and managing their own learning and teaching.

The conception of leadership as an enabling, empowering source of change was absent, however, from most improvement studies (Fidler 2001). In the UK, familiar modes of headship, usually perceived as paternal and controlling, seemed to be at variance with the culture and structures associated with school improvement. In the US, however, new leaders were found (Bass and Avolio 1994) or imagined (Covey 1992) who could transform the purpose, motivation and morality of their organizations, and inspire their colleagues to attain remarkable levels of achievement (Burns 1978: 20).

Transformational leadership

As the pace and demands of education reform have accelerated, the catalytic role of leaders in bringing about transformational change has been increasingly emphasized. Michael Fullan (2003) exemplifies the depth of ambition that permeates education policy in many countries, and the faith that is placed in leaders to manage people to achieve outstanding goals. He believes we need 'large-scale, sustainable reform and improvement . . . I am talking about system transformation' (ibid.: xiv). His confidence in leadership is based on Collins' (2001: 14) analysis of 11 'great' US companies, selected from the Fortune 500 because their financial success was sustained over a period of 15 years. Collins describes this elite group as 'Level 5 leaders' whose personal humility and professional will enables them to build 'enduring greatness'. Fullan (2003: 11) argues that transformation can be achieved by comparable school leaders as they inspire teachers to become immersed in 'disciplined, informed professional enquiry . . . [aimed at] raising the bar and closing the gap by engaging all students in learning'.

This optimism about leaders and their potential impact on long-standing social problems has been an important influence on government policy and research in the UK and elsewhere. It shaped the decision to launch the NCSL, in 2000, and has informed public service reform more generally. Leaders are recommended to adopt styles and strategies to induce heightened motivation and change, especially in student outcomes. They are encouraged to transform their organizations by galvanizing effort around ambitious goals and offering intellectual stimulation and individualized support (Gold *et al.* 2003; Leithwood and Riehl 2003: 2–3).

The theoretical framework adopted by the NCSL is derived from Hay McBer, a consultancy firm commissioned by the Teacher Training Agency (TTA) in 1996 to create the Leadership Programme for Serving Heads (LPSH). The underlying research is surprisingly dated. In 1968, George Litwin and Robert Stringer of the Harvard Business School ran an experiment with business students to discover how leadership style impacted on the work environment, which they termed the climate, and how that climate influenced performance and motivation. Three simulated defence contractors (*Booker*, *Balance* and *Blazer*) competed to construct radar units for the government. Each firm had a president with his own calculated managerial style. The experiment lasted eight days, during which time the government demanded new products and insisted on tight deadlines, pressurizing the presidents and employees to combine innovation with low cost.

Booker was run to emphasize the need to control and influence others; *Balance* was directed to accentuate informality and warm personal relationships; *Blazer* was managed informally but with rewards for high standards and performance. The climate of each company was measured on six dimensions, with employees asked to rate the degree to which they were expected to comply with rules; the amount of responsibility they were assigned; the emphasis managers placed on quality and standards; how far rewards exceeded criticism for mistakes; the extent to which goals and objectives were clear; and how much team spirit was encouraged. Each student's motivational profile was assessed before and after the experiment to measure how far their commitment was aroused by the company's leadership approach.

The experiment showed that leadership styles could indeed influence organizational climate, worker motivation and organizational performance (Litwin and Stringer 1968). *Blazer* aroused the achievement motive through a combination of informality, involvement and an emphasis on excellent performance, and was easily the most successful company. In contrast, *Booker*'s tightly regulated environment prompted employees to strike, causing the experiment to end after eight days rather than the intended ten.

David McClelland (1987), closely associated with the Hay Group, has also investigated motivation and why leadership styles have such an impact on behaviour. Earlier research instruments were burdened by too many motives, while attempts to code responses were unreliable (Murray 1938). McClelland aimed to identify the fewest motives that, in combination, could explain the most. He believed three social motives (achievement, affiliation and power) were responsible for 80 per cent of behaviour (NCSL 2003b).

McClelland and Burnham (1995: 6) conclude that successful, power-motivated managers influence subordinates by creating climates that arouse their social motives, especially the need for achievement. Authoritarian, bullying or controlling styles and behaviour stimulate compliance or, as in the case of the *Booker* strike, resistance. Equally ineffective are leaders who need to be liked. Because they focus on promoting warm, friendly relations, and worry more about themselves than the needs of the organization, performance is poor, as demonstrated by the *Balance* company.

These insights into styles, organizational climate, motivation and embedding mechanisms provide, therefore, the best foundation we have for the claim that leaders can transform organizations and drive followers to higher levels of performance, productivity and achievement.

Distributed leadership

Critics point to the potentially totalitarian implications of transformational leadership, despite the moral enthusiasm of its advocates. Although a leader's vision is no less subjective and fallible than a follower's, managers control the agenda and its implementation. There is little scope to question or challenge a headteacher. Followers risk losing influence, the prospect of advancement and even their jobs if they resist being drawn into a particular project, or fail to respond to motivational leaders (Allix 2000).

The government's advocacy of strong leadership has also been criticized for its reliance on heroic, even military, models that seem at odds with the participative values of the school improvement tradition, as well as the HRM belief that ownership enhances motivation. As late as 2001, heads were being invited to play an heroic, solo role in transforming their schools, even though this can undermine attempts to build healthy, democratic communities. A 'bastard' variant of leadership (Wright 2001) seemed to be driving a managerial agenda concerned with raising standards at all costs. As a result, the NCSL, opened by Tony Blair in 2002, was urged to devolve the moral dimensions of leadership to schools, and to promote far more distributed models of leadership practice (ibid.).

Another source of concern has been the lack of evidence that transformational leadership 'brings about anything but modest improved consequences for pupil outcomes' (Gold *et al.* 2003). The performance tables show a widening rather than a narrowing achievement gap between the most and the least successful schools, while disadvantaged students continue to lag behind. Educational leaders seem unable to replicate the productivity gains reported for business and commerce. Leadership effects have been consistently reported as small, mediated and difficult to detect (Hallinger and Heck 1998; Mabey and Ramirez 2004). Where is the promised transformation?

Perhaps influenced by these considerations, the NCSL has been at pains since 2001 to promote a less heroic, miracle-working version of headship, and to encourage an approach that is not linked to status or embodied in a single individual, but dispersed or shared throughout the school (Gold *et al.* 2003). Although *distributed*, *devolved* or *shared* leadership is not a new or clearly defined phenomenon, there is widespread support for the idea that leadership is 'an emergent property of a group or network of interacting individuals' (Gronn 2003) and that 'varieties of expertise are distributed across the many, not the few' (Bennett *et al.* 2003: 6–7). The NCSL has consistently promoted a distributed version of leadership that aims to enhance school capacity through organizational learning (Maden 2001; NCSL 2001, 2003b).

An NCSL-sponsored study of 11 schools in three English LAs produced a developmental sequence of six models of distributed leadership (Figure 4.1, from MacBeath 2005: 357). Schools evolve through stages over time, so the six categories described in the figure are not fixed or mutually exclusive. These models were subsequently tested with teachers and headteachers, and then published by the NCSL as a professional development activity (MacBeath 2005).

Spillane *et al.* (2004) confirm the validity of this approach. In their view, we should analyse leadership activity, not the actions of individual leaders. Leadership practice is the interaction of leaders, followers and their situation when tasks are performed (see Figure 4.2 from Spillane *et al.* 2004: 11).

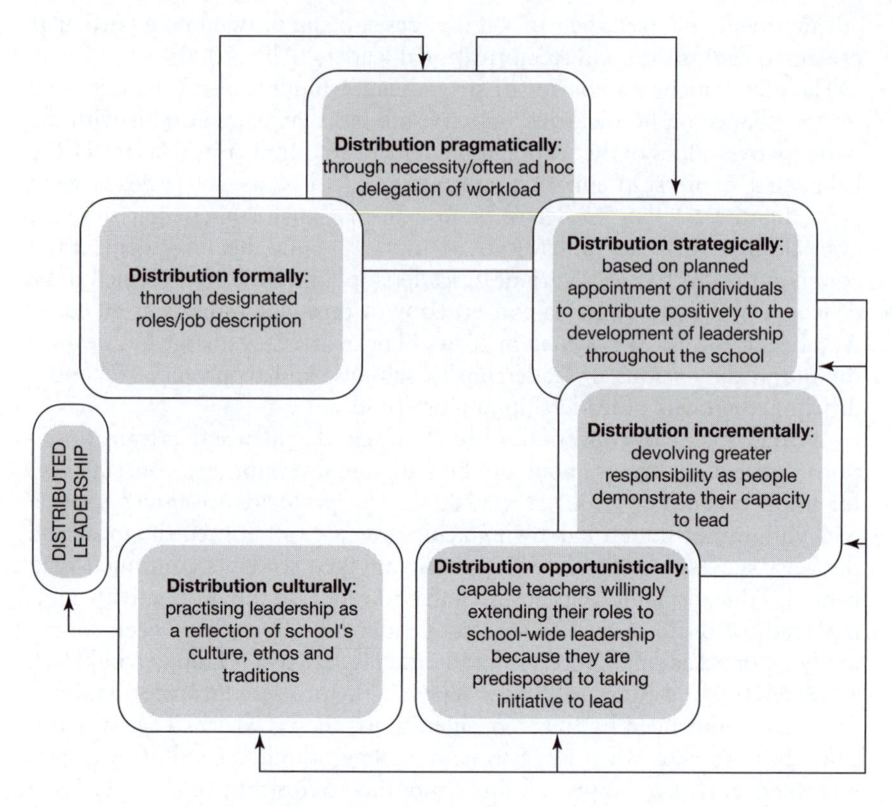

Figure 4.1 Six models of distributed leadership

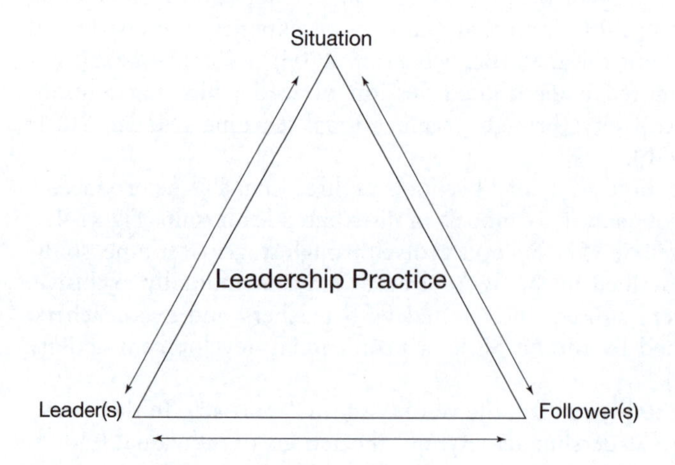

Figure 4.2 Leadership practice

Defined in these terms, distributed leadership is consistent with the school improvement tradition, with its emphasis on teachers working collaboratively to increase motivation and commitment, and with an HRM model that sees empowerment throughout an organization as a major source of energy and productivity.

Reforming social organizations

Despite the promise of these refined and improved models, there is a risk of overestimating the extent to which leadership practice can control the complex combination of variables that shapes the internal structure of schools, or the 'increasingly wild and unpredictable social environment' that impacts on the world of teachers and children (Ball 1987: 10). How can leaders or followers be sure that actions will produce the desired result if the links between variables within a system are irregular and non-linear (Radford 2006)?

Sarason (1996) notes the number and complexity of the different systems that have to change before improvement efforts can succeed. Kotter (1996) shows how the unexpected connections between variables can frustrate change, and has identified eight recurrent obstacles that cause most reform initiatives to fail. As Fullan (1982: 84) acknowledges:

> It is easier to put a person on the moon than to attain the goal of raising reading levels across the country, because the factors keeping reading at its current levels are innumerable, different in different situations, constantly changing, and not conducive to altering on any wide scale.

Social organizations are inextricably involved in society, and are not easily converted into instruments for changing social relationships and altering the processes of cultural reproduction (Bernstein 1970).

A further problem is that the current emphasis on leadership has given the misleading impression that school leaders stand outside the black box of reform, shaping changes without themselves being changed. There is evidence, however, that leaders have life cycles of their own that influence their attitudes and behaviour. As time passes, heads lose their initial idealism and progress through a period of development and consolidation to autonomy, followed by single-loop learning and disenchantment (Day and Bakioğlu 1996). This is also true for groups and teams. In the formative period, there is an emotional focus on issues of inclusion, power, influence, acceptance, intimacy and identity. As a group progresses to maturity, however, the focus shifts to preserving the group and its culture, with creativity and member differences being seen as a threat (Schein 2004).

Optimism about available leadership models should be qualified, therefore, by an awareness that:

- social organizations are complex and embedded in the wider society;
- leaders and followers are subject to life cycle-related changes that may compromise their sustained effectiveness;
- the impact on outcomes may be smaller than expected.

The case studies presented below describe two contrasting schools where major change programmes have been sustained for more than 15 years. Each investigation is based on repeated interviews with 20 participants over a six-year period. In this way, substantial empirical data have been gathered about how staff, students and governors perceived their improvement journeys. Very few studies have revisited the same schools a number of years later, so the stories told here represent an unusual opportunity to review evidence about the validity of the claims made for transformational and distributed leadership (Gray 2001).

Case study 1 examines how far a long-serving head at Norcross School in the north of England was able to mobilize his colleagues to make a real difference to student outcomes, despite the social disadvantage experienced by the local community. Can transformational heads close the achievement gap? *Case study 2* investigates the impact of changes in leadership and direction on Felix Holt School. Are transformations sustainable despite individual and group life cycles?

Case study 1: overcoming social disadvantage at Norcross School

This case study is based on work by Barker (2009).

Norcross School is located in a former coalfield, with high social deprivation and limited employment opportunities. When John Turner was appointed head, the pupil roll had fallen from approximately 1,800 to less than 1,000 in under 10 years. About 30 children a year migrated from the area to neighbouring schools.

Colleagues admired John Turner's passion and intense, hands-on commitment. They said he was first to arrive and last to leave. He worked tirelessly for the good of the school, motivating others through his charisma and example. Accessible to staff and students, he walked the classrooms and corridors, and supervised breaks in the windswept grounds.

He at once embarked on a host of reforms to raise achievement. Many parents did not value education and condoned their children's absence for less than convincing reasons. A 'positive culture' group was established to identify ways to celebrate student achievement. A new school day and timetable were introduced. Policies for marking and homework were given a high priority. Progress was checked against agreed performance indicators, including examination results and student planner completion rates.

By Turner's fourth year, an upward trend in GCSE results had emerged. Results in mathematics improved immediately after a new head of department was appointed. Indifferent teachers were squeezed out, and the climate became uncomfortable for anyone not committed to student achievement. The head delegated responsibility; standards were emphasized repeatedly; rewards, praise and celebration became a way of life; team spirit soared, especially as the school began to succeed; and the only rules were those needed to ensure clarity and consistency.

After an Ofsted inspection, new improvements were introduced under the title 'Raising Expectations Mark 2'. The head challenged truancy and absence, which were as high as 80 per cent in some Year 11 forms. A governor committee was set up; individual poor attenders and their families were targeted for letters and the Educational Welfare Officer visited; a class register system was introduced.

Benchmark data were gathered for every student, and individual attainment monitored against estimated grades. Senior managers supported every curriculum area, working with heads of department, observing lessons, and helping colleagues improve their methods. SMT members mentored Year 11 students, and primary liaison was extended to include cross-phase language development. By 1997, Ofsted concluded that better teaching was producing a steady improvement in results.

Performance trends at Norcross are presented in Figure 4.3. The dotted line shows a hypothetical *natural* trend for GCSE results, calculated to match the average percentage obtaining 5+ A*–C grades at comparable local schools, based on eligibility for free school meals (FSMs). Before the head's arrival, results at Norcross were well below those obtained at neighbouring schools serving similar villages.

At first, Norcross accelerated, catching up with its rivals. After this, however, the school struggled to maintain parity with national increases in results. In other words, once schools return to their *natural* trend line (a prediction based on the percentage eligible for FSMs), further measurable

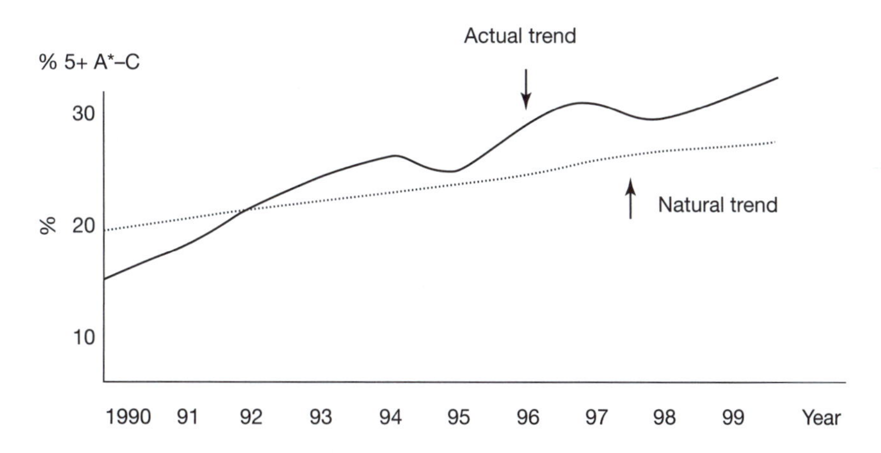

Figure 4.3 GCSE trends at Norcross

improvements in GCSE outcomes are exceptionally difficult to achieve without a substantial change in intake.

Despite this discouraging finding, the head pressed on, attending LPSH in 1999. LPSH data (processed on behalf of NCSL by Hay Diagnostics) suggested that he had created an outstandingly positive organizational climate at Norcross, while interview data confirmed that in his tenth year he continued to be an exceptional motivating force.

However, teachers were quick to identify an important obstacle that Turner had not tackled. In conversations with a visiting consultant, they described one deputy as an amiable but limited man who avoided work. Another was seen as someone who 'stores grievances; he glares at you, people are fearful and wary of him'. There were complaints that this deputy 'is nasty for the sake of being nasty; he humiliates people for being late'. The head was liberated when he read the consultant's report: 'This is a paradigm buster. I've just assumed the SMT couldn't change.' Within 18 months, two members of the SMT had departed, and a new structure, with assistant heads reporting directly to the head, was established.

Four years later, in 2005, the changes in the SMT were perceived very positively. An assistant head said the departure of the deputies had been pivotal, creating cultural change and enabling the school to move in new directions. Senior management was highly rated, and responsibility was dispersed widely through the school.

Yet although results have improved, teachers believe there are definite limits to what can be achieved in this former coalfield area: 'We're going in the right direction but you are working with definite limitations.' The annual GCSE 5+ A*–C percentages achieved between 2002 and 2005 (see Table 4.1) broadly confirm this picture, with steady but slow progress that lags behind local and national averages.

Discussion

John Turner emerges from this account as an exceptional leader who has won the respect and trust of his colleagues and students over a period of 16 years. He has sustained his enthusiasm despite the unpromising social and economic environment of the former coalfields. There is no sign of his losing direction or lapsing into disillusionment, unlike heads in other studies (Weindling and Earley 1987; Day and Bakioğlu 1996). On the contrary,

Table 4.1 GCSE higher grades at Norcross: recent trends

Year	*2002*	*2003*	*2004*	*2005*
Norcross percentage of 5+ A*–C	34	30	33	39
Percentage below local average	6	10	8	6
Percentage below national average	18	23	21	17

his LPSH data after ten years confirmed his continued ability to create a strongly positive climate and to motivate his colleagues. The school community perceives him as an energetic figure whose vision and optimism have provided energy and reassurance in difficult times.

Although Turner displays many characteristics found in transformational leaders (Judkins and Rudd 2005), his long-term tolerance of a dysfunctional SMT suggests that fully distributed, facilitative leadership, in the terms defined by the NCSL, can be difficult to achieve. At Norcross, it is reported to have developed only recently. For ten years, the head was inclined to consult and delegate rather than facilitate. Decisions were made 'at more senior levels' and staff exercised initiative within 'clear areas of responsibility' (NCSL 2004: 16). Judged on many criteria, nevertheless, Norcross is a school transformed, far better led and managed than at any time in its recent history. The intake has improved, partner schools are better and the results are on an upward trajectory. There is high-quality teaching and learning. John Turner has applied a rigorous regime of target-setting and monitoring of the type recommended by government agencies, while Ofsted inspections have praised his success.

Despite Turner's sustained ability to energize colleagues and create internal structures to raise expectations and celebrate achievement, the data show that the dominant influence on student outcomes remains 'extreme social disadvantage' (DfES 2003b: 1). The local context has exerted a greater influence on results than other organizational variables. Although Norcross is just one school, and alone neither confirms nor refutes claims that exceptional leaders can change the system, this finding is consistent with reports that relative underachievement is common to areas with 'relatively high levels of deprivation' (DfES 2001: v) and justifies pessimism about the prospects for transforming results (Mortimore and Whitty 2000).

Norcross suggests that even when an inspiring leader has implemented government recommendations in full, endemic social and cultural problems continue to shape student performance. The head mobilized 'the passion and commitment of teachers' and since 2002 has distributed leadership effectively, but still the achievement gap has not been closed (Table 4.1). On the contrary, this study corroborates others (Bell *et al.* 2003) that have found school leaders to have no more than a small, indirect and mediated impact on examination results.

Case study 2: leadership succession and change at Felix Holt School

This case study is based on work by Barker (2006).

The headline numbers at Felix Holt School, located in an older industrial part of the Mid Valley but also near affluent villages and suburbs, suggest that a transformation has taken place. Since 1992, the number on roll has risen from 550 students to 1,200, while the GCSE 5+ A*–C score has risen sharply. After a period of slow decline under a long-serving and disillusioned head, two very different leaders have driven Felix Holt forward.

Arriving in 1992, Brian Tyzack was seen as a 'new broom sweeping clean, very young, all guns blazing, very enthusiastic'. He was 'like Lenny Henry turning round a failing school . . . he was a good communicator, a salesman; he tackled graffiti, excluded a few children to make the point that poor behaviour would not be tolerated and was hands-on about the school'.

He visited every primary school and announced, 'I've not come to be in charge of a failing school.' He supported the staff 'to the hilt, regardless'; he knew everyone and was determined to reverse the school's reputation as a place you went to 'because you couldn't get in anywhere else'. Relationships with inherited senior managers were less positive, however, and several years passed before the head found a congenial inner group of colleagues.

The school became 'a children's school', and public formalities (like standing up in assembly) were scrapped. Pupils remember that he was 'constantly around the school, knew everyone's name, was very active'. Tyzack had a laugh and teased the children, but also purged poor behaviour and rooted out disloyal and idle staff. He was 'ruthless' and challenged departments that 'had nothing happening'.

The school decided to pursue grant-maintained status (GMS), seeing it as a way to avoid closure. The old guard moved on or retired, while new managers arrived to run the sixth form, technology and pastoral care. Newly recruited teachers were promoted. A system of departmental review was introduced, and pupil data were collected. The new head of technology 'took charge of pastoral care and had a major impact on parents and children to whom he related well'. Another internal promotion was placed in charge of primary liaison and helped the steady rise in numbers.

Staff were convinced that GMS 'helped get the basics right – the mould was broken'. Extra funds were available and 'dilapidated buildings started to look fantastic'. GMS also led to a more active and committed governing body. The new chair became particularly proactive.

The head recognized that GMS had enhanced his 'chief executive' role. His attitude was 'I'm running a business'. A new sports centre project, funded by selling off part of the grounds, became intrinsic to the head's vision. As the scope, complications and costs of the proposed centre grew, however, the head 'detached himself emotionally from the project' and said that he felt he 'couldn't do more'. The chair of governors encouraged Tyzack to take extended leave to recover from his evident exhaustion. A year tutor felt that the head was 'beginning to lose momentum . . . there were explosions, things were never stable'. Colleagues felt that he chose the right time to move on, for himself and for the school.

Brian Tyzack was reputed to have 'turned the school round', with the numbers at 11+ up from 74 in 1993 to 186 by 1998; the ability profile had been raised; and the public reputation of the school had been transformed.

On the other hand, the GCSE 5+ A*–C percentage in 1998 placed Felix Holt bottom of the local league.

Although Felix Holt was oversubscribed for the first time in its history that autumn, and 'a brighter, more middle-class intake' was recruited from local primaries, the arrival of the new head, Steven Stuart, in January 1999, could have jeopardized all that had been achieved. Stuart was not perceived to be as dynamic as his high-profile predecessor, and his speeches at public events sounded nervous. According to one teacher, 'the head's confidence took a real bashing' as a member of the SMT set out to undermine him. A year head reports that 'warring factions were obvious to the staff'.

Youthful, inexperienced colleagues were recruited to fill the gaps left by departing older teachers. By 2003, only two middle managers had been in their current posts more than three years. There was high staff turnover and a 'huge arrival of young innovators'. Student and staff numbers rose sharply.

Stuart decided not to compete with his predecessor's 'one guy on a white horse' leadership style. The school needed professional systems, he believed, not a charismatic performance, so he set out to be 'straight and supportive'. A long-serving science teacher noticed that in Brian Tyzack's time there was 'one person at the top' whereas the new head 'split the workload among the managers'.

The sudden improvement in GCSE results (up from 13 per cent in 1998 to 42 per cent in 1999) two terms after Stuart's arrival was probably due to the better-quality students Tyzack had managed to recruit from local primary schools for the September 1994 intake. Stuart and the governors interpreted the results as evidence that the school had been transformed.

Steven Stuart engineered a loyal, committed team able to drive the school forward, and prompted the departure of less useful colleagues. By the summer of 2002, the entire inherited SMT had been replaced, including the business manager. As the head began to trust this new team, colleagues noticed continuous dialogue becoming a feature of his approach.

The school is heavily oversubscribed each year. After radical restructuring, the sixth form has expanded from 64 students in 1998 to 203 in 2003. An English teacher reflects, 'Children see the school as high-achieving and valued; they are told it so often that they perform to expectations.' As a Year 9 pupil said, 'If you don't do well, people will be disappointed . . . it's motivating but also it's pressure.'

Discussion

Like John Turner, Brian Tyzack was perceived as a charismatic leader, with a strong emphasis on behaviour, attendance, targets and standards. A new staffing structure, together with systems for developing the curriculum, and for monitoring teaching and learning, built capacity for later improvement. Tyzack was an inspirational 'salesman' who roamed the school to find out what teachers needed, and made them 'want to work for him'. Unlike

Turner, Tyzack was more of an heroic 'mould-breaker' than a source of strength for others. There were eight redundancies among the 'old guard', suggesting resistance rather than improved commitment and motivation. Tyzack's galvanizing impact and opportunistic plunge into GMS, together with the sports centre project, show that he resembled one of Belbin's *shapers* rather than a facilitative, NCSL-type leader concerned to work through others. New arrivals led change initiatives but a stable team was slow to emerge, perhaps because Tyzack, as a shaper, was 'impatient and easily frustrated', even prone to aggression (Belbin 1981: 59).

His *frontiersman* style was different from approved transformational models. At the time of his departure in 1998, Tyzack displayed marked symptoms of disenchantment, and his personal life cycle was at variance with the school's. His *shaper* method had outlived its usefulness and his 'resonance' had faded. The visible transformation of Felix Holt seemed to be wrapped up in the distinctive personality of the head, while the examination results were no better than before. When Tyzack departed suddenly, his achievements seemed intangible and vulnerable. The long-term value of his mould-breaking contribution would have been lost but for the tenacity of his successor.

At first, Steven Stuart seemed to lack charisma and found himself in conflict with other senior managers. Some of the people brought in by Brian Tyzack resisted the new head and were obstacles to his plans. Stuart deliberately adopted an approach that contrasted with the imagery of a 'guy on a white horse'. Instead of relying on style and emotional 'resonance', he mobilized various sources of power to undermine and remove problematic people and structures, while maintaining an unobtrusive personal demeanour. High levels of staff turnover created an opportunity to establish effective teams and systems.

Stuart was persistent in creating enduring management structures and processes, and was successful in exploiting the benefits of the improved reputation and intake achieved by Tyzack. He operated from a deeper position than his predecessor, aiming to empower rather than overshadow his colleagues. He began to distribute responsibility through a trusted team but within a delegated rather than a facilitative framework (John 2007).

The remarkable improvement in GCSE grades (from 13 per cent in 1998 to 72 per cent in 2006) demonstrates the success of the two heads in creating the conditions for transformation. Felix Holt was once a small, underperforming school; it is now twice as big and its results (see Table 4.2)

Table 4.2 GCSE higher grades at Felix Holt: recent trends

Year	*2003*	*2004*	*2005*	*2006*
Felix Holt percentage 5+ A*–C	51	57	68	72
Percentage above local average	–7	–1	+7	+8
Percentage above national average	–2	+3	+12	+14

compare favourably with those of other schools, locally and nationally. Tyzack's reputational breakthrough enabled more and better students to be recruited from mixed and highly mobile local communities. The school was fortunate, therefore, that successive heads possessed skills and qualities well suited to the internal and external environments in which they found themselves, and that the potentially disruptive consequences of changing heads were contained.

Felix Holt also illustrates how a leader's life cycle, departure and replacement may influence the conditions for improvement. Rather than exuding beams of emotional energy that provide a consistent source of stimulus for their colleagues, the two heads' motivational impact fluctuated as they passed through individual phases of initiation, development, autonomy and disenchantment. Ebbs and flows of leadership energy, at all levels within an organization, are an underestimated influence on improvement trajectories (Goleman *et al.* 2003). In the right circumstances, with the right leaders, schools can recreate themselves and transformation can be sustained over time, but success is very far from certain, and may be limited by all-pervasive social conditions or undermined by unexpected events.

Conclusion: leaders and change

Respondents at Norcross and Felix Holt confirm the importance of leaders in developing their organizations. All three heads succeeded in creating a climate that had a marked effect on how teachers and children felt about themselves and their schools. At their best, the heads enabled a high proportion of their colleagues to feel part of a special, rewarding journey. The variations in personality and behaviour between John Turner, Brian Tyzack and Steven Stuart suggest that there is no simple formula or template for transforming schools, only 'a magic about a fine leader in action which the College cannot bottle' (NCSL 2006a). Brian Tyzack, in particular, had an explosive, challenging style that he could not have learned on an LPSH programme. Steven Stuart consciously chose not to be a charismatic leader, and worked behind the scenes to achieve many of his improvements. Some people succeed by being triumphantly themselves, while others adopt a self-conscious mix of selected styles.

As Felix Holt shows, success is never secure or guaranteed, because the cast of players in the staffroom changes over time to produce unpredictable micro-political manoeuvres with incalculable consequences. Individual and group life cycles can interrupt the best-laid plans and may jeopardize an apparently well-grounded transformation. The risks of leadership succession are unjustly neglected in the improvement literature.

These case studies also encourage scepticism about the ability of transformational leaders to bring about remarkable improvements in results, or to close the gap between advantaged and disadvantaged groups of students. John Turner displayed all the characteristics associated with transformational leadership and produced changes that were admired by colleagues and successive inspection teams. Even so, deprivation continued to be the main influence on student achievement at Norcross.

After five years of Brian Tyzack's transformational drive, there was no evidence of an impact on GCSE performance at Felix Holt. By the time the examination results did improve, Felix Holt was a different school, with twice as many students and staff, and a completely new set of people. Brian Tyzack and Steven Stuart have transformed the school to the point where it makes little sense to compare results from the small, run-down version of Felix Holt that existed in 1992 with its present incarnation as a large specialist science college with excellent facilities and resources.

The case studies also confirm that the level of trust required for distributed leadership and effective teamwork is not easily established (Fullan 2003). John Turner worked round two frustrating deputies for ten years before he was able to develop a distributed leadership approach. Brian Tyzack battled with the 'old guard' and introduced new people to run key initiatives. Steven Stuart engaged in deep micro-political manoeuvres before he was able to engineer a loyal and committed SMT. Strong leadership of the type recommended by the government in the late 1990s seems to have been the default mode for all three heads (DfEE 1997). Much of their distribution of leadership seems to have been opportunistic or incremental rather than cultural or strategic (see Figure 4.1). At none of these schools was a collaborative culture fully established. Instead, responsibility for the curriculum and pedagogy was delegated along traditional lines. The next chapter considers the role of groups and teams in developing distributed leadership and collaborative cultures in educational settings.

5 Empowering groups and teams

(with Dave Allman)

Self-managing teams

This chapter examines claims that self-directed or self-managing teams have the potential to empower employees and increase their motivation so that organizational performance and productivity are enhanced. Examples of successful teamwork in business and commerce are reviewed and the potential benefits for education are considered. A case study of teamwork at Felix Holt, an English comprehensive, illustrates the advantages and limitations of self-managing teams within prevailing structures and conditions.

The self-directed or self-managing team, described by *Fortune* magazine as 'the productivity breakthrough of the nineties', is now widely established in business, with at least 90 per cent of North American organizations operating some type of self-managed work team. Empowerment through self-management has been established as a powerful way to mobilize the workforce in the quest for improved quality and productivity. Traditional organizations, outsmarted by more agile competitors in a turbulent environment, have turned to their employees, encouraging a high degree of involvement in which the workers make decisions for themselves (Elmuti 1997; Fisher 2000). Expectations are very high, encouraged by the 'possibility that a team will generate magic – producing something extraordinary, a collective creation of previously unimagined quality or beauty' (Hackman 2002: viii). Tom Peters, the best-selling author and business guru, now regards self-management as the basic organizational building block (Elmuti 1997).

Self-directed teamwork is seen as a revolutionary approach to management that stands traditional human resource practice on its head. Whereas traditional work groups expected to be told what to do, self-directed teams take the initiative. While traditional work groups sought individual rewards, blamed others and acted competitively, self-directed teams focus on team contributions, develop solutions and cooperate. They continually improve and innovate, but without demanding more resources, as traditional work groups were wont to do. They work proactively to avoid emergencies and save money by improving quality (Elmuti 1997).

Successful empowerment has been found (Brower 1995) to depend on self-directed teams that:

- have the authority to make many, though not unlimited, decisions;
- are accountable for their actions and outcomes;
- are aligned in terms of vision, mission, values and goals at all levels, in every function, team and individual;
- are aligned along three dimensions: (1) internally, (2) horizontally with customers, suppliers and other functions, and (3) vertically with the direction of the parent organization;
- have the ability to do their usual work in addition to directing themselves.

Educators who believe that distributed leadership and collaborative cultures have the power to transform our schools and colleges are encouraged by the strongly positive experience of self-directed teams in business and industry over the past 15 years (NCSL 2004; MacBeath 2005). The self-directed team seems to have the potential to liberate teachers and support staff from established, hierarchical structures, and to empower them to enhance the student experience.

Teamwork

The advantages of teamwork are well known. Any individual, including the boss, has a limited impact on outcomes, but with teamwork the potential effects are multiplied. Team members possess a variety of expertise, skills, personalities and abilities that complement one another and create a task-related team dynamic. The pooling of energy and expertise produces an outcome that is greater than the sum of individual actions, and stimulates learning. Teams can tackle a greater range of problems, generate peer pressure and commitment, and place the responsibility for identifying and solving problems with those who are closest to them (Morrison 1998; Bennett *et al.* 2003; Bush and Middlewood 2005).

Teams are not automatically successful, however. From a survey of 6,000 respondents, LaFasto and Larson (2001: xii) conclude that:

- team members can be either collaborative and easy to work with, or dysfunctional and counterproductive, thereby diminishing and even ruining the team effort;
- good teams are highly dependent on relationships, which can be simple and easy or complicated and hard;
- what matters in the end is whether the right decisions are made fast enough;
- team leaders can either help or hinder a team's performance;
- an organization's environment can either encourage or discourage working together easily in terms of management practices, systems and rewards.

It seems that organization members are not always convinced that teams work better than the alternatives. When organizational conditions are unfavourable, teamwork does not flourish. For those directly involved, personal styles, capabilities and preferences can make team membership feel risky or uncomfortable (Castka *et al.* 2001). A study of 111 teams in four organizations found that the level of employee empowerment depended on the actions of external leaders, the responsibilities given to the teams themselves, the team-based human resource policies adopted, and the social structure of the teams (Kirkman and Rosen 1999). The single most important way to increase group effectiveness, however, is to set clear group objectives. This is because the clarity or specificity of goals predicts group performance outcomes (Curral *et al.* 2001). In addition, five conditions are essential for team success (Hackman 2002):

- having a real team;
- having a compelling direction;
- an enabling team structure;
- a supportive organizational context;
- expert team coaching.

Teams in education

Despite the hierarchical structure of schools and school systems, distributed leadership and teamwork are well established in one form or another. Senior managers and their colleagues have long espoused the idea of a community of professional practice, where involvement, cooperation, participation, delegation and effective two-way communication are the essence of good management (Weindling and Earley 1987; Bell 1992). School leaders report themselves as being at various points on a spectrum of distributed leadership, and few would now argue for a more paternalistic or authoritarian style.

In fact, empowerment seems to start at the top, with effective heads extending their own influence by sharing their responsibilities with a supportive group of colleagues. A key factor distinguishing effective heads is their readiness to risk losing control by sharing and delegating tasks. The degree to which the head is prepared to share impacts on the extent to which individual members of the team contribute, and on the level of team synergy that develops (Wallace 2001).

The culture of teamwork that has developed in many schools seems to involve a tension between two apparently contradictory beliefs. Typical senior leadership team (SLT) members accept the management hierarchy, with the head enjoying differential status, salary and accountability levels, but they also believe in their own entitlement to make an equal contribution to team decisions. Despite this tension, delegation, distribution and consultation have become accepted norms, and these depend on the operation of a wide variety of teams for their success.

The shift towards distributed leadership and teamwork has proved just as challenging for middle managers. Their roles and responsibilities have grown to include (Dew 2000):

- maintaining focus on mission;
- managing the feedback systems;
- defining team boundaries;
- raising the bar;
- involving teams in strategy;
- assessing team performance;
- mediating conflict;
- championing cross-functional efforts;
- coaching the coaches;
- assuring recognition.

Such an extensive remit requires post-holders to cope with more significant ambiguities and tensions than those found in a functional, task-based culture.

Whereas traditional managers were admired for their decisiveness and ability to direct subordinates, empowering team leaders have the much more difficult task of motivating their colleagues and encouraging them to make their own decisions. In schools and colleges, especially, middle leaders have constantly to switch roles and lines of accountability between different aspects of their work (Brower 1995; Wise and Busher 2001). They are expected to fulfil at least four operational roles and to provide leadership in each of them (Morris and Dennison 1982: 40):

- a professional role as a classroom teacher;
- an organizational role within the department;
- a corporate role within the school as part of the administrative structure;
- a personal role.

As intermediaries in an externally driven structure, middle managers also experience uncomfortable tensions when they are obliged to justify directives from above or defend their team against challenges and threats from without (McConville 2006). Flexing between roles, they seek space within a loosely coupled system to reconcile competing demands and priorities (Weick 1988). External accountability requirements and the internal pressures they create can reduce or subvert the empowering potential of teamwork. Permanent teams operating in these conditions may become defensive and resistant to change, limiting the middle manager's room for manoeuvre and scope for leadership (O'Neill 1997).

The NCSL's *Leading from the Middle* programme (NCSL 2007) encourages development in five key areas to help middle managers overcome these difficulties:

1. leadership of innovation and change;
2. knowledge and understanding of their role in leading teaching and learning;
3. enhancing self-confidence and skills as team leaders;
4. building team capacity through the efficient use of staff and resources;
5. active engagement in self-directed change in a blended learning environment.

Team empowerment also depends upon a range of organizational conditions, some of which can be significant sources of frustration. The degree of trust between leaders and followers is perhaps the most important of these. The intimacy, cohesion and directedness of the successful team are undermined whenever an individual member ceases to be worthy of trust. A team member may be insufficiently competent at assigned tasks, or not deliver what has been promised or agreed. The individual may fail to maintain high standards of confidentiality and truthfulness, or be less than committed to team goals. A single obstacle of this nature is sufficient to derail an entire change initiative, and may render one or more teams unproductive and disrupt the work of the whole organization (Kotter 1996; Reina and Reina 1999).

Lack of trust may be compounded when team members adopt divergent social styles or have incompatible personal characteristics. For instance, the different individual social styles adopted by members of administrative teams have been blamed for the frustration, unresolved conflict, hidden agendas, unspoken questions, and confusion about decisions and goals at many community colleges in the US (Darling and McNutt 1996). Team members seem to perform better when they share common characteristics, while interpersonal attraction may aid group cohesion and promote positive team processes (Van Vianen and De Dreu 2001).

Unfortunately, teams that achieve a high degree of consensus run the risk of *group-think*, manifested in a reluctance to examine alternative goals and practices. Strong cohesion can make it difficult to induct new members and to avoid inter-group rivalry and ill-feeling (Morrison 1998). On the other hand, differences in individual motivation and behaviour can also compromise teamwork. People vary considerably in their desire for responsibility or autonomy in decision-making. Not everyone is eager to be empowered. A given leadership style may encourage self-leadership in some but leave others confused and insecure (Yun *et al.* 2006).

Size is another influence on team effectiveness. Larger teams, especially those concerned with change and innovation, can struggle to agree on shared objectives. The more people there are in a team, the harder it is to involve them all, and to build trust (Curral *et al.* 2001). Interviewed during a study of team effectiveness, the head at one school declared:

> I have always stuck out against a larger team because I couldn't see how I could make it workable on a regular basis. I couldn't imagine how

> I could have regular and meaningful meetings with seven or eight people . . . I don't think you can have genuine discussions in a group that size.
>
> (Wallace and Huckman 2003: 232)

There are questions, too, about the extent to which the benefits of group synergy apply to a profession that 'is almost invariably a solitary activity' (O'Neill 1997: 83). Teaching itself is not a team job; an individual adult most often works only with a group of children. How relevant, then, is the concept of the self-directed team to a group of employees who have day-to-day responsibility for managing themselves, and who work with little direct supervision (O'Neill 1997; Fisher 2000; Vogt 2003)?

Group formation and development

Whatever their operational conditions, successful teams also depend on complex, often unseen, processes of formation and development. Human groups pass through various stages and cycles that have great significance for their behaviour and produce remarkable fluctuations in energy and performance. There is, for example, a tendency for a newly formed group to rely on its leader. Yet as members become familiar with one another, they emphasize the group itself and their commitment to one another. Later, as the group begins to perform, the emotional focus shifts towards accomplishing the mission and maintaining harmonious working relationships. At this point, member differences are valued because they are seen to contribute to group effectiveness. As the group matures, however, members know who they are and where they are going, so regard new ideas and internal differences as threats to be overcome rather than as learning opportunities (Schein 2004).

Bruce Tuckman's (1965) famous stages of group formation and development have clear implications for performance:

1. *Forming*. Individuals join the group. During the induction process, they meet and form relationships with others who vary in age, experience and career development.
2. *Storming*. New groups 'shake down' as roles are assumed, agreed or decided. Members test and practise various working methods. Tensions and conflicts are resolved and group identity is established.
3. *Norming*. The group achieves operational efficiency. Roles are enacted. Work is completed. 'Norms' are established in terms of behaviour and working practice. Individual and group attitudes and aspirations are aligned.
4. *Performing*. With experience and expertise, peak performance is achieved. Effective teamwork, developed over time, enables individuals to achieve more than if they were working in isolation.

Although Tuckman later added a fifth stage to describe the closure and mourning of a mission, it is tempting to consider an alternative *fading* stage, where *organizational pathos* sets in and tiredness, stress and over-familiarity reduce the advantages of a group's maturity and experience. At this point, members sense they have 'seen it all before', so work begins to lose the buzz necessary for high performance (Tuckman and Jensen 1977; Hoyle 1986; Barker 2001).

The Development cycles model (Figure 5.1) illustrates the implications of these stages for a typical school. There are many overlapping groups of varying size, including, for example, the SLT, the whole-staff team, subject departments, pastoral teams and short-life task groups (e.g. school production, curriculum review). Each has its own life history and has arrived at a stage of group development that reflects the arrival time and mutual accommodation of its leader and followers. At the same time, however, there is constant interaction between the teams, and frequent disturbance as individuals seek to influence one another, the work of a particular group and the overall mission. The stages themselves are not fixed, and teams progress through alternating phases of inertia and revolution in their work behaviour.

The model in Figure 5.1 suggests that, even with distributed leadership and a strong commitment to teamwork, it is not easy to micro-manage these complex relationships in order to secure continuous, sustained improvements

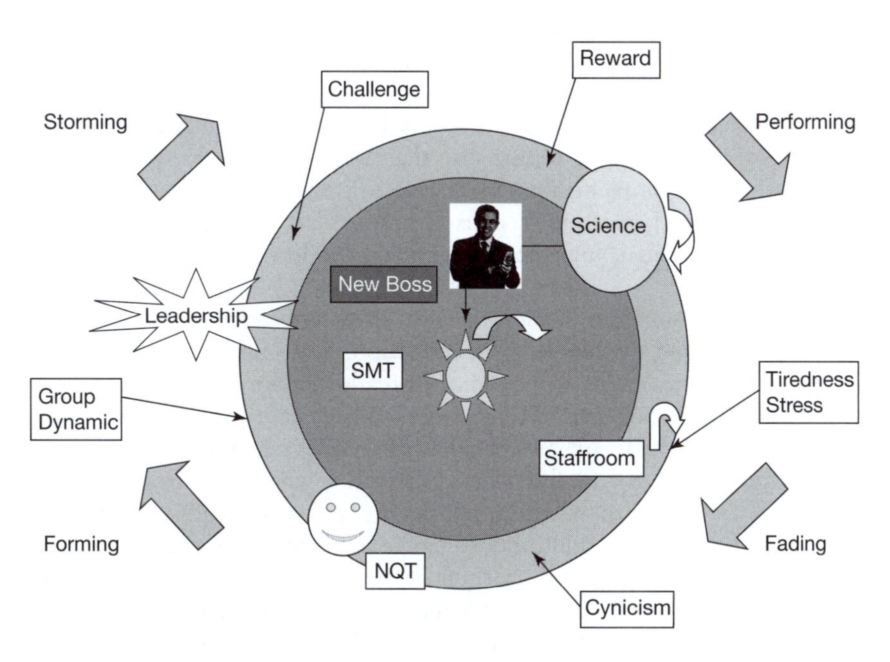

Figure 5.1 Development cycles model

in performance, especially as there is a continuous risk of group maturity leading to *fading* performance and reduced learning capacity (Wallace 2002).

Team roles

Belbin's (1981) research into effective teams may offer a solution to this problem. One hundred and twenty teams competed in business games, with the membership of each varied to test the value of particular combinations of skill, intelligence and psychological make-up. Team members were found to contribute in distinctive ways, and it became clear that a balance of skills and styles was more important for success than outstanding intellectual ability. Eight team roles were identified as important for effective teams:

1 chairman – sets objectives, values contributions;
2 company worker – practical organizer;
3 shaper – drives and challenges;
4 plant – develops imaginative ideas;
5 resource investigator – explores opportunities;
6 monitor-evaluator – assesses ideas and progress;
7 team worker – promotes team spirit;
8 completer-finisher – sees things through.

Belbin found that the winning teams had a spread of mental abilities, a spread of personal attributes, a distribution of member responsibilities that matched their different capabilities, and the ability to recognize and adjust for imbalances in the group. In other words, team effectiveness depends on members recognizing and adjusting to their relative strengths so they adopt appropriate and complementary roles. Selecting a winning team is, therefore, an intricate operation, requiring considerable skill. If the people and the roles are right and aligned, high performance will follow (Belbin 1981; Fisher *et al.* 2001).

With the assistance of widespread psychometric testing, Belbin's team roles have entered the language of education. SLT members tested on the Myers–Briggs Personality Type Indicator readily acknowledge that they are 'company workers' or 'completer-finishers' (Fisher *et al.* 2001). Nonetheless, there is growing evidence that specialized team roles may not be as important as previously thought. Belbin was researching when organizations were relatively static, and managers could devote their time to the problems of closed systems. Today, continuous change is inevitable, so team members should devote more energy to learning. Multi-skilled, flexible teams may be better than specialized, role-centred ones. Moreover, the idea of specialized team roles does not seem consistent with empowerment (McCrimmon 1995).

Case study: improving teamwork at Felix Holt School

How important are distributed leadership and teamwork for school improvement, and how far is the potential of the self-directed team frustrated by current structures and conditions? After several years of disappointing results, the head and his senior colleagues at Felix Holt School contrived to appoint new heads of faculty in three key areas: science, English, and information and communication technologies (ICT). An unpublished study by Dave Allman dating from 2007 investigates the roles, styles and strategies adopted by these new appointees as they worked to enhance teamwork and improve student results. His analysis provides a glimpse of the shifting calculations leadership team members made as they embarked on changing middle management structures and personnel. It also illustrates just how complex and unpredictable are the processes of team-building and development.

Failing departments

Senior managers at the school had been concerned about science and English for several years, partly because the Key Stage 3 and GCSE results in these core areas were improving less rapidly than elsewhere, and partly because the old subject leaders were not contributing to the school's overall development as expected. The science faculty seemed entrenched and complacent. Teachers were pleased with the relatively high level of achievement at GCSE and saw no reason to embrace change. The head of faculty played only a limited role in writing the successful bid for specialist Science College status, and discouraged his colleagues from innovations that would dilute tried and trusted methods. Although there was an effective liaison programme with local primary partners, few teachers promoted science beyond their own laboratories. An Ofsted subject-specific inspection found that the pace of change at Key Stage 3 was too slow, and that specialist status was having little impact on the rest of the school. Although one or two teachers acknowledged, privately, that the faculty had stagnated, there were no signs of significant change before the Ofsted subject inspection. Immediately after the report was received, the old head of faculty retired, six months earlier than expected. James, the Key Stage 4 coordinator at that time, was appointed acting head of faculty.

In the English faculty, five very different leaders in as many years had rendered relationships between colleagues dysfunctional. Personal animosities seemed more important than the classroom. Teaching was poorly organized, with individuals working in isolation and deciding their own priorities. Schemes of work and resources were inadequate. Although Felix Holt had a plausible cross-curricular literacy policy, there was no consistent drive to improve practice. Moreover, the 2005 Ofsted inspection commented on the need to improve students' literacy skills and their ability to learn independently. After previous difficulties in finding suitable applicants for the head of faculty position, the SLT decided to advertise the latest vacancy as an assistant headship, with responsibility for English. When William arrived, one term before the start of Allman's study, he found his new colleagues ground down by the lack of direction, structure and resources, and well aware of the need for change.

Shibata, the third appointee, was put in charge of a newly created faculty for professional studies. The departure of the disorganized head of ICT and one of his colleagues provided an unexpected opportunity to merge ICT with business and vocational education. It was hoped that the new head of professional studies would build an effective team to deliver ICT across the curriculum.

Perceived solutions

The three curriculum areas presented a familiar set of challenges for senior managers hoping to sustain improvement across the curriculum, despite constant arrivals and departures, the shortage of high-quality recruits, and the failing or fading missions of middle leaders. The long-serving head of science had run out of steam and was entrenched in previous practice. The five heads of English in five years had failed to establish credible strategies and imploded in various ways. Relationships in both faculties were deteriorating, with the result that individual teachers occupied isolated, defensive positions and lost the ability to work and learn together. Moreover, despite their strategic significance, science and English did not interact constructively with the rest of the school. In ICT, the head of faculty lacked the skills to build a broad-based team able to teach the subject across the curriculum, and, anyway, there was significant resistance to the idea.

Confronted with increasing evidence of relatively poor performance (Ofsted, test and examination data), the SLT were swift to diagnose middle management failure as the primary cause. Poor or tired leaders were perceived to be responsible for dysfunctional teams that could not collaborate effectively. Opportunities to change middle leaders were seen as critical moments in the improvement journey and grasped, accordingly. The head of science was confronted with negative data; the status and pay of the head of English was raised to attract a high-quality candidate; ICT was merged into a new faculty.

In all three faculties, the SLT expected to delegate sufficient authority to enable the new leader to recreate the faculty's mission so that it matched the school's goals and targets. The SLT aimed to provide additional curriculum time, equipment and resources, and other support, as needed. The deputy head also arranged to mentor the newcomers as they worked to build coherent, collaborative teams. Felix Holt's internal monitoring systems were designed to check their progress towards the intended, sustained improvement in student outcomes. Leadership was distributed, therefore, to the extent that James, William and Shibata were given the authority and control to improve teamwork, efficiency and results.

Allman's interviews with these three heads of department, their subject staff, and members of the SLT, including the headteacher, provide a detailed portrait of a 12-month period when team-building and harmonious collaboration were the primary concern of all involved. Allman's respondents in the three faculties are consistent in describing relatively swift progress towards more effective teamwork, with early hesitation and doubts about the need for change dissolving into enthusiasm for well-led, well-organized faculties, with a growing capacity for self-improvement. Rather than mourning the loss of an allegedly golden era, teachers in science, English and professional studies at Felix Holt praise their present leaders, to whom faintly heroic halos are attached (Hoyle 1986).

Science

Allman's unpublished study describes James's leadership journey in terms of four overlapping phases, as follows.

Shadow of the old leader

James tried to encourage people who wanted to innovate, taking it upon himself to act as a catalyst for improved practice. The old head of faculty allowed him to run science-across-the-curriculum workshops but seemed more concerned with abdicating his own responsibilities than empowering his Key Stage 4 coordinator. He also blocked fundamental change to the practices he had established over time. At this stage, James did not have permission to set a new direction.

Licensed leader

As acting head of faculty, James adopted a tentative, experimental approach to leading the team of which he had so recently been a member. Aware of the adverse impact of the Ofsted inspection and the abrupt departure of the old head of faculty, he adopted a gentle style, seeking to understand how each person was thinking, 'prodding' and 'drip-feeding' those who seemed receptive to change. He walked round the department in the mornings, checking preparations for the day and making sure his colleagues were happy. There was a sense of urgency about basic faculty organization following the change in leadership, but James was also conscious that he had to be seen to deliver on Science College goals.

Authoritative leader

As he grew in confidence in his relationships with colleagues and was confirmed as the permanent head of faculty, James began to lead with greater authority. He found that his slightly shell-shocked colleagues appreciated the extra structure and direction he provided, and welcomed his determination to draw the faculty together so that the strengths of each individual could be deployed to best effect.

Invitational leader

Towards the end of the year, there were signs that James was building an invitational culture. Teachers were moving from the frozen condition engendered by the old head of faculty towards a more fluid, exploratory mode where they volunteered readily for tasks and activities that used to be reserved for the head of faculty, and James himself as Key Stage 4 co-ordinator. All the staff now seemed to have permission to fulfil an extended professional role.

Allman concludes that by the end of the year, faculty members were positive about James's leadership, had accepted the past, and were at ease with the majority of changes that had taken place. They were confident that the faculty had been primed for success in the coming academic year. The head, however, was less certain that improvements in team morale would translate into better student outcomes. In his view, 'the jury is out'.

English

Although William was appointed as an assistant head, with an established track record in middle management, his initial approach to the English faculty was as cautious as James's in science. Aware of the bitter history, he adopted a collegiate style, aiming to nurture, goad and gently push his new colleagues forward. He was encouraging and non-confrontational, and adapted his interpersonal behaviour to get the best out of each member of his team. Teachers saw him as 'genteel' – a person who respected others as people and as professionals. His priority was to build a shared vision and to help teachers contribute to its implementation. William was clear that trust is the foundation for effective teamwork.

In the early stages, he placed a strong emphasis on curriculum planning, new schemes of work, and good-quality resources, so that there was a secure base from which teachers could develop confidence in themselves and the team. William saw what he termed 'proximity' as essential for team-building. Accordingly, he arranged for a room to be converted into a departmental work area. One teacher said that bringing everyone together in one room was the most important thing William had done. Others reported that the morale of the faculty had been turned round. William was seen to encourage individuals and to enthuse the team. The head was impressed, saying, 'Within six months, William has turned the personnel issues round in his department by force of leadership, by consideration, and by getting them all to see how they can work together.'

William's professional expertise gave him a flying start with the wider question of literacy across the curriculum. He was seen to possess a knowledge and understanding of intervention that had been missing before. Even so, respondents were unsure whether literacy was better taught as a result of these activities. Success seemed to depend as much on the attitude of other faculty leaders as on William's own drive and enthusiasm.

Within the faculty, however, English teachers were certain that William's calm, can-do style had enabled them to develop schemes of work, lesson plans and resources that were bound to have a major impact on student performance, although this would take time to work through. Meanwhile, the faculty has become an effective team, conscious of its professional efficiency, and ready to contribute to whole-school themes such as literacy.

Professional studies

Although he was appointed to a new faculty with a demanding mission, Shibata experienced few of the initial interpersonal complications that were present in science and English, and was not obliged to move with undue caution or sensitivity. Instead, he embarked on what the head described as 'nothing short of a revolution'. He introduced an entirely new suite of qualifications at Key Stage 4, persuaded the SLT to make ICT compulsory for all students in Years 10 and 11, and had a major impact on the delivery of cross-curricular ICT.

Shibata was seen as a remorselessly positive and optimistic operator – a strategist who was also an agitator, prepared to make things happen and to support teachers with ideas. According to one deputy head, 'the word "can't" doesn't come into his vocabulary'. He adopted a systematic approach to change, deliberately encouraging a competitive environment where his colleagues could shine. Senior managers commented on important changes in attitude stemming from this activist style. One said:

> He has succeeded in motivating and getting the commitment of his staff; he has actually got them all going forward in the same direction. Evidence of that is that they are willing to come to work in their time off and work above expectations in order to secure really strong pass rates.

New schemes of work were created for Key Stage 3 to accommodate a doubling in curriculum time, while non-specialist ICT teachers were trained to support this expansion and to ensure high-quality provision at all times. A dynamic cross-curricular team was established, something that in the past had existed in name only. Teachers reported that Shibata had opened up ICT for every subject, and commented on the increased numbers coming through.

This success was said to stem from an enthusiastic faculty head who was also a good manager of people, able to give 'a kick up the backside' when required, but eager to praise, as appropriate. Shibata remarked on his own impact, saying, 'Are they disgruntled? I don't think so. Are they tired? Yes, I think they are very tired with the pace of change – they are not used to it, but I don't think I have disgruntled people out there.'

Shibata attributed his own success to 'knowing when to win, when to lose, and when to block'. Faculty members were content that sound foundations were being laid for a long-term sustainable curriculum that would be enriching for all students, whatever their ability.

Distributed leadership and teamwork

Felix Holt provides an example of the strategic distribution of leadership, with the SLT consciously appointing 'individuals to contribute positively to the development of leadership throughout the school'. Interventions were required in science, English and ICT because the school's culture of distribution was insufficiently strong to sustain these subject teams when faculty managers lost direction or failed. A critical Ofsted report revealed that the science team was frozen into a defensive posture, while the English faculty seemed to have become incapable of working collaboratively. The ICT team was not effective in helping other faculties with the integration of computer-related learning. School policies (Literacy, Science College) had limited impact because the relevant faculty teams were not engaged with their colleagues in other areas and tended to operate in isolation.

The science faculty also illustrates the impact of development cycles on individuals and teams. The head of science was a respected middle manager, but after many years in post his sense of mission and direction had faded. Consequently, team members were reluctant to respond to the opportunities generated by the school's success in winning specialist science status. Group dynamics became unproductive and members of the team admitted that they were 'shambolic' and had 'stagnated'.

The SLT was unable to improve effectiveness while the three faculties were trapped in the *mourning* or *fading* stage of their respective development cycles. New leaders were needed to rebuild faculty coordination, cohesion and commitment. All those involved in the study plainly believed that positive teamwork was an essential precondition for improvement. Although these teachers spend a considerable part of each day working alone with children, they are adamant that a sense of team identity, direction and respect are vital for success. The intense demands of the performance agenda seem to have increased teachers' awareness of their physical isolation and their need for collaborative, collegial relationships.

The stories of the three faculties show the role played by middle managers as enablers of distributed leadership and teamwork. James, William and Shibata inherited *fading* teams but within months all three faculties are reported to have achieved operational efficiency (*norming*) and to have had the capacity to achieve peak performance (*performing*). All three leaders made getting people on board a priority, but combined consideration for individual needs with a determination to align their faculties with school goals. The leaders' styles varied considerably, but each gave a high priority to creating a shared purpose and direction to inform effective teamwork.

Their efforts were strongly supported by the SLT, especially the deputy head, who mentored the three faculty heads, working with them to shape strategy and ensuring appropriate resources were available. New schemes of work, examinations and resources provided security, while a volunteer culture was encouraged. Under their new leaders, the teams developed positive identities remarkably quickly. Within them, individuals were given permission to innovate and take risks. As confidence grew, the teams were better integrated horizontally (with other faculties) and vertically (with the SLT). Professional studies began to drive ICT across the curriculum, while English began to make the school's literacy policy a reality.

Although distributed leadership was probably not embedded in the school's culture, ethos and traditions, the new faculty heads were given enough authority and trust to restore organizational health. During the first year, the three faculties began to develop the characteristics associated with self-directed teams. Each team was increasingly ready to:

- show initiative;
- focus on team contributions;
- concentrate on solutions;
- cooperate;
- improve and innovate;
- work with what it had;
- take steps to prevent emergencies;
- save money by improving quality.

The faculty teams were operating, nevertheless, within limits defined by hyper-accountability, with its performance-related rewards and sanctions, and narrow focus on tests and examinations. Goals and targets were set and driven from the top, so middle managers were self-directed only in relation to means, not ends. Innovation, creativity and learning were valued only in so far as they generated very specific changes in the results profile – that is, more GCSE C grades (Mansell 2007). This form of empowerment, constrained by an externally imposed definition of quality and progress, seems inconsistent with the measurement principles believed necessary to increase the effectiveness of self-directed teams. These are that:

- the purpose of the measurement system should be to help a team, rather than top managers, gauge progress;
- teams should play the lead role in designing their own measurement systems;
- teams should adopt only a handful of measures.

Short-term, preconceived goals restrict individual and group learning, and encourage teams to persist with predictable, standardized solutions (Meyer 1998). The next chapter explores how much more self-directed teams can contribute, when teachers have permission to reach beyond their current boundaries and begin to understand the complex systems that shape educational processes.

6 Designing learning organizations

Improving social organization

This chapter explores the potential of the learning organization for education. Can the ideas developed pre-eminently by Schön (1973), Senge (1990, 1999) and Argyris (1993, 1999) help heads and teachers transcend policy and institutional constraints, and stimulate them to find new and better ways to enhance outcomes? Can individuals and schools recreate themselves as learning organizations, able to build their capacity for change and improvement, as well as increase their bottom-line results? As there are few real-life empirical examples of successful learning organizations (Infed 2007), this chapter also investigates the case of The Shire School to discover the extent to which the promise of Senge's (1990) *The Fifth Discipline* can be realized in an educational setting.

Leaders in education are increasingly committed to the idea that organizational development is the natural way to improve performance and survive in a turbulent climate (Holton 2002). Despite a lingering nostalgia for the apparently stable conditions of the post-Second World War period, heads and their colleagues accept that change is an intrinsic feature of modern life and believe their task is to invent and develop social systems that bring about 'their own continuing transformation' (Schön 1973). As seen in previous chapters, a number of current policy strands point towards new forms of social organization in which distributed leadership, teamwork, professional development and coaching build the capacity for lasting improvement. Schools are beginning to transform themselves (Hampton and Jones 2000; Barker 2005, 2006, 2007).

These experiments are constrained and frustrated, however, by the effectiveness framework that governs the school system (Fenwick 2007). Targets, inspection and performance tables define public expectations and obscure the qualitative improvements in student experience achieved by determined and adventurous schools (Fielding 1999). The improvement tradition provides consistent evidence regarding successful schools and colleges, but leaders are distracted by an insistent performance agenda that emphasizes productivity as the ultimate measure of learning (Southworth

2000; Fenwick 2007). Obliged to operate within a government-regulated environment, educators seem to lack the entrepreneurial freedom that enables multinational companies to pursue long-term changes in behaviour and culture, rather than immediate results.

Even so, concepts associated with the learning organization have become immensely popular and attractive for two reasons. First, they challenge conventional wisdom about management, learning and change. Second, they promise to empower us as leaders and learners. Characterized by distributed and egalitarian power based on members' knowledge, the learning organization asks us to reject heroic bosses, father figures and rigid hierarchies (Dixon 1998).

We are invited to become open-minded leaders ourselves, ready to challenge, but also alert to the organizational learning that assists the work of groups and teams. We are advised to distrust our own experience and the incremental, single-loop learning that often flows from it. The metaphors of the learning organization represent a vision of change, development and transformation. They suggest schools should be seen as dynamic, unpredictable and complex social organisms, able to learn and adapt through their interaction with the wider world (Coppieters 2005). This is in stark contrast with effectiveness research that describes schools in terms of set factors and characteristics but is unable to explain how failing and stumbling organizations can become success stories (Lodge 1998). The best-practice solutions that less effective schools and colleges are encouraged to adopt or copy seem a poor substitute for organizational learning.

Although the transformational possibilities of this mix of empowerment, teamwork and participation have attracted 'fervent interest' (Stewart 2001: 141), some authors have drawn attention to what they perceive as the dark side of the learning organization. While advocates claim that this model is the antithesis of the traditional bureaucratic organization, offering a dreamlike ideal or new workplace paradise, critics are concerned that Senge's concepts may be used to create totalitarian environments and lead to a 'nightmare of exploitation' (Driver 2002: 34). Postmodern, so-called *greedy* corporations are accused of exploiting 'the intimacy of social relations to achieve organizational goals' (Blackmore 1999: 37). So, while this chapter draws upon data from The Shire School case study to illustrate the benefits of learning organizations, the following chapter draws upon the two UAE case studies to highlight the risks associated with transformational projects where performance and productivity are overemphasized.

Organizational learning and the learning organization

Despite the obvious appeal of its essential paradigm, the learning organization remains strangely inaccessible, partly because there is little consensus in terms of definition, conceptualization and methodology, and partly because the key ideas are often expressed in ambiguous or metaphorical language that practitioners do not find especially useful (Tsang 1997; Tosey 2005). For example, some writers use the terms *organizational learning* and *learning organization* interchangeably, whereas others, such as Örtenblad (2001), distinguish between them. Unfortunately, however, the distinctions they make are not always consistent from one author to another.

The most straightforward approach is to see *organizational learning* as an existing process that changes the behaviour of individuals and groups. As a consequence of *organizational learning*, organizations are able to become *learning organizations*, meaning that members learn continuously, and thus efficiency and innovation are improved (Reynolds and Ablett 1998; Finger and Brand 1999; Armstrong and Foley 2003).

The relationship between individual learning and organizational learning is another unresolved issue. Only individuals can learn in the conventional sense, but learning organizations are more than the sum of their members' knowledge and experience. According to social complexity theory, individual learning may take place at many levels and become encoded in the organization's memory as 'theory-in-use' (Garavan 1997; Tosey 2005; Antonacopoulou 2006; Fenwick 2007). Organizations can exhibit learning abilities, such as competency acquisition, experimentation, boundary-spanning and continuous improvement. They can also accumulate knowledge in files, rules, roles, routines and procedures. Even so, Argyris (1999) is certain that the system cannot be altered without fundamental changes in individual behaviour, regardless of how difficult these may prove to bring about in an unsatisfactory organizational climate.

The principles

Peter Senge (1990: 3) envisages individual learning as the first stage in a liberating project in which people 'continually expand their capacity to create the results they truly desire, where new and expansive patterns of thinking are nurtured, where collective aspiration is set free, and where people are continually learning to see the whole together'. The learning process begins when individual members of the organization embark on a self-reflective journey to clarify what really matters to them, and to achieve a deeper vision of the future. Five disciplines are recommended as fundamental to organizational learning:

- personal mastery;
- mental models;
- building a shared vision;
- team learning;
- systems thinking.

The purpose of *personal mastery* is to see reality as objectively as possible, and to use the creative tension between where one is and where one wants to go as a source of energy and direction. The main obstacle is that deeply ingrained assumptions and internal pictures of the world are very often ill-adapted to new situations. This prevents us learning from our mistakes. Influenced by these *mental models*, people tend to reason defensively and engage in *single-loop learning*. This is when organization members encounter new problems and seek incremental, logical solutions based on past learning. Assumptions and beliefs, described by Argyris as 'theory-in-use', can limit thinking and lead to unrecognized errors (Argyris 1993; Larsen *et al.* 1996). Senge (1990) insists that the discipline of working with mental models involves rigorously scrutinizing our internal pictures and models, and being prepared to accept criticism without becoming defensive.

The next concern of the learning organization is to align the individual dreams and goals of all members through the discipline of *building a shared vision*. Senge (1990) envisages a process in which guiding practices are used to build shared pictures of the future. Success for the organization depends on the ability of members to develop trust in one another and to hold a shared picture of the future. This vision-building discipline is based on individual dreams and goals, clarified through the practice of personal mastery. Visions should not be sold by charismatic leaders, but should instead originate in the minds of participants. This is very different from the NCSL's emphasis on outstanding headteachers using their impact and influence to deliver a compelling vision derived from their own personal values and passionate commitment (NCSL 2003b).

Team learning builds on the disciplines of *personal mastery* and *building a shared vision*. It aims to develop a group's capacity to achieve desired goals and results. The discipline begins with dialogue, an activity in which team members suspend their assumptions about each other and enter into a process of 'thinking together' that helps them to recognize the destructive patterns of interaction that undermine learning (Senge 1990). Team learning is more difficult than individual learning, so the skills of team learning need to be practised if individual and organizational effectiveness are to be improved. The extent to which individuals adopt defensive routines that limit their ability to learn as a team is easily underestimated (Garavan 1997). Teams can, nevertheless, develop trust and openness in communication and relationships, and, eventually, a strong capacity for coordinated action. When this stage is reached, the intelligence of the team far exceeds the intelligence of individual members (Senge 1990).

Senge (1990) uses 'the beer game' to illustrate the barriers to effective learning, for individuals and for teams. The beer game was developed at Massachusetts Institute of Technology in the 1960s. It involves three positions – a retailer, a wholesaler and a brewery marketing director – each working to maximize their profit. In week 1 of the game, the retailer finds that his beer sales have unexpectedly doubled, and therefore doubles his next order. However, because it takes the wholesaler four weeks to deliver an order, and the brewery two weeks to brew the beer, the system does not cope well with this increase in demand. The problem is compounded by the fact that the three positions do not communicate directly with each other, only via an order-sheet. By the end of the game (when four months have supposedly passed), all three players are blaming each other for (1) not having been able to meet the increased demand in the early weeks and (2) having ordered or produced far more beer than they can sell in the later weeks. The game provides a classic illustration of how people fail to learn from their mistakes. According to Senge (1990), this is because:

- the players become their positions, and do not see how their own actions affect other positions;
- when problems arise, the players blame each other; other positions, or even the customers, become the enemy;
- when the players get proactive and place more orders, they actually make matters worse because they ignore the two/four-week time-lag;
- over-ordering builds up gradually, so they do not realize how exposed their position has become until it is too late;
- they do not learn from experience, because the most important consequences of their actions occur elsewhere in the system;
- the teams running the different positions become consumed with blaming other players for their problems, precluding any opportunity to learn from each other's mistakes.

The solution, for Senge (1990), is to emphasize 'the primacy of the whole'. Individuals, groups and organizations should stop imagining that the world is made up of separate, unrelated forces and focus instead on the system as a whole (Larsen *et al.* 1996). The discipline of *systems thinking* provides, therefore, a conceptual framework that expands our picture of the world and enables us to see interrelationships (rather than simple causes and effects) as well as the consequences of our actions for other parts of the system.

Together, Senge *et al.*'s (1997) five disciplines enable individuals and groups to strengthen their learning by using a range of strategies and tools. In this way, they are able to create flexible, responsive and highly effective organizations. Argyris and Schön (1978) believe three levels of organizational learning are necessary for the development of new solutions and, hence, successful adaptation. First, organizations should aim to improve current ways of working. This is *single-loop learning*. Then, they should have the ability to question and challenge established habits and patterns. This is *double-loop learning*. Finally, they should become self-conscious about the processes of single- and double-loop learning. It is tempting to call this *triple-loop learning*, but Örtenblad (2001) labels it 'deutero-learning'.

Characteristics of learning organizations

One of the difficulties in defining learning organizations is that the self-reflective journey envisaged above is continuous but incomplete. The five disciplines describe complex processes of learning that are best understood in terms of a *voyage* rather than a *destination*. Senge is not writing about a condition that can be attained, or a goal that can be reached. The learning organization represents, instead, an ideal state that people desire and pursue, even though the reality may prove elusive (Tosey 2005). As a result, definitions of successful learning organizations can sometimes seem generalized, and difficult to identify in real-life contexts. For example, Infed (2007) lists six characteristics commonly found in the literature on successful learning organizations. Learning organizations:

1 provide continuous learning opportunities;
2 use learning to reach their goals;
3 link individual and organizational performance;
4 foster inquiry and dialogue, creating a climate where it is safe to share and take risks;
5 embrace tension as a source of energy and renewal;
6 are aware of, and interact with, their environment.

Similarly, Garvin (1993) identifies five main activities that characterize learning organizations:

1 systematic problem solving;
2 experimenting with new approaches;
3 learning from past experience;
4 learning from the best practices of others;
5 transferring knowledge quickly and efficiently throughout the organization.

Lists like these indicate the kinds of activities that lead to organizational learning, but practitioners seeking to embark on their own journeys are unlikely to find them helpful. Australian teachers who were actively engaged in creating learning communities, for example, provided researchers with a mixture of definitions that suggested an inadequate understanding of the concepts involved. They were committed to innovation and were eager to adopt the idea of the learning organization as a philosophical basis for action, but their use of imprecise terms enabled many different approaches to be accommodated. Even in a general, non-school context, the concept of a learning organization has proved difficult to operationalize (Voulalas and Sharpe 2005).

Leithwood *et al.* (1998: 77) have developed a detailed specification of the characteristics of schools as learning organizations. Their list (Figure 6.1) is

School vision and mission
- clear and accessible to most staff;
- shared by most staff;
- perceived to be meaningful by most staff;
- pervasive in conversation and decision-making.

School culture
- collaborative;
- shared belief in the importance of continuous professional growth;
- norms of mutual support;
- belief in providing honest, candid feedback to one's colleagues;
- informal sharing of ideas and materials;
- respect for colleagues' ideas; support for risk-taking;
- encouragement for open discussion of difficulties;
- sharing success;
- commitment to helping students.

School and structure
- open and inclusive decision-making processes;
- distribution of decision-making authority to school committees;
- decisions by consensus;
- team-teaching arrangements;
- brief weekly planning meetings;
- frequent problem-solving sessions among sub-groups;
- common preparation periods for teachers needing to work together.

School strategies
- use of a systematic strategy for school goal-setting, involving students, parents and staff;
- development of school growth plans;
- development of individual growth plans;
- defining priorities for action;
- periodic review and revision of goals and priorities;
- well-designed processes for implementation of specific initiatives.

Policy and resources
- sufficient resources to support professional development;
- availability of a professional library and professional readings circulated among staff;
- availability of computer facilities;
- access to technical assistance to implement new practices.

Figure 6.1 Characteristics of schools as learning organizations

cited and reproduced by both Southworth (2000) and Coppieters (2005), who confirm its validity in the light of other studies.

As we have seen, the learning organization is engaged in a continuous dialectical process that precludes easy definition. Hence, even well-grounded, specific descriptions like these have their limitations. The investigator needs the equivalent of a video camera to capture the complex, organic unfolding of organizational learning, and may require the techniques of action research to provide a fully satisfying account of the layered changes that contribute to new forms of social organization (Phillips 1993). The case study that follows aims, therefore, to describe the transformation of The Shire School from the point of view of participants, and to consider the extent to which developments there, since 1995, match the expectations set out in Leithwood *et al.*'s (1998) list. Do the ideas of the learning organization make sense in a real-life school?

Case study: The Shire School

This case study is based on work by Barker (2007).

The Shire School was selected as a suitable case study because there is strong, triangulated evidence that the school has been transformed since 1995 and that much of its progress has been achieved through organizational learning, stimulated and encouraged by Sara Thomson, the present head-teacher. The inspection conclusion that there were 'no major issues for action' (Ofsted 2000: 8) was unusual, especially for a state comprehensive, and suggested that it would be worthwhile to study the processes of change and improvement at the school. The Shire School was also listed as 'out-standing' by Her Majesty's Chief Inspector (HMCI) in 2002.

Seventeen staff members were interviewed in June 2005. The sample was inevitably constrained by the availability of particular individuals, but as far as possible it reflected the total population of the school staff in terms of age,

Table 6.1 List of interviews with Shire School staff

Interview (role, interview date, number of years' service)	*Code in text*
(1) Administration, 21.06.05, 14 years	1Ad
(2) Administration, 21.06.05, 16 years	2Ad
(3) Assistant Head, 21.06.05, 14 years	3AH
(4) Assistant Head, 21.06.05, 8 years	4AH
(5) Assistant Head, 21.06.05, 8 years	5AH
(6) Deputy Head, 22.06.05, 6 years	6DH
(7) Head, 22.06.05, 10 years	7H
(8) Head of Department, 21.06.05, 7 years	8HoD
(9) Head of Department, 22.06.05, 13 years	9HoD
(10) Head of Department, 22.06.05, 2 years	10HoD
(11) Head of Year, 21.06.05, 12 years	11HoY
(12) Head of Year, 22.06.05, 25 years	12HoY
(13) NQT, 21.06.05	13NQT
(14) Teacher, 21.06.05, 2 years	14T
(15) Teacher, 21.06.05, 2 years	15T
(16) Teacher, 22.06.05, 11 years	16T
(17) Teacher, 22.06.05, 7 years	17T

gender, length of service, role (teaching or administration) and status. Table 6.1 gives details of who was interviewed (column 1) and the codes assigned to them (column 2) in order to safeguard anonymity. For example, 7H refers to the headteacher. Interviews lasted approximately 30 minutes each and were semi-structured around a range of issues relating to leadership and transformation.

In addition, classes were observed in order to gather evidence about the impact of organizational characteristics on learning and teaching. A sample of eight classes across the age and ability range were visited, with half-lessons being observed in English (3), mathematics (2), science (2) and geography (1). The choice was constrained by the timetable and other teacher commitments on the chosen day. Other sources of information for the study include the Ofsted (Ofsted 2000) inspection report, online performance data (BBC 2005; DfES 2005), the school's self-evaluation form (SEF), a research paper presented by the head (Thomson 2006) and the school brochure.

Progress at The Shire School

Under the leadership of the present head, The Shire School has developed a reputation as a successful 11–18 foundation comprehensive serving a rural and generally prosperous community in southern England. In 2000, 11 per cent of students were eligible for free school meals (FSMs), compared with a national mean of 16.5 per cent (Ofsted 2000; Gorard and Taylor 2001). Students are now drawn from 26 primaries and from three neighbouring counties. The school has benefited from many Labour Government initiatives since 1997, including gaining Language College status (achieved in 2002) and Leading Edge status (achieved in 2004). This enhanced framework has facilitated numerous collaborative partnerships, especially around the leisure centre and the Language College (7H, 6DH).

Evidence from the case study is used to evaluate how far the principles and characteristics of the learning organization (as found in the literature and discussed above) have been developed in practice at The Shire School. To what extent have Sara Thomson and her colleagues encouraged organizational learning, and how far has this contributed to the school's apparent transformation?

Vision and mission

Sara Thomson's family upbringing and Christian faith are the bedrock of her vision: 'The traditional values associated with religion are what most parents want for their children . . . heads are the last bastions upholding those traditional values – you can be pushed away from them' (7H). Sara's sense of purpose for the school is designed around the themes of 'friendship and knowledge', which is 'translated through the vision statement to mean that everyone can make academic progress' (7H). The head's ability to communicate this philosophy, motivate her colleagues and inspire their commitment to improvement is widely recognized (15T). Her vision for the school 'feeds down; she's a very strong leader who has driven the school forward through all the changes that we've had' (17T). At her interview prior to appointment, she 'promised to make this the best in the area' (7H), and ten years later is still perceived to be 'very driven and determined . . . like a dog with a bone . . . keeps at it all the time, she's adamant' (13NQT).

Respondents see her as 'the driving force behind all the improvements' (4AH) and are clear about their 'ultimate goal . . . to maximize pupil progress'. They 'never lose sight of the big picture about why we are here' (3AH) and believe that there is a 'sense of a shared determination to do the job right and be happy doing it' (6DH). An intangible ethos is reflected by 'fantastic relationships in all sorts of ways, at all sorts of levels' (3AH). According to one teacher, the head's personal qualities have enabled her to be 'successful in bringing in the same kind of people, who share that view, who fit into the whole scheme of things' (14T).

School culture

The Shire School is said to have a strongly collaborative culture, based on an open and friendly approach that 'makes the staff feel safe' (10HoD). Everyone is committed to the school, and to each other. People 'are always coming up with ideas; there's a steady strand of ideas to how we're to achieve the vision' (13NQT). Senior managers have a supportive, open, non-critical attitude. According to one head of department, 'nobody points a finger; sometimes you make a mistake, you may feel bad about it, but the focus is on the solution'. The absence of a blame culture encourages people to be honest. As a result, staff 'are happy to say whether it works or not' (10HoD). Even those familiar with The Shire School are constantly surprised by the strength of mutual support available:

> Having taught in five schools, I think it is amazing! The students are so friendly and open and not afraid to give an opinion, but they are also respectful – when you ask, people do it – staff the same. This is totally different from everywhere else I've been.
>
> (10HoD)

Continuous professional development (CPD) is woven into the fabric of the school. There is an extensive CPD programme, regarded by one interviewee as 'a real strength and an improvement since the last Ofsted . . . there's lots of in-house training . . . training on discipline, on what makes a good lesson, INSET [in-service training] days used well to target key areas'

(5AH). Newly qualified staff commented on the 'fantastic induction programme' (14T) run by the deputy, praising, in particular, the open forum, where they could be honest about their feelings and problems. Colleagues are pleased that the 'teachers lead the INSET' because they believe people are 'far more likely to take on board the advice and adopt the practice' (5AH) when recommendations come from within. The administrative team is fully included in the programme and participates in regular training and development, particularly to equip individuals for new roles under *workforce remodelling* (see Chapter 9).

The calm, friendly ethos leads to 'really superb' pastoral care and exceptionally good relationships between students and teachers (17T). The Shire School has 'not lost that sense of closeness between teachers and students that you might get in a larger school', and everyone is committed to helping pupils succeed (17T).

The head and leadership team are seen to work well together in establishing priorities for development, and this has produced a collaborative, mutually supportive approach that 'has made the school what it is' (2Ad).

School and structure

When she was appointed, the head quickly assessed her colleagues and built her plans around their potential for growth:

> I did an analysis of their capacity for change – who wanted to change and progress; I worked out a see-saw model, intuitively assessing their reactions and responses. Who is moving in my direction? I worked closely with those who looked like wanting movement, for example the head of languages, who said we would be ready to go for Language College status in three years.
>
> (7H)

She provides 'clear leadership' and has 'the balance right between giving people responsibility and allowing them to exercise it' (11HoY). She has a strong 'people instinct' and is a 'good personnel person' (5AH).

The head's strategy is to 'grow' leaders within the school, challenging people early in their careers with extra opportunities and responsibility. All of the SLT were internally promoted, after showing their personal qualities and ability to contribute in other positions. The SLT was described as a 'well-oiled machine' (13NQT), remarkable for its efficiency and helpfulness.

According to one assistant head, target-setting also contributes to the effective distribution of authority and responsibility: 'Leadership is widely dispersed across the school – huge responsibility is given. Target-setting can give people more autonomy and highlights the excellent job that the vast number of departmental people are doing' (4AH).

The leadership team 'make sure that we go through the middle managers – we trust the middle managers . . . give them responsibility for a chunk of the curriculum' (5AH). Consequently, middle managers feel 'empowered to do things' (5AH). Teachers in different departments describe similar experiences of trust and collaboration:

> The head seems to pick out the ones who are good; you know they are going to be reliable or trustworthy.
>
> (8HoD)

> The head of department . . . always expects good results from us, but we all expect good results from ourselves anyway.
>
> (14T)

> I get the feeling she trusts in the teachers' judgement and independence, though we work as a team. Things get said and they get done and integrated in policy.
>
> (15T)

Departments are held accountable, however, and operate within a clear framework of policies and expectations. All subject staff follow the same guidelines on reporting, target-setting and other key areas.

This distribution of responsibility is also associated with participatory decision-making. Teachers feel 'part of the process rather than someone who has to do as they are told' (8HoD). For ordinary members of staff, it is never a case of Sara and 'the rest of us' because 'we are there as a group . . . I never get the feeling that I'm being ordered or told' (13NQT).

Interviewees feel involved at departmental level. When a new scheme of work was introduced, for example, subject staff felt 'we were all involved' (14T). One department head was said to be 'democratic, organized' so that everyone feels 'you can contribute'. Middle managers were perceived to be 'open to other people's ideas', although 'everything is very structured' and 'people have clear responsibilities' (13NQT).

School strategies

Senior staff emphasize the importance of a systematic approach to establishing goals and priorities, and of monitoring, evaluation and marking. An assistant head claims that the target-setting process has been an important vehicle for coaching. A comprehensive mentoring programme has 'made it clear to all explicitly what we are here for: moving forward and working hard'. The deputy head has introduced tracking systems that have increased staff accountability as well as enhancing everyone's commitment (4AH). She reflects that,

> [w]e have learned a lot about what works in terms of what raises pupil attainment, and what you mustn't do, like losing sight of students as individuals. Data is only useful in terms of helping individuals. You mustn't convert the school into an examination factory and lose the quality of relationships and sense of purpose.
>
> (6DH)

Students are monitored three times a year; tutors monitor those with difficulties in one or two subject areas; heads of year pick up individuals with wider issues; and there is a formal mentoring system that uses value-added data. Although the school has organized a large number of interventions, the effort is concentrated on 'the right students in the right subjects'. Pastoral staff are accustomed to their role in academic monitoring and mentoring, so the school's 'energy is used in a focused manner' (6DH).

Priorities and goals for individuals and groups are constantly reviewed, and appropriate strategies for improvement are implemented. An action plan has been established to improve life for students in lower ability groups, for example. Peer mentoring was introduced as part of a collaborative Leading Edge project to help gifted and talented students, as well as underachieving boys. As a result, students have been involved in a summer school, team-building exercises and website design. Each of the schools involved sent a pupil representative to help (6DH).

Policy and resources

The infrastructure has been greatly improved in order to support professional development and enhance methods of teaching and learning. Every teacher now has a designated classroom, so there are 'no itinerant teachers who are all over the shop' (4AH). According to one head of department, a 'fantastic building' has made a 'big difference to the feel of the place' (8HoD). Electronic whiteboards, wireless laptops and new software have 'radically changed the way we teach' (4AH) through their interactive, creative potential (17T). Two and a half full-time technicians now support the network.

One head of department explained that,

> I can show images . . . you can do so much with video clips . . . you can get on the Amnesty website, show prison, show a letter to write . . . my NQT has been doing brilliant work with it, designing starters and plenaries using wireless.
>
> (8HoD)

Learning and teaching

Inspection and observation reports provide evidence that the school's development has had an important impact on the quality of learning and teaching. In December 2000, inspectors found that teachers had very high expectations for pupils of all abilities and achieved high standards of academic performance through very good teaching (Ofsted 2000). The head of English, like other middle managers, was said to provide a very good example that was having an impact on standards. Skilful questioning encouraged pupils to extend and develop their answers (ibid.).

One of the authors observed lessons and had conversations with staff and students as they worked, and can confirm the quality of life in the classroom. Students were punctual, attentive and well behaved. With only one minor exception, classes waited quietly for teachers to begin lessons and responded eagerly to questions and tasks. Lessons were exceptionally well planned and documented, with a consistent emphasis on learning objectives and frequent reference to schemes of work. The goals of each activity were communicated clearly, using a variety of media (blackboards, whiteboards, PowerPoint slides, wall charts). The skills and knowledge to be acquired were explained in relation to previous learning and future needs. Practical activities and group tasks were managed so that changes of pace and direction engaged and motivated students of all ages and abilities. All the observed lessons combined accessibility with challenge (author's notebook, 6 October 2005, various entries).

One girl commented that she likes 'all the teachers, they're all cool, only one or two grumpy ones', while a boy confided that 'Shire kids are nice kids, there's no bullying'. Another student felt the teachers 'are so good, I feel sorry for my friends who tell me about other schools . . . our maths is at a level to challenge us but we can still do it' (author's notebook entry, 6 October 2005).

An English lesson shows how the school climate encourages inventive teaching. Students from Year 11, equipped with prepared poems and carefully planned learning activities, worked in groups with Year 7 children. The two groups were given name badges and introduced to one another. They quickly generated a steady buzz of explanation and discussion about a wide variety of poems. The teacher moved between tables with a clipboard, recording oral contributions but also pausing to explain the difference between a simile and a metaphor. She commented that the format had created 'so many opportunities to score points . . . their oral grades have rocketed up' (author's notebook entry, 6 October 2005).

Transformation?

The Shire School has been transformed on many levels. The school has become 'bigger, more popular, the results are very good; surrounding villages hear about it and that's when you pull in the more middle-class people' (16T). Since 1994, the school roll has increased from just under 600 pupils to over 900; the sixth form has more than doubled in size; the number of candidates entered for A/AS examinations has risen from 26 to 62; and the GCSE cohort has climbed from 94 to 133. Since 1995, the average verbal reasoning quotient of the students has risen from 92 to over 100 (Thomson 2006). An enhanced reputation has attracted more capable staff (11HoY) as well as an improved intake. Overall, a virtuous circle of success has developed (Thomson 2006).

However, in terms of test and examination results – the government's favoured measures of success and effectiveness – the evidence of transformation is more equivocal. A good part of the 4 per cent increase in the proportion of students achieving five or more GCSE higher grades (GCSE 5+ A*–C) between 1994 and 2005, relative to the local authority mean, can be explained by changes in the student intake, as evidenced by the improvement in the average verbal reasoning quotient.

Sara Thomson and her colleagues seem to have led, modelled and encouraged organizational learning with characteristics similar to those identified in the literature. The Shire School provides teachers and students with 'continuous learning opportunities', and they 'use learning to reach their goals'; they have created a 'climate where it is safe to share and take risks' (Infed 2007). The school experiments with new approaches, learns from past experience and transfers knowledge quickly through the organization (Garvin 1993). The vision is clear, accessible and shared; the culture is collaborative and supportive. Leadership is distributed and decision-making is devolved to those who take responsibility at the relevant level. Individual, group and school growth plans shape priorities and provide a framework for new initiatives. School-based, school-led professional development is the catalyst for innovative teaching that impacts directly on the classroom (Leithwood *et al.* 1998). A climate has been created that encourages double-loop learning, while individual behaviour is better than teachers have experienced elsewhere.

Schools as learning organizations

The virtuous circle identified at The Shire School confirms that, in the right conditions, the learning organization is a relevant and useful concept for school and college leaders as they seek alternative, more profound approaches to organizational improvement. Sara Thomson and her colleagues seem to have transcended the policy constraints associated with 'hyper-accountability' (Mansell 2007: 16) and to have avoided the narrowing, limiting effects of the test-driven culture. Deep, learning-based changes seem to have produced important qualitative improvement, although, unsurprisingly, these have had a relatively limited impact on test performance. While outcomes are measured exclusively through the medium of tests and examinations, it will remain difficult to recognize the real progress that is achieved in the quality of classroom experience.

A rare example of a successful learning organization like The Shire School is insufficient, however, to silence the critique of performativity. There is growing evidence that educational workplaces have become debilitating hothouses where every innovation is designed to extract more effort and commitment from participants. Results data, for example, are now used in over 20 different ways to increase performance and productivity (Mansell 2007). It is right, therefore, to explore the argument that the learning organization is just another device to control and manipulate organization members. The following chapter does just that.

7 *Greedy* organizations

Introduction

As a counterbalance to Chapter 6, this chapter reviews the arguments and evidence against, rather than for, the learning organization. It examines the central paradox that modern institutions seem to promise emancipation but at the same time create mechanisms for the suppression rather than the actualization of self (Giddens 1990; Symon 2002). In the previous chapter, we saw how Sara Thomson, an outstanding head, transformed The Shire School over a number of years. Better results started to attract a higher-ability intake from more committed families, as well as more capable staff. Success bred success, and, over time, a virtuous learning cycle was established whose impact extended well beyond test results. In this chapter, we consider an alternative conceptualization of the learning organization – one in which human capital theory is taken to extremes, and teachers' souls are captured by managers obsessed with productivity and efficiency rather than social justice (Fenwick 2007; Fielding 2006). We end by considering which of Driver's (2002) two memorable metaphors does better justice to the concept of the learning organization – 'Utopian sunshine' or 'Foucauldian gloom'.

Intensification of work

The Europe-wide experience of increased work intensity over the past 20 years, especially in professional organizations, has encouraged a critical view of modern, so-called *greedy* organizations. Pressured by fierce competition in global markets, companies are believed to have reduced costs and raised quality by introducing a mix of strategies to increase worker productivity and performance. This has produced a rise in reported work strain and a fall in job satisfaction, especially for professional workers, whose discretion in carrying out daily tasks has been reduced (Green 2004, 2006, 2008).

A nationwide survey by Cambridge University, based on over 300 in-depth interviews with men and women employed in a wide range of industries and occupations, found that job insecurity increased throughout the 1990s, especially among professional workers. More than 40 per cent said that management could be trusted 'only a little' or 'not at all', while three-quarters believed that management and employees were not 'on the same side'. Job insecurity and work intensification were associated with poor general health and tense family relationships. Over two-thirds said they 'always' or 'regularly' worked longer than their basic working hours (Burchell *et al.* 1999).

This unfortunate combination of increased workplace efficiency and declining job satisfaction seems to stem from important changes in technology and organization. New, expanding ICT has enabled managers to exert close control over work schedules, to coordinate workflow so that gaps and downtime are reduced, and to monitor output. Deficiencies in work quality are more easily traced to individual workstations. Appraisal and performance management systems monitor employees over a medium-term horizon. Laptops, e-mail, the Internet and mobile phones maximize the time available for work on trains, planes and at home. Data and information are constantly accessible, anywhere. Especially in the public sector, managers can use these data systems to raise the pace of work by speeding up the flow of customers in need of service (Green 2004).

Technological change is reinforced and made powerful by the spread of human resource policies designed to involve employees in the organization and to increase their identification with company objectives. New HRM strategies seem to have been effective in soliciting extra effort from employees. Just-in-time production methods, Total Quality Management and teamwork have spread throughout industry, while employees are empowered through mentoring schemes, company meetings and training designed to increase commitment (Green 2004).

Performativity

Developments in education seem consistent with trends identified in the wider economy. Indeed, work intensification in Britain in the 1990s was 'strongest by far in the Education sector', and school teaching remains an 'exceptionally high-effort' occupation (Green 2008: iv).

Education reform, stimulated by an acute awareness of the success of other countries in raising their levels of skill and knowledge, has introduced a new architecture of controls designed to discipline and regulate schools. Within a framework of performance management, teachers are encouraged to set aside their own personal beliefs and commitments in favour of producing better and better test and examination results. The *performative* creature of this regime seeks excellence and success as defined by official measures, even while others experience feelings of inner conflict, confusion and resistance (Blackmore 1999; Ball 2003; EOC 2007).

The feelings of insecurity and burnout reported by some teachers seem to be linked to increased work demands and external accountability. One primary teacher reflected:

> I don't have the job satisfaction now I once had working with young kids because I feel every time I do something intuitive I just feel guilty about it. 'Is this right; am I doing this the right way; does this cover what I am supposed to be covering; should I be doing something else; should I be more structured; should I have this in place; should I have done this?' You start to query everything you are doing – there's a kind of guilt in teaching at the moment. I don't know if that's particularly related to Ofsted but of course it's multiplied by the fact that Ofsted is coming in because you get in a panic that you won't be able to justify yourself when they finally arrive.
>
> (Jeffrey and Woods 1998: 118)

Another teacher, Marion, found herself in head-on collision with Ofsted because she was opposed to the values imposed by inspectors. Accountability took on a life of its own as she found herself 'just doing things for someone else to read'. Even when she was at home, ill, Marion tried to catch up with the accountability paperwork for the inspection (Troman 2000: 346).

Successful teachers and principals seem to survive by keeping two sets of books: one based on their private version of a good school or classroom, and the other carefully adjusted to prescribed curricula, external lists and the criteria against which they will be judged (Barth 1990). This double life leads to dissonance and exhaustion, as teachers struggle to reconcile official priorities with their experience of what matters for their own students and community (Barker 1999; Gunter 2001). Teachers seldom feel in control of their work, and it seems all-absorbing and ever more demanding. To busy classroom teachers, school leaders can seem like missionaries of an oppressive regime concerned only with targets, productivity and performance. Ours has become a high-risk society where anxiety and dread have replaced trust (Giddens 1990; Ball 2003). This is the context for fears that the learning organization may generate a 'nightmare of exploitation' where individual desire, passion and energy are abused for organizational ends (Blackmore 1999; Driver 2002).

Power and organizations

The central complaint about Peter Senge's account of the learning organization is that he underestimates the significance of the power that pervades our institutions, while his desire for transformative experience brings him dangerously close to the *wind of totalitarianism*. As organizations cope with turbulence and change, those with their hands on the levers of power find themselves in a privileged position they are unlikely to relinquish (Coopey 1995; Fielding 2001). Managers have an important role in shaping vision and goals, and may be reluctant to raise inconvenient questions about prevailing norms, policies and practices (Antonacopoulou 2006; Antonacopoulou and Chiva 2007). Instead, transformational techniques are adopted to mobilize workers for ends they are obliged to accept. Employees may be empowered, but only to the extent that they learn how to achieve organizational goals more effectively. They are not in a position to question the validity of the targets prescribed for them by external agents and their own immediate line managers. Organizations are driven by their bottom line, not the dreams and aspirations of employees (Driver 2002; Symon 2002).

With the agenda so clearly controlled by the leaders and managers, who aim to empower their colleagues and stimulate organizational learning, the opportunity to develop personal mastery and to question deeply ingrained assumptions seems limited. Team dialogue is unlikely to lead schools to abandon testing or to dump the dubious educational practices associated with it when a fierce disciplinary apparatus ensures that compliance, not learning, is the priority. As one teacher confided to a visiting journalist, as she prepared her class for the Key Stage 2 tests:

> I might not agree in principle with what we are doing, but we have to do it. . . . It is narrowing what they learn, there's no doubt about it. The children are aware they are not getting through the whole curriculum. We do music, but not design and technology. History and geography also go by the board to some extent.
>
> (quoted in Mansell 2007: 30)

The teachers quoted seem highly motivated and committed, even though the values and practices they have been asked to espouse create inner conflict. Their own beliefs are at variance with official doctrine, but they have internalized the performative agenda nevertheless. These teachers constantly interrogate themselves, being prepared to complete 'accountability paperwork' at home and abandon the rest of the curriculum for the sake of test results, so vital are they for the school's survival in the marketplace. Their dilemma seems to stem from an agenda that incorporates at least as much coercive persuasion as empowerment. Organizations like this are easily compared with prisons, from which teachers may be unable to escape (Schein 1999; Perryman 2006).

False consciousness

A different, but related, concern stems from the learning organization's reliance on dialogue and discussion. Critics worry that members seem to live in a state of false consciousness, where their implicit assumptions and beliefs distract them from an objective view of reality. The world is presented as a 'beer game' (see p. 82) in which players make decisions based on imperfect knowledge and are unable to recognize the systems to which they themselves belong. There is a unitary, positivist reality out there to be discovered through the five disciplines, above all by team dialogue that leads to double-loop learning. In the learning organization, disagreement stems from our failure to align our mental models, to build a vision and to see the whole pattern of change. When people learn to question their fundamental assumptions, they should become free to develop better ways of framing and solving their organizational problems (Fenwick 2007; Fielding 2001).

The onion-peeling process of deconstruction is, however, exceptionally demanding. Many individuals are not comfortable with critical self-reflection. They are equipped with elaborate psychological defence mechanisms to protect themselves from unpleasant and threatening information. Managers are adept at suppressing ideas that may threaten the status quo, and are inclined to promote socially acceptable ideas. People also have an internal compass or 'theory-in-practice' that is resistant to disconfirming data and acts as a serious obstacle to double-loop learning (Fenwick 2007; Easterby-Smith 2004).

This resistance suggests that there is more to learning than simply removing our false perceptions and mistaken assumptions. A one-dimensional, positivist view of reality provides an incomplete account of how meaning arises from social interaction, and does not adequately explain the divergent interpretations that shape human behaviour. People have real interests and differences, as well as mutual misunderstandings and misperceptions (Blumer 1969; Greenfield and Ribbins 1993; Fielding 2001). Educational goals are inescapably diffuse and diverse, so attempts to reduce them to a single, compelling vision must be at the expense of valid, legitimate alternatives (Hoyle 1986). The totalitarian risk of shared visions like this is that employees are expected to commit themselves without reservation to aims and goals that may be very different from their personal values and beliefs. The eventual result may be teams that are trapped in conventional thinking and plagued by inner doubt.

Characteristics of *greedy* organizations

The human disadvantages of managerial techniques designed to improve efficiency and effectiveness are well documented, while the characteristics of modern, *greedy* organizations are described in the literature with reasonable consistency. In these organizations, managers:

- endorse human capital theory – people are seen as a key resource in the search for increased productivity, efficiency and competitive advantage (Fenwick 2007);
- use new technology to manage, control and monitor workflow and job performance (Green 2004);

- adopt HRM practices (appraisal, mentoring, training, quality circles, workplace meetings, flexi-time) to increase identification with organizational goals (Green 2004);
- exploit individual desires, passion and energy for organizational ends (Blackmore 1999);
- use ICT to facilitate flexible working and ensure efficient use of available time (Green 2004);
- encourage a long-hours culture (EOC 2007);
- emphasize individual and group targets and performance (Ball 2003).

In England, relentless student testing and school inspection regimes can turn some state schools into *greedy* organizations with leaders who display all the characteristics listed above. In other phases of education, and in other countries, additional or different factors may be at work. In the United Arab Emirates (UAE), for example, very specific sponsorship laws allow all employers to exploit expatriate staff, to varying degrees (depending on the sector). Within UAE higher education, cutting-edge technology provides further scope for the development of *greedy* organizations, as does the intense institutional rivalry manufactured by senior leaders, both local and expatriate. Case studies of Rihab University and Al Fanar College illustrate this point.

Case studies: Rihab and Al Fanar in the United Arab Emirates

Eighty per cent of UAE employees are expatriate guest workers on fixed-term contracts, under the sponsorship of an Emirati employer. This sponsorship can be terminated at any time for any reason (though three months' salary in lieu of notice may be payable). Employers can also ban certain types of employees from taking another job in the UAE for a year after their sponsorship has been cancelled. Employees and their dependants then have 30 days in which to leave the country, no matter how many years they have lived in the UAE. Expatriate lecturers on three-year renewable contracts with federal colleges and universities may enjoy competitive tax-free salaries, small class sizes and state-of-the-art facilities, but they have absolutely no job security.

The research reported here, and in Chapter 10, is based on a four-year study of two federal HEIs given the pseudonyms Rihab University and Al Fanar College (see Mercer 2007 for further details). As well as participant observation and documentary research, 38 individual interviews were conducted with three senior managers (equivalent to deans), six middle managers (equivalent to deputy deans) and 29 teachers. All 38 interviewees were expatriate guest workers from Western countries. Some had worked in the UAE for only a few months. Others had worked there for over 15 years. To provide as much anonymity as possible, quotations have not been attributed to particular (coded) respondents, some levels of the hierarchy have been conflated under the umbrella terms *middle* and *senior* management, and all respondents have been referred to as *she* even though some of them were male.

Most interviews lasted between 45 minutes and an hour, but a few lasted much longer. Although the study was loosely focused on appraisal, a grounded theory approach was followed (Glaser and Strauss 1967; Strauss and Corbin 1990), so the data were very wide-ranging. When the data were re-analysed in the light of the literature on *greedy* organizations, both institutions – but particularly Al Fanar – were found to display many of the characteristics outlined on pp. 99–100.

Lecturers were required to be on-campus from 08.00 until at least 16.15 (longer if there was a staff meeting), with their arrival and departure observed by guards on the gate. Despite spending over 40 hours on-campus, lecturers often took work home, partly because the students expected them to be available for consultations throughout the day and partly because the open-plan offices shared by 30 people made it hard to concentrate. At the time of the study, Rihab University boasted state-of-the-art technology. Every classroom had a data projector and ports for 24 laptops; every student was required to buy a university-approved laptop, and every staff member was given one. At first, teachers felt excited by the new technology, but it quickly became oppressive in two ways. First, students expected to use their laptops every lesson, even when teachers thought the learning objectives would be better achieved without them. Second, there was a certain amount of pressure from both managers and fellow teachers to see who could use their laptop to best effect. People usually left at the same time, and, with open-plan offices, not many wanted to be seen locking their new toy away for the night. Once at home with the laptop, only the most self-disciplined and self-confident teachers did not succumb to some late-night tinkering with the following day's material.

Al Fanar was not as technically advanced as Rihab, and still used staff desktops and student computer labs rather than individual laptops. Accordingly, there was less pressure to spend hours developing sophisticated lessons using the latest technology. However, other features of the *greedy* organization were very much in evidence. The college was part of a national network of similar institutions, and every semester the results from standardized tests were compared across the system, as were graduate employment rates every year. Staff at Al Fanar were left in no doubt about the importance of getting the college high up in these performance tables. One of the middle managers described the college as,

> patriarchal . . . system-driven . . . admin-driven . . . fear-driven, a lot of the time, as well . . . fear in the sense of doing what is expected by [the Emirati Minister of Higher Education] for example, rather than what might be the best decision to make . . . fear of poor results, fear of being outstripped in the results table by another college, fear of not placing your students in jobs.

In similar vein, a senior Al Fanar manager openly acknowledged that 'we're an exam-driven institution . . . nothing else', led by an expatriate college head who would 'lash out at the teachers' if the exam results were comparatively low. In her opinion, the college head knew that low scores were not caused by poor teaching, but merely reflected the fact that many students entered the college with low levels of attainment. She said, 'As an intelligent, educated man, he [the college head] doesn't believe what he is saying but he wants to have this public bashing [of teachers].' The senior manager was aware that the head's strategy contradicted the rhetoric on HRM, but added:

> Perhaps he is right because all it does is make us more determined than ever . . . he could say, look what I've done, I've been nasty . . . for the last two years and . . . [this year's] results are the best in the system.

Interviewees at both institutions also highlighted how the sponsorship rules allowed and even encouraged exploitation. Twelve teachers mentioned the ease with which staff could be instantly dismissed. Three typical comments are as follows:

> The notion that we're on probation for one year is farcical, because we're always on probation in the sense that we can have our contracts terminated any time.
>
> I mean the kind of culture that it is here – people can get sent home any day for any reason.
>
> In my opinion, the problem is the society. Or a set-up where your job and your right to live in the country, and your children to go to school, and have a house, depends on your job. And if you lose your job, you've got no recourse. You can't go to any industrial tribunal to get it back. You have to hand over your house, the school, and leave the country in most cases, unless you find another [job]. And that employer can control whether you can move to another country or not. . . . It's because of the sponsorship system . . . which I don't think is conducive to good management practices.

Similar feelings were expressed by six of the nine managers. A senior Rihab manager talked of not being able to protect her faculty from decisions made by those above her, saying:

> I think this is a very uncertain place to work in. I have never been in a place where I think there is so much uncertainty. . . . This is the first time . . . where I couldn't protect the faculty. . . . And I just don't like that feeling. Not that it's paternal. I don't mean it in a paternal way, I mean it in the way of management, in the sense that they can't come and dismiss you without my being involved and either agreeing or trying to

> defend you or whatever. There is no appeal process here, which is such a big thing in American universities now.

The senior Al Fanar manager mentioned earlier was even more forthright, saying, 'Each college is a little dictatorship . . . one wrong word and we could all be out . . . all power is in the hands of one person [the head of the college] and nobody else can affect that decision.'

Although some teachers suggested poor performance would go unnoticed so long as the teacher was compliant and did not 'rock the boat', this was not a view shared by the managers themselves. Indeed, four of them said identifying any weakness in a teacher would be enough to get them sacked. In the words of one Al Fanar middle manager:

> Instead of allowing time for problems with one particular teacher to work themselves out, PD [professional development], support, help and so on, depending again on who's up at the top . . . the minute anything, any problem, is mentioned at appraisal, it's bye-bye.

Likewise, a senior Al Fanar manager talked about devising a very successful action plan that greatly improved a probationary teacher's performance, only to have the head of the college dismiss the teacher anyway. In her words, 'identifying them as being at risk has more or less been their death-knell'.

Two Al Fanar middle managers justified this policy by claiming that student learning would be compromised while a weak teacher was being developed. The first of these managers had been appointed less than a year ago, and was clearly torn between the highly developmental environments she had presided over elsewhere and the highly judgemental environment she was now expected to endorse:

> We don't really have the environment in which you can work with somebody and develop them. So, to a certain extent, we are saying to people, this is the level of performance we expect, right from the beginning, and through our appraisal system, we are looking to see if you meet that standard, and if you don't, there's not an awful lot we can do about it, really. . . . I think it's political basically. They pay good salaries and they can afford to – they say, OK, you know, we'll give you this, but this is what we expect in return. And we're not really interested in having to develop people because we can get other people who are as good or better. I think it's simple economics . . . I have mixed feelings about that. Because in previous organizations I've worked for, it's not been like that, and we have worked with people. And I think, you know, it's obviously much more preferable to work with people and develop them. The problem is that while you're doing that, students can be suffering. And I think that's fair enough, you know, if it might take somebody a year to come up to an acceptable standard of teaching,

> and in the meantime, the students could be getting more from another teacher who's already there.

The second manager, who had been in the college system for many years, suggested that students' experiences in state schools were so 'paltry' that only 'the best' teachers would do. In her words:

> The stakes here are higher because our learners have so many difficulties and because they are not independent learners and because they are so immature. . . . We need better teachers, it's as simple as that. Students in other areas, or other countries that could get away with an average or even a mediocre teacher, it just doesn't happen here. They have to have the best, if we're going to succeed.

Although the staff collectively were viewed as a vital resource, individual teachers were highly expendable, and those at the top would not hesitate to remove anyone whose performance was merely average. Such ruthless pursuit of the competitive edge is obviously damaging to those teachers who are sacked – one interviewee called it 'a very significant . . . human tragedy'. Just as importantly, though, it raises questions about the sustainability of the teaching profession, and whether government organizations have any obligation to develop the next generation of teachers. Is it right that some institutions can cherry-pick those they judge to be the best just because of their greater financial bargaining power and/or allegedly more disadvantaged students? For *greedy* organizations such as Al Fanar, the answer, it seems, is a resounding yes.

In defence of the learning organization

While it has to be conceded that the quite distinctive UAE sponsorship laws have encouraged the emergence of *greedy* organizations like Al Fanar, reformed education systems all around the world are using new technologies to gather, monitor and evaluate performance data, and then applying rewards and sanctions to the winners and losers. Schools and colleges operating within such an environment are bound to display at least some of the behaviours found in *greedy* organizations. Even schools like Norcross, Felix Holt and The Shire (discussed in Chapters 4, 5 and 6), with their transformational leaders and thriving collaborative practices, have internalized the performative agenda to some extent.

Each school emphasizes individual targets and encourages teachers to adopt a variety of tactics to improve test scores. Each leadership group has stitched a never-ending quest for better results into the organizational DNA, and has aligned the school's mission with official requirements, especially those of Ofsted. The imposed pressure to increase test and examination scores obliges school managers to emulate their commercial counterparts, and leads them to drive their organizations towards explicit, measurable goals and objectives. Under these conditions, the mission is more likely to produce an increase in work intensity and double vision than a sense of empowerment and personal fulfilment (Ball 2003).

Even so, Senge would argue that imposed visions and instrumental goals are inconsistent with the five disciplines. In other words, schools cease to be learning organizations when they allow inquiry, dialogue and learning to be suppressed by the fear of external evaluation. The blind pursuit of test results is a classic example of single-loop learning. Existing knowledge (best practice) is applied with remorseless logic. In England, for example, Year 6 students spend months practising for Key Stage 2 tests in literacy and numeracy, while history, geography and design technology 'go by the board' (Mansell 2007). Yet the result is only a modest rise in test scores, to be set against a considerable impoverishment of the student experience.

Senge may have paid insufficient attention to the pervasive influence of power in organizations, but there is nothing in his work to encourage 'bastard leaders' whose aim is to impose a managerial project on their colleagues (Wright 2001). Senge (1990: 340) is unequivocal that our traditional view of leaders as special people who set the direction, make decisions and energize the troops is 'deeply rooted in an individualistic and non-systemic world view'. Myths about heroes who rescue their people from circling enemies encourage short-term, present-tense thinking that blinds us to systemic forces and blocks collective learning. Deep and lasting behaviour change grows from changes in the theories that people use, and in the learning systems of the organization, not through any quick-fix gimmick improvised by a daring leader (Argyris 1999: 67).

This is not to discount entirely the suggestion that learning organizations may increase the power and control available to those at the top. The processes of individual and team learning have to be managed, and there is no guarantee that dialogue will lead to democratic outcomes or empower subordinates. The essential problem is that we do not fully understand the complex phenomenon of team learning. Senge believes that until there is a satisfactory theory of what happens when teams learn, and we have more reliable methods for building teams capable of learning together, the outcomes of team learning are likely to remain a product of 'happenstance' (1990: 228). For the time being, therefore, the learning organization should be seen neither as a workers' paradise nor as a psychic prison, but as an alternative paradigm – a vision of a participatory form of organization that has the potential to challenge the top-down managerial structures that dominate today's schools (Driver 2002).

Ambiguous learning

Although exciting ideas often end in disappointment (Tosey 2005), the learning organization remains a powerful metaphor. The imagery of a learning journey reminds us that virtuous circles like that at The Shire School are possible, even in climates dominated by top-down managers, standardization and narrow targets. The open, collaborative, double-loop learning of the learning organization stands in sharp contrast with the closed, single-loop learning of the so-called effective school. An alternative narrative, where learning rather than testing is the central concern, may help expose the limitations of the official model, and encourage all those who demand more from education than just a result. A worrying question remains, however, about the extent to which an apparently insecure and anxious society can cope with organizations that are 'dynamic, unpredictable and complex social organisms' (Coppieters 2005: 129). Is the journey too demanding for those who have grown accustomed to bureaucratic solutions?

Dream or nightmare?

The evidence of this chapter is that both dream and nightmare are possible. Some honest endeavours have succeeded in generating a virtuous circle despite a discouraging contemporary environment. Other journeys, even if they began with a determined effort to involve and empower people, quickly lapsed into managerial projects driven by results. The margin between learning and exploitation may be smaller than it seems. The questions below seem critical for organizations that wish to improve their ability to learn:

1. What was the starting point for your journey, in terms of organizational learning and individual learning?
2. How strongly did people work through the stages of organizational learning towards the learning organization? Did they allow enough time? How did they deal with pressure?
3. How were organizational goals and ends decided – by an alignment of vision through systems thinking, or by management's emphasis on the bottom line?

Part III

Contemporary practices in human resource management

8 Selecting and developing professionals

Introduction

This chapter investigates the training, recruitment, selection, induction, development and departure of teachers and school leaders. It argues that although warnings of widespread teacher shortages are justified in parts of the developing world, they are overstated elsewhere. It highlights how *performativity* is limiting the focus of teacher induction and professional development, thereby jeopardizing their potential benefits.

Similar concerns are raised about the preparation, induction, development and departure of school leaders. The head's remit has expanded exponentially in the past 30 years, with the result that heads are now held accountable for a huge range of school outcomes. While schools face little difficulty in appointing deputy and assistant heads, fewer and fewer people aspire to headship. Most potential candidates remain unconvinced by the government rhetoric portraying heads as inspirational instructional leaders, transforming the quality of student learning through the magic of distributed leadership. Instead, they see incumbents working long, unsociable hours at the behest of a flawed government agenda that drowns them in bureaucracy and bombards them with change initiatives. They witness what little space heads have to pursue their own vision for the school, and hear of how easily heads can be reallocated or dismissed. They also note that most heads retire early, unwilling or unable to keep up the pace. Until these systemic failures are addressed, government initiatives to tackle the crisis in headship supply will have little enduring impact.

The alleged crisis in teacher supply

Over the past 20 years, there have been countless reports of an impending crisis in the supply of state-school teachers. Many of these reports have been critiqued by Gorard *et al.* (2006) and shown to rely on samples of the total population and/or respondent self-report, such as asking heads how hard it is to fill vacancies. Rather than use such incomplete and anecdotal evidence, Gorard *et al.* (ibid.) grappled with a multitude of large-scale national datasets from both the UK and the US. Using figures from the UK's Office for National Statistics, the Department for Children, Schools and Families (or its predecessors), the Universities' Council for the Education of Teachers (UCET), the School Teachers' Review Body (STRB), the Teacher Training Agency (TTA) and the Office for Standards in Education (Ofsted), they conclude that there is no evidence of a crisis in teacher supply. In fact, in England in 2004 there were more teachers than ever before, and pupil–teacher ratios were close to their lowest-ever levels – lower, at secondary level, than in the Netherlands, New Zealand, Canada and South Korea. Turnover and teacher vacancies had certainly increased, but this merely reflected an overall expansion of the profession, fuelled by higher government spending. Moreover, the relative absence of teachers aged 30–39 was not a demographic time bomb, as so often suggested, but merely an enduring fact of life, indicating the propensity of female teachers to take time out to raise families. In other words:

> There was no especial crisis at the turn of the century, and there is none now. There is no retirement time bomb, no mass exodus of disillusioned teachers, no drop in teacher quality or qualifications, and no worsening shortage, and no lack of new trainees.
>
> (Gorard *et al.* 2006: 130–1)

Certainly there are shortages in particular subjects (such as maths and science) and particular geographical areas (such as inner London and south-east England), but there is no robust evidence of a national crisis. Nor are these recruitment difficulties unique to education. There are simply not enough maths and science graduates to go round, and in fact schools and colleges are doing rather well by recruiting approximately half of them.

Nonetheless, three issues remain. First, ethnic minorities continue to be significantly under-represented in the teaching profession (Guarino *et al.* 2006; Bush and Moloi 2008). Second, the most disadvantaged schools have the greatest difficulty recruiting and retaining staff (Ingersoll 2004; Guarino *et al.* 2006; Borman and Dowling 2008). While average turnover might be 5 per cent per year, in high-poverty schools it can easily reach 20 per cent, leading to 'the stratification of educational opportunity' (Ingersoll 2004: 3). Third, the academic credentials of those choosing to teach are comparatively low. In the US and the UK, for example, students enrolling on teacher education courses generally have lower school-leaving exam results and/or lower degree classifications than their non-teaching contemporaries (Gorard *et al.* 2006; Guarino *et al.* 2006). Whether or not this adversely affects student outcomes is debatable, however, as the art of teaching depends on far more than intellectual ability.

Thus, talk of a national crisis in teacher supply is unwarranted in the US and the UK. Elsewhere, though, the situation is truly dire. Many developing countries have experienced both an exponential increase in demand, as they implement policies on universal education, and a simultaneous decrease in supply, as they struggle with disease, civil war and migration to the West (De Villiers and Degazon-Johnson 2007). In sub-Saharan Africa, an additional 14–25 million teachers will be needed in order to meet *Education for All* targets, but in countries such as Kenya, Zambia and Namibia, more teachers die each year of HIV/AIDS than graduate from teacher training colleges (Moon 2007). The problem is compounded by the fact that even though qualified teachers are paid less than those in other salaried occupations (Eraut 2000), many governments say they can-not afford the wage bill. So, unqualified teachers are employed instead, at a third to a half of the price, and put in charge of primary classes with 70–120 students (Sinyolo 2007). In this way, 'teachers are in the process of disappearing to be replaced by largely untrained para-professionals' (Moon 2007: viii).

While authors in the West claim that HEIs make a distinctive and essential contribution to teacher preparation, developing countries find this model prohibitively expensive (Lewin 2002). It may well be the case that HEIs have more time than schools to train teachers, better access to the latest research, and a longer tradition of critical reflection (Pring 1999; Williams and Soares 2000; Taylor 2007), but in the developing world it makes little sense for children to miss out on schooling just so potential teachers can undergo years of pre-service training (Lewin 2002).

Teacher recruitment and selection

In the UK, qualified teachers can apply for any vacancy, and schools can appoint any applicant. Elsewhere, the situation is very different. In the Middle East, for example, strict sponsorship rules prevent expatriate teachers from applying for other jobs, and in Israel, Singapore and China, heads have no say in the teachers government officials assign to them. Although in the short term, allocating teachers to schools may overcome the recruitment difficulties faced by schools in deprived areas, in the long term it is not an effective solution. Depending upon a society's cultural norms (individualist or collectivist) and the prevailing economic climate (expanding or contracting), teachers unhappy with their assigned school may ask to move or even change profession. Only in highly collectivist societies or places with limited alternative employment are teachers likely to stay at schools they hate – and even then, their negativity must surely affect their students.

On the other hand, allowing teachers and schools a completely free choice presents its own challenges. It seems the selection criteria heads use are at best inconsistent, and at worst arbitrary. Heads say they look for prior teaching success, good character (however it be defined), strong classroom management skills, the ability to work with diverse learners, and excellent interpersonal skills (Guarino *et al.* 2006). Although shortlisting panels favour applicants who have majored in the relevant subject, high test scores or a prestigious *alma mater* confer no advantage (Balter and Duncombe 2005). Prospective employees might be asked to teach a demonstration lesson or present a teaching portfolio, but conventional interviews still carry the most weight. Rather worryingly, empirical studies show that the decisions thus reached are 'generally' influenced by factors unrelated to job performance, and 'generally' fail to comply with employment law (Delli and Vera 2003: 147; Young and Delli 2003).

One such unrelated, but very significant factor is the candidate's expected salary. Where schools manage their own budgets, hiring decisions are likely to take account of not just how well someone will do the job, but how expensive they will be to employ (Carter 1997; Guarino *et al.* 2006). We have already seen (in Chapter 7) how one hirer at Al Fanar in the UAE justified recruiting only the best teachers money could buy. Although few hirers would put it so bluntly, many selection decisions are influenced, at least to some extent, by financial considerations.

Teacher induction

The nature and purpose of induction are viewed differently in different countries (Howe 2006; Wang *et al.* 2008), depending on the type of pre-service education available. In France, Germany, Belgium and Chinese Taipei, for instance, beginning teachers have had a whole year's internship, whereas their counterparts in New Zealand may have spent just four weeks in schools (Howe 2006). Induction is also affected by historical traditions. Typically, in the US, beginning teachers are given the most challenging classes, fewer classroom resources, more teaching hours and more extra-curricular duties than veteran teachers (Howe 2006; Borman and Dowling 2008), which perhaps explains the county's relatively high attrition rate whereby 22 per cent of teachers leave within the first two years (Smethem 2007). By contrast, beginning teachers at primary schools in deprived areas of New Zealand report very high levels of satisfaction with their induction programmes, rating them 3.71 out of 4. This may explain why these schools have lower attrition rates than schools in wealthier areas.

Beginning teachers require both professional and organizational socialization. They need to develop their identity as a teacher *and* find their feet within a particular institution. Being socialized into a particular discipline or subject area may also be important for secondary schoolteachers and those in tertiary education. Ideally, induction should focus on subject-specific pedagogy (Wang *et al.* 2008) and involve a mentor in the same field (Guarino *et al.* 2006). The mentor should receive specific training for the role, and both mentor and mentee should be allocated sufficient time for mentoring. Beginning teachers should be 'introduced early on to the skills of inquiry and given many opportunities to develop the habits of critical colleagueship' (Howe 2006: 295). Induction should enhance their commitment, develop their capacity to 'self-author', and equip them to be at the vanguard of change (Tickle 2001). It should attend to their personal and emotional needs as much as their professional and technical ones (Jones 2002; Findlay 2006). The process should involve the whole school, rather than just one mentor, and it should be strongly supported by the leadership team (Wang *et al.* 2008). Beginning teachers should have ample opportunity to observe colleagues and, when they themselves are observed, the focus should be on development, not evaluation (Dymoke and Harrison 2006; Wang *et al.* 2008).

Sadly, empirical studies indicate that few beginning teachers experience this kind of exemplary induction. In many cases, they are expected to achieve certain standards or competencies by the end of their induction, making their mentor both guide and judge (Jones 2002; Findlay 2006; Dymoke and Harrison 2008). The whole process then becomes assessment driven, and narrowly focused on observable classroom behaviour, even though much of a teacher's work is done outside the classroom (Tickle 2001). The generic standards or competencies apply to all beginning teachers, taking no account of their diverse life histories, subject specialities and school contexts (Findlay 2006). They enshrine a reductionist, minimalist role for the teacher (Tickle 2001; Findlay 2006), and, being 'rooted in a bureaucratic-managerial approach to teacher development', they encourage neither self-monitoring nor critical reflection (Dymoke and Harrison 2006: 80). Teachers who pass are relieved, but they learn very little and resent the added stress (Jones 2002). Teaching is not the only profession to maintain a traditional rite of passage, but the research cited above indicates that, too often, the dead hand of assessment stifles growth and development at the very moment when beginning teachers ought to be feeling nurtured and inspired.

Teacher development

According to Day (1999: 4):

> Professional development consists of all natural learning experiences and those conscious and planned activities which are intended to be of direct or indirect benefit to the individual, group or school and which contribute through these, to the quality of education in the classroom. It is the process by which, alone and with others, teachers review, renew and extend their commitment as change agents to the moral purposes of teaching; and by which they acquire and develop critically the knowledge, skills and emotional intelligence essential to good professional thinking, planning and practice with children, young people and colleagues through each phase of their teaching lives.

This conceptualization of professional development is very helpful – so much so that it was adopted by the CPD Review Group (2005a and b) – because it highlights natural learning experiences as well as conscious, planned activities. Although this chapter focuses more on the latter than the former, it is important to remember that professionals learn six times as much through non-formal as through formal means (Becher 1999). Likewise, we must not forget that learning can be unintended as well as non-formal, a good example being the 'hidden' curriculum that is acquired surreptitiously, unconsciously or from peers (Knight *et al.* 2006).

Although, by definition, non-formal learning cannot be guaranteed, there is much schools can do to facilitate it. Creating a culture in which staff believe their ideas will be valued is absolutely vital, but so too is simply providing adequate space and time for interaction. For this reason, it is impossible to overestimate the importance of having a staffroom where all staff feel welcome (regardless of their role) and which provides sufficient comfortable seating, appropriate free refreshments and well-organized, professionally oriented notice-boards. In similar vein, it is best not to cram mandatory professional development days so full of scheduled activities that teachers get no time to chat informally about their work.

With regard to formal CPD, one of the most obvious but least effective types is the one-off short course attended by individual teachers from different schools. Although such events enable colleagues to network, teachers are unlikely to change their practice as a result (Wang *et al.* 2008), and even if they did, the rest of their school would not benefit (CPD Review Group 2005a). So, a much better model is to combine external expertise with peer support, by ensuring at least two teachers from the same school are involved. The focus should be on content (what students are expected to know) rather than teaching strategies per se (Penuel *et al.* 2007), and it should incorporate active experimentation rather than just reflection and discussion (CPD Review Group 2005a). Examining student work collaboratively in relation to expected standards of achievement presents a particularly rich learning opportunity (Ingvarson *et al.* 2005).

In addition, any CPD programme should allow time for feedback and follow-up. Ideally, teachers should be observed by both their peers and an external expert as they try out new ways of working, because such 'at-the-elbow' coaching and support is crucial to embedding innovation (Ingvarson *et al.* 2005).

The CPD on offer should be differentiated to take account of a teacher's personality, current motivation, job description, school circumstances and career stage. In the first three years, for instance, CPD may need to build a positive professional identity and increase classroom competence; in the years before retirement, for those coping with declining health, fatigue and/or disillusionment, it may need to promote resilience and sustain commitment (Day and Gu 2007).

A balance has to be struck between the needs of the country, the school and the individual (Bolam and Weindling 2006), but the more control teachers have over the focus, pace and scope of their CPD, the more they and their students are likely to benefit (CPD Review Group 2005b). On the other hand, learning organizations need to coordinate their CPD opportunities meticulously to ensure they are consistent with the core values of the institution, and promote the greatest synergy. CPD opportunities also need to be carefully evaluated.

Guskey (2000) suggests a fivefold hierarchy of impact:

- Level 1 relates to the participants' reactions – whether they are satisfied with the content, the process/pedagogy and the context (e.g. the size of the training room).
- Level 2 relates to what the participants think they have learned in terms of cognition, affect or behaviour.
- Level 3 relates to organizational support and change – whether the school values CPD, in general, and supports the specific changes being advocated as a result of it.
- Level 4 relates to the participants' actual use of new knowledge and skills, measured a reasonable time after the CPD has ended.
- Level 5 relates to student outcomes – though of course it is virtually impossible to prove that a specific instance of CPD caused a particular student outcome.

To this typology, Muijs and Lindsay (2006) add an important, but often overlooked, consideration: value for money. Their research with 223 CPD coordinators and 416 teachers shows that CPD in English schools is rarely evaluated in terms of these five levels. Most often it concentrates on Level 1 (participant satisfaction); sometimes it encompasses Level 2 (participant learning) and value for money; only very rarely does it encompass Levels 4 (actual behaviour) or 5 (student outcomes). As a result, schools may be unwittingly squandering their precious resources on forms of CPD that have limited impact on teachers, let alone students.

In addition to this lack of rigorous evaluation, the prevailing policy context is seen by some as counter-productive (Purdon 2003; Kennedy 2007). Just as the transformative potential of induction can be choked by the spectre of assessment, so too can the power of CPD be stifled by a standards-based approach aimed at compliance and conformity. The rhetoric on CPD paints a rosy picture of teachers working collaboratively to develop genuinely innovative solutions to their most pressing problems. The reality, it is claimed, is a 'managerial conception of professionalism' (Kennedy 2007: 108) in which state-sponsored CPD serves only to ensure that individual teachers meet and maintain prescribed standards at various points during their career. Coaching and mentoring programmes act 'as transmission belts for the replication of competency-based approaches to teaching' (Stevenson *et al.* 2007). Nobody gets inspired, and many choose to leave.

Teacher retention

In the UK, large numbers of would-be teachers never make it into the classroom. Nearly half of all PGCE applicants are rejected (Gorard *et al.* 2006); 12 per cent of those who are accepted leave without completing the course; 30 per cent of those who graduate from a PGCE do not go into teaching (Smithers and Robinson 2001). Of the 70 per cent who do get teaching jobs, 18 per cent leave within the first three years – a few because they never intended to stay long, but most because they are disillusioned. Thereafter, attrition stabilizes at about 14 per cent per annum, a rate higher than the average for all occupations (11 per cent) but similar to that in law enforcement, nursing, social work, the military and engineering (Guarino *et al.* 2006; Borman and Dowling 2008). Attrition begins to rise again when teachers become eligible for early retirement, and a relatively generous pension (Borman and Dowling 2008), leading to what has been called a U-shaped curve.

Naturally, not everyone who resigns is dissatisfied with teaching. Over half take up positions elsewhere in education and many leave to raise children. Nonetheless, for the long-term health of the profession it is important to investigate what makes some people so unhappy that they leave.

According to a survey by Smithers and Robinson (2001), secondary school teachers in England and Wales leave because of workload (58 per cent), pupil behaviour (45 per cent) and government initiatives (37 per cent), while primary teachers leave because of workload (74 per cent), stress (26 per cent) and government initiatives (16 per cent). A similar study by Guarino *et al.* (2006) found that US teachers likewise resign because of poor student discipline, but instead of workload or government initiatives, these teachers complain of low salaries and a lack of support from the school leadership.

The evidence on whether higher salaries would encourage more teachers to stay is mixed. Generally, people who go into teaching are motivated more by intrinsic factors, such as job satisfaction and a desire to share their knowledge, than by extrinsic factors, such as salary or status (Gorard *et al.* 2006). On the other hand, there is some evidence that higher salaries would (1) encourage graduates with better qualifications from more selective institutions to consider teaching as a career (Guarino *et al.* 2006), and (2) encourage teachers with more than five years' experience to stay on (Borman and Dowling 2008). What it would not do is stop teachers leaving within the first five years, or retain those who leave because the other factors noted above become intolerable. To keep this latter group in teaching, governments would need to reassess the work they ask teachers to do and reduce the frequency with which new initiatives are introduced. School leaders would need to allow teachers more input and more decision-making powers, and communities would need to promote good behaviour in their young people more actively.

Leadership supply

While the crisis in teacher supply may have been overstated, there is strong evidence that fewer and fewer teachers aspire to headship. Assistant and deputy head positions are generally not hard to fill (Howson 2008a) but headship shortages have been reported in many countries, including England and Wales (Howson 2003, 2005, 2007, 2008a), the US, Canada, Australia and New Zealand (Hansford and Ehrich 2006). Women and those from ethnic minorities are under-represented at headship level (Coleman 2007; Howson 2008b). Ironically, less successful schools that are most in need of strong leadership find it hardest to recruit (Stevenson 2006; Higham *et al.* 2007; Howson 2007).

Although heads generally describe themselves as satisfied (Hansford and Ehrich 2006; NCSL 2006b), teachers in Australia claim to be deterred by the long hours, night-work and conflicting demands from different stakeholders (Hansford and Ehrich 2006). Similarly, non-heads in England and Wales are put off by the heavy workload, initiative overload, excessive accountability and an insufficient pay differential, especially in the primary sector (Smithers and Robinson n.d.). Non-heads also note that it is much easier for the governors to sack the head than it is for the head to sack a teacher (Higham *et al.* 2007). Non-heads in the US mention the same worry about losing their job, alongside stress, inadequate funding, educating an increasingly diverse population and shouldering responsibilities that once belonged to the home or community (Fink and Brayman 2006).

Since heads themselves are 'overwhelmingly positive about their role' (NCSL 2006b: 3), one obvious response to the shortage is for them to publicize the perceived rewards more frequently, particularly to those in their own schools with headship potential. Another, more radical, solution would be for the government to curtail 'its reforming zeal and policy of pressure from the centre' (Smithers and Robinson n.d.: v). This would not only reduce heads' workload but also create space for individual heads to exercise their own values, instead of having ill-considered initiatives constantly imposed upon them. Earley and Weindling (2007) also contend that the role would be more attractive if prospective heads were better prepared and actual heads better supported. This suggestion will be explored further in a section titled 'Leadership development' (p. 121) – but it is somewhat surprising, given that the NCSL already offers a wide range of CPD for both these groups, one element of which, the National Professional Qualification for Headship (NPQH) is mandatory.

Leadership recruitment and selection

Heads, like teachers, are prepared and selected differently in different countries, such diversity being rooted in the unique political, economic, social, cultural, historical, professional and technical circumstances of each nation

(Bolam 2004). In most cases, heads are self-selected volunteers, but in China, for instance, they can be appointed against their wishes (Su *et al.* 2000). Normally, but not always, heads have teaching experience. In some developing countries, heads are appointed because of their political affiliation and may never have set foot inside a classroom (Oplatka 2004). It is also technically possible in England and Wales for someone without teaching experience to become a school leader. The NPQH is usually taken by qualified teachers, but it has been successfully completed by a handful of school business managers (SBMs). Teaching unions are divided over whether such people should be allowed to become heads, with ASCL saying yes and NAHT saying no (Higham *et al.* 2007). A fuller discussion of the arguments for and against can be found in Chapter 9, but given how difficult it is for some schools in deprived areas to appoint any sort of head, widening the potential pool to include SBMs may offer a pragmatic, if far from ideal, solution.

Prerequisites and selection criteria differ in other ways, too. In Africa, outstanding classroom practitioners are often appointed to headship irrespective of their leadership potential (Bush and Oduro 2006). In South Korea, it is not teaching expertise that counts, but length of service; potential heads need at least 20 years' experience (Kim and Kim 2005). In England and Wales, the NPQH, a practice-oriented qualification, is mandatory, while in the US and Singapore, a university Master's degree is needed (Huber and Pashiardis 2008).

The key decision-makers also vary from place to place. Heads in England and Wales are hired and sometimes fired by a particular school's board of governors. Each governing body has between 9 and 20 members, including representatives nominated by parents, school staff (both teaching and non-teaching), the LA and the local community. Their work is unpaid and their training patchy. Supporters of the appointment system claim it endorses community engagement and democratic choice; critics claim it leaves the most important decision a school will ever make in the hands of a group described by the NCSL (NCSL n.d.b: 4) as 'well-intentioned, dedicated, but essentially amateur'.

By contrast, in parts of the US, Canada and Australia, district education boards appoint heads for a period of three to five years and can reallocate them to different schools at will. Earley and Weindling (2007) contend that such short-term contracts prevent heads from stagnating after too many years at the same school. Fink and Brayman (2006) disagree. They claim that having several heads in quick succession is bad for schools, because innovation never becomes embedded. Accordingly, they advocate ending the so-called game of chess in which districts 'move their principals around like pawns to maintain the illusion of improvement' (ibid.: 85).

A compromise position might therefore be to allow heads to remain in post for a minimum of three years (barring gross misconduct), so they have time to embed changes without fear of dismissal or transfer; to allow extensions beyond three years by mutual agreement; and to set a limit on tenure at any one school. The length of this limit may need to vary, depending upon the school's circumstances and the head's enthusiasm. Earley and Weindling (2007) suggest that performance usually plateaus after seven years, so a maximum of eight might be reasonable.

We noted earlier how heads use inconsistent and/or arbitrary criteria when choosing teachers. This is also true of some headship selection. Twenty-seven years ago, Morgan *et al.* (1983: 62) observed secondary headship appointments in 26 local education authorities (LEAs) and came to the conclusion that most elimination criteria were inconsistent or irrelevant, and that personality at interview 'dominated decisively'. The situation has certainly improved since then, but some governing bodies still rely on instinct and gut feeling (NCSL n.d.b: 4). There is also a persistent tendency to choose someone who is perceived to match the school's current requirements rather than considering the kind of leader the school might want in the future (Morgan *et al.* 1983; Fink and Brayman 2006; NCSL n.d.b).

Leadership preparation and induction

While the preparation and induction of novice teachers can usually be divided into two distinct phases, one in a teacher training institution and the other in a school or college, the preparation and induction of leaders is much more diffuse because leadership can be exercised in different ways and at different points within a single career. Indeed, the NCSL's Leadership Development Framework lists five stages of school leadership (emergent leadership, established leadership, entry to headship, advanced headship and consultant leadership) and provides an ever-expanding suite of CPD programmes to support each stage (NCSL n.d.a). At one end of the spectrum is *Leading from the Middle*, a programme for teachers experiencing their first formal promotion to head of department (for instance). At the other is *National Leaders in Education*, a programme for outstanding school leaders keen to support other schools in difficulties.

The NCSL was established in 2000 and officially opened by the then prime minister, Tony Blair, in 2002. Its main goal is to 'provide a single national focus for school leadership development, research and innovation' (NCSL 2002: 9). Supporters claim it is 'the most impressive organisation of its kind' (Caldwell 2006: 185), providing 'the most comprehensive and sophisticated national school leadership development model in the world' (Bolam 2004: 255). Thousands of teachers have taken NCSL courses in the past decade, and its reach is undeniably impressive.

Nonetheless, reservations have been voiced about the NCSL's 'unhealthy domination' (Bush 2005: 23) of the sector, particularly its exclusive control over the NPQH. It has also been criticized for its lack of intellectual rigour and limited engagement with research and theory, especially when compared with the Master's degrees required elsewhere. Finally, the fact that it was set up by the Labour Government and receives millions of tax pounds compromises its independence, and renders it vulnerable to political whim (Bush 2008).

The NPQH, run by the NSCL, has been criticized for its focus on the achievement of the *National Standards for Headteachers*. These identify 'the knowledge requirements, professional qualities . . . and actions' heads are said to need in order to fulfil their core purpose (DfES 2004: 5). The standards are organized under six non-hierarchical headings, namely:

1 shaping the future;
2 leading learning and teaching;
3 developing self and working with others;
4 managing the organization;
5 securing accountability;
6 strengthening the community.

We have already seen how achieving QTS can dominate the beginning teacher's induction year, to the detriment of other types of growth. In the same way, critics of the NPQH decry its close association with the *National Standards*, arguing that this link encourages compliance rather than critique (Gronn 2003). In other words, because NPQH participants want to achieve accreditation, they might passively accept everything the course teaches, rather than questioning whether the content is genuinely evidence based or appropriate for their particular context. Similar criticisms have been voiced in New Zealand, where, despite huge variations in school context (including the existence of rural primary schools where the principal is the only teacher), the government commissioned the Hay Group to identify the *generic* skills, knowledge, attributes and competencies needed by first-time heads, from which it then developed a national programme of headship induction (Brundrett *et al.* 2007).

In its defence, the NCSL can argue that NPQH has been comprehensively redesigned twice already (in 2001 and 2008) and that it has published six 'focus pieces' detailing how the *National Standards for Headteachers* have been contextualized by school leaders in urban primary schools, *extended schools* (meaning schools that provide a range of services, such as childcare), nursery schools, rural schools, small schools, and schools with a religious foundation. Nonetheless, the NPQH is still accredited, and the *National Standards* still apply to all headteachers 'irrespective of phase and type of school' (DfES 2004: 5). Critics remain doubtful as to whether this type of competency-framed, government-controlled CPD can ever 'develop the kind of reflective knowledge and higher order cognitive abilities that will undoubtedly be required by leaders in the increasingly complex world of educational leadership in the 21st century' (Brundrett *et al.* 2007: 31–2). Something more differentiated, less prescribed and more intellectually rigorous than the NPQH may be necessary. Indeed, now that the DCSF (2007) expects all teachers to achieve a Master's degree, the NPQH's very limited engagement with theory and research looks increasingly hard to justify. So long as it does not deter too many potential heads, a more flexible combination of postgraduate study, practical training, school-based mentoring and external placement might provide a better preparation.

Leadership development

Once heads are appointed, levels of support vary (Ofsted 2002). PricewaterhouseCoopers (2007) found that between 2004 and 2007, 7 per cent of heads had not had any CPD at all, a finding they contrast with other professions where a certain amount of annual CPD is mandatory. While noting that most heads are satisfied with their CPD, the PricewaterhouseCoopers (2007) report calls for a stronger focus on developing soft skills, such as relationship-building and team-working, and attributes such as self-awareness and resilience. This is to be combined with more innovative modes of delivery, such as secondment into business, cross-sectoral mentoring, work-shadowing in other sectors, international exchanges, and study and research opportunities. In line with earlier research, the report also highlights the enormous benefits heads derive from peer support networks, and mentoring by experienced practitioners.

As a helpful counterpoise to the NCSL's rhetoric, Bolam (2004) reminds us that transformational leadership cannot be expected of every school leader even some of the time, let alone all of the time. Indeed, in the developing world, headship is often an administrative function, with limited scope for instructional leadership, either because all such decisions are taken centrally or because heads spend all their time trying to ensure staff and students have access to basic necessities like food, water and shelter (Oplatka 2004). Leaders everywhere need to be mindful of their national, local and institutional contexts, and use their professional judgement within the constraints of their unique circumstances. Training courses therefore need to equip heads with a range of feasible strategies and a framework within which to choose the most appropriate course of action in a given situation (Bolam 2004). Relentlessly promoting a narrow, idealized form of leadership is unhelpful, even demoralizing, for those heads whose circumstances make it impossible for them to live up to such expectations.

The weaknesses Muijs and Lindsay (2006) identify with regard to the evaluation of teacher CPD are also evident in the evaluation of leadership CPD. Leithwood and Levin (2008) list several leadership CPD evaluation frameworks, each of which incorporates one or more of the following six variables:

1. participant satisfaction;
2. qualities of effective programmes;
3. changes in participants' knowledge, skills and dispositions;

4 changes in leadership practices in schools;
5 changes in classroom conditions;
6 improved student outcomes.

Because variables 5 and 6 (which investigate changes in classroom conditions and student outcomes, respectively) are methodologically problematic, Leithwood and Levin (2008) contend that it is 'reasonable' to limit evaluation to models 3 or 4 (which investigate changes in leadership capacity or actual practice). However, model 1 (which simply asks about participant satisfaction) is 'the most commonly used', despite being 'the least valuable' (ibid.: 284).

Leadership departure

In England and Wales, the majority of heads, once appointed, remain at the same school until they retire (Earley and Weindling 2007). Two-thirds take early retirement before the age of 60 (Higham *et al.* 2007). The relatively generous pension provision may be one factor behind this early exodus, but heads also cite the long, unsociable hours, the endless paperwork and their disenchantment with the standards agenda (Fink and Brayman 2006). Day and Bakioğlu's (1996) research suggests heads pass through four stages – from initiation, to development, to autonomy, and then disenchantment. Opinion is divided over whether government policies are ameliorating or exacerbating the natural tendency for enthusiasm and effectiveness to diminish over time when a person stays in the same role.

Earley and Weindling (2007) contend that heads have a 'shelf-life' of seven to eight years, after which their performance normally plateaus. Their proposed solution is to offer limited-tenure headships of (say) five years. For some heads, this type of portfolio career may well be attractive, but others will be reluctant to forgo the security of job tenure. In addition, although changing jobs may rekindle a head's enthusiasm, age may prevent a similar renewal of energy. Moreover, if the root cause of a head's disenchantment is a clash of values, no amount of movement within the public education sector will restore the head's commitment to government policies they believe are ineffective or even unjust.

Conclusion

This chapter has focused on the selection and development of two groups of staff, namely teachers and school leaders. Learning organizations are meant to be inclusive, so all staff should be selected and developed with equal care. However, resources are always finite, and undeniably some categories of staff are likely to have a greater impact on student learning than others. School business managers and teaching assistants now have a wide range of structured CPD available to them, reflecting the emerging importance of these roles (explored further in Chapter 9). While it is unrealistic to expect that the opportunities afforded to cleaners and lunchtime supervisors will be quite as extensive, it is also unfair to assume they have no CPD needs at all. As ever, a balance needs to be struck between the needs of the organization and the desires of the individual, between the idealism of lifelong learning for all and the pragmatism of a limited CPD budget.

9 Remodelling

New learning and teaching teams

The National Agreement

As mentioned in Chapter 2, the national agreement on *Raising Standards and Tackling Workload* (hereafter *The National Agreement*) (DfES 2003a) was signed on 15 January 2003 by the English Department for Education and Skills, the Welsh Assembly government, five of the six unions representing teachers and headteachers, three unions representing support staff, and the organization representing teachers' employers. However, the largest education union, the NUT, refused to sign for reasons explained below. *The National Agreement* set out a seven-point plan designed to reduce the number of hours teachers and school leaders worked, and to improve pupil outcomes (ibid.: 52).

Under the terms of the agreement, teachers' overall hours were to be reduced. They were not to undertake administrative and clerical tasks routinely, or cover for absent colleagues. They were to receive guaranteed planning, preparation and assessment time (PPA) within the school day. School leaders were to receive dedicated time for their leadership responsibilities. Unnecessary paperwork was to be reduced. Personal assistants, cover supervisors and higher-level teaching assistants (HLTAs) were to be introduced, alongside business and personnel managers from outside education. To support these changes, additional resources and national change management programmes would be introduced, and progress would be monitored.

A three-year timetable was outlined. From September 2003, teachers should not perform routine clerical and administrative tasks, and teachers with leadership responsibilities should receive dedicated time for this; from September 2004, teachers should not have to cover for colleagues, beyond an initial maximum of 38 hours per year. From September 2005, all teachers should get 10 per cent PPA time and be excused from invigilation, while heads should get dedicated headship time.

A key driver behind *The National Agreement* was the independent report into teacher workload commissioned by the DfES from Pricewaterhouse-Coopers (2001). This indicated that teachers worked very intensively during term-time, averaging 52 hours per week, whereas other UK professionals worked only 45 hours per week. Weekly averages for those with leadership responsibilities were higher still, with heads said to work 300–400 more hours per year than managers in other sectors. The report also noted that teaching staff undertook some tasks that did not require the expertise of a qualified teacher. Four solutions for providing non-contact time were offered, namely:

1. reducing pupil taught time;
2. increasing pupil–teacher ratios and/or new approaches to timetabling;
3. recruiting additional teachers;
4. supporting learning through staff other than teachers.

The government embraced the fourth suggestion, and began remodelling the school workforce in new and highly controversial ways.

A note on terminology

The school sector has struggled to find suitable terms for employees who do not hold QTS – not least because such staff perform a wide range of functions, some of which are held in higher regard than others. *The Deployment and Impact of Support Staff in Schools* (*DISSS*), a national five-year (2003–8) study commissioned by the DfES, identifies seven different categories, as follows (Blatchford *et al.* 2006: 7):

1. teaching assistant equivalent (teaching assistant (TA), learning support assistant (LSA) for special educational needs (SEN) pupils, nursery nurse, therapist);
2. pupil welfare (Connexions personal adviser, education welfare officer, home–school liaison officer, learning mentor, nurse and welfare assistant);
3. technical and specialist staff (information and communication technologies network manager, ICT technician, librarian, science technician and technology technician);
4. other pupil support staff (bilingual support officer, cover supervisor, escort, exam invigilator, language assistant, midday assistant and midday supervisor);
5. facilities staff (cleaner, cook, and other catering staff);
6. administrative staff (administrator/clerk, bursar, finance officer, office manager, secretary, attendance officer, data manager, examination officer, and personal assistant (PA) to the headteacher);
7. site staff (caretaker and premises manager).

These terms are not universally accepted, however. Those labelled *teaching assistants* by the *DISSS* study are termed *classroom assistants* by both the Scottish government and the staff themselves (Wilson *et al.* 2002, 2003).

This reflects the fact that in Scotland the remit of such staff is more limited. Whereas the law in England and Wales was changed in July 2003 and July 2004, respectively, to allow TAs to assume responsibility for whole classes without the presence of a qualified teacher, in Scotland classroom assistants continue merely 'to support the teacher by relieving him/her of unnecessary tasks that are not related directly to the process of learning and teaching' (GTCS 2003: 6).

Likewise, the term *bursar* is viewed in some quarters as outdated, because it can imply a narrow focus on finance, whereas the remit of the school business manager (SBM) is much wider (O'Sullivan *et al.* 2000). Indeed, financial management is the subject of just one of 12 chapters in a recent book written for SBMs (Keating and Moorcroft 2006). Within the opening part of the book (entitled 'Skills and technical competencies'), financial management sits alongside chapters on managing risk, ICT, facilities, human resources and office systems. Also included, however, is a part entitled 'Thinking strategically', with chapters on strategic management, managing school improvement and performance, and change management. Such chapters will, no doubt, interest the 50 per cent of secondary SBMs and 17 per cent of primary SBMs who operate at a strategic, rather than operational or tactical, level (Aldridge 2008).

Indeed, in recognition of their expanding role, members of the National *Bursars* Association voted to change their name to the National Association of *School Business Management* in November 2008 (NASBM 2008). Although the NCSL is still referring to the *Bursar* Development Programme containing a Certificate, a Diploma and an Advanced Diploma of *School Business Management*, it surely cannot be long before the word 'bursar' is dropped. Clearly, terminology matters because of the connotations words convey, but there is still some way to go before the field can claim an agreed nomenclature.

The scale and scope of workforce remodelling

Although schools had previously employed secretaries and caretakers, the 1981 Education Act introduced additional staff into classrooms. Such staff, known as *welfare assistants*, were employed to support specific students with SEN as they transferred from special schools to mainstream settings (Swann and Loxley 1998; Bach *et al.* 2006). The 1988 Education Reform Act again increased the number of support staff in two ways. First, staff previously employed by the local education authority, such as cleaners and caterers, became employees of the school. Second, as schools became responsible for a much larger budget, they needed more administrative staff to oversee and record how it was spent. So, even before *The National Agreement*, the number of support staff was rapidly increasing.

As is shown in Table 9.1, the number of teachers in England increased by a modest 5 per cent between 1997 and 2002. In the same period, however,

Table 9.1 Number of full-time equivalent employees (in thousands) in LA-maintained schools, academies and city technology colleges in England

	1997	*2000*	*2001*	*2002*	*2003*	*2004*	*2005*	*2006*	*2007*	*2008*
Teachers	400.3	405.8	411.3	420.8	425.0	429.6	434.2	438.4	439.3	441.2
Total support staff	133.9	162.0	186.3	213.9	223.7	241.5	265.9	289.1	308.2	326.6
Teaching assistants	60.6	79.0	95.0	105.4	121.3	132.2	147.2	153.5	163.8	177.0
Other support staff	73.3	83.0	91.2	108.4	102.5	109.2	118.7	135.6	144.4	149.6
Total workforce	534.2	567.8	597.6	634.6	648.8	671.1	700.1	727.6	747.5	767.7

Source: Department for Children, Schools and Families (2008: Table 1).

the number of FTE support staff increased by 60 per cent. When the figures for TAs are separated out, the increase is an even more striking 74 per cent. In one sense, therefore, *The National Agreement* is simply continuing this trend of small annual increases in the number of teachers but large annual increases in the number of support staff, especially TAs. In the five years following *The National Agreement* (2003–8), the number of teachers rose by only 16,200, but the number of support staff rose by 102,900 and the number of TAs rose by 55,700.

What makes workforce remodelling contentious, therefore, is not so much the increase in the number of support staff, per se, as the ensuing changes to their remit; tasks that were once the preserve of a qualified teacher are now being opened up to those without QTS. This begs some fundamental questions about the nature of teaching, the nature of educational leadership and who is best placed to enhance pupil learning. In this way, remodelling is part of 'a grand narrative' (MacBeath and Galton 2007: 33), the site of 'a very complex struggle over ideas and territories; the amount and deployment of resources; and the culture and practices of professionality' (Gunter 2007: online). Two flashpoints illustrate the issues, and accordingly they are explored in more detail in what follows. The first concerns whether heads need QTS, and the second concerns whether people without QTS should take responsibility for whole classes.

Heads without QTS?

In a much-quoted report into school leadership, the private consultancy firm PricewaterhouseCoopers notes that it is not a legal requirement for the head of an English state school to have QTS, merely 'custom and practice' (2007: 105). The report also notes how in Sweden, for example, heads require 'educational knowledge and practice', but not QTS per se. This leads the report's authors to conclude that,

> [t]here should be no barriers for individuals with the relevant skills to take on the leadership role as long as there is always a senior qualified teacher on the team to act as the 'lead learner' and direct teaching and learning within the institution.
>
> (ibid.: 111)

A year later, this contention was put to the test when Peter Noble was appointed chief executive of the Richard Rose Federation in Carlisle and given overall responsibility for two newly formed secondary schools, Central Academy and Morton Academy. Mr Noble, a former NHS executive and head of a university medical faculty, had never worked in a school before. The academies' sponsors – the chief executive of a lorry firm and a property developer – appointed him because they wanted an expert in change management and human resources (Stewart 2008). Sadly, despite being supported by two heads with QTS, Mr Noble left after just five months, following a damning Ofsted emergency inspection (Marley 2009a). Those such as the Association of Teachers and Lecturers (ATL), who oppose the appointment of heads without QTS, claim that this unfortunate incident proves their point. Those more receptive to the idea, however, emphasize that one of the supporting heads with QTS also left, and that even Mr Noble's successor, Mike Gibbons, said there had been too much government pressure to open Central Academy a year earlier than planned (Marley 2009b). So, although it is unlikely that another state school will appoint a leader without school experience any time soon, the argument about QTS is far from over.

Indeed, a recent poll in *School Financial Management* (SFM n.d.) indicated that 44 per cent of respondents were in favour of SBMs becoming heads, and 56 per cent against – though, of course, the SFM readership is a rather skewed sample. Similar ambivalence is displayed by Moorcroft and Summerson (2006: 271) when they describe SBMs becoming 'Joint Chief Executives' as 'a step too far for the foreseeable future (although legitimate as part of a futuring exercise)'. The ASCL, however, is more encouraging. It maintains that, while business leaders from outside the school sector should never be appointed to headship, outstanding SBMs with NPQH could be (*Leader* 2007). This seems a sensible middle course, given that the NPQH is an overt acknowledgement of the successful candidate's immediate readiness for headship (NCSL n.d.c) *and* open to staff without QTS. Currently, only a handful of SBMs have been awarded the NPQH, but as the number increases, so too will the pressure to appoint at least some of them to headship.

Teachers without QTS?

QTS has never been a requirement in the UK private sector, and even within the maintained sector, people without QTS can still be employed to teach if they have trained overseas or there is no qualified teacher available. Workforce remodelling, however, takes the deployment of staff without QTS to a new level. Heads, at their discretion, can use such people to teach whole classes when their regular qualified teacher is absent. This applies to absences necessitated by the requirement to provide teachers with 10 per cent PPA time, as well as absences resulting from CPD attendance and illness. This is the reason the NUT refused to sign *The National Agreement*, calling it 'A price too high' (NUT 2003).

The National Agreement stresses that 'teachers and high level teaching assistants are not interchangeable' (DfES 2003a: 12), as do subsequent government pronouncements (Miliband 2003: 5). Unfortunately, however, the demarcation between those with and without QTS remains far from clear, and the frequent comparisons with the medical profession obscure rather than illuminate the perceived difference.

For example, in 2001, Estelle Morris, the Secretary of State for Education and Skills, foresaw a position whereby, within the next five to ten years,

> our best teachers have a status and a role which makes them more like consultant doctors than either junior doctors or nurses, responsible for the most difficult teaching tasks and also for the organization of other teachers and teaching assistants.
>
> (2001: 18)

Unfortunately, such a comparison is informative only if both speaker and audience agree on the criteria for judging the 'best' teachers and the 'most difficult' teaching tasks. This is far from being the case. Likewise, Doug McAvoy, the General Secretary of the NUT, explained the union's opposition to *The National Agreement* by suggesting that 'the government is asking the theatre sister to take over the brain surgery' (BBC 2002). Perhaps with this comment in mind, David Miliband, Minister of State for School Standards, later reassured his audience that 'no one suggests that nurses should do brain surgery. But no brain surgeon would work without a nursing team' (2003: 5). Again, such comparisons work only if the tasks performed by teachers and TAs can be as easily delineated as those performed by brain surgeons and nurses. This is manifestly not so, as illustrated by the considerable overlap between the 33 Professional Standards for QTS (TDA 2007) and the 33 Professional Standards for Higher Level Teaching Assistants (TDA n.d.a). There is also the anomaly that TAs, unlike nurses, are completely unregulated; there are no mandatory qualifications, and no previous training or experience is required. Moreover, the three-day preparation course (TDA n.d.b) and half-day assessment visit (TDA n.d.c) required for the award of HLTA status are not remotely comparable to the training and assessment undertaken by fully qualified nurses.

Comparisons with the medical profession are disingenuous because teaching is not a *classical* profession (Hargreaves and Goodson 1996; Gillard 2005). As we saw in Chapter 3, it does not enjoy the same autonomy as the older professions of law, medicine and divinity, particularly in England, where entry and progression are controlled by the TDA, and teachers' work is heavily constrained by the National Curriculum, the National Strategies, Standardized Assessment Tests (SATs) and Ofsted (Wilkinson 2005). Nor can its practitioners lay claim to a specific body of *formal knowledge* – 'general, abstract, theoretical knowledge of the kind acquired in universities' (ibid.: 432). Whereas in the 1970s, university departments of education all taught four key disciplines (psychology, philosophy, history and sociology), nowadays there is no consensus about the core knowledge teachers require (ibid.). Instead, *The National Agreement* refers only vaguely to 'the extra range, experience and complexity of understanding reflected in their [teachers'] higher qualifications' (DfES 2003a: 12). Even before workload remodelling, McNamara (1993: 282) recognized 'that the formal knowledge base for their [teachers'] professional practice is weak and this enables outsiders to intrude upon their work in the classroom'. More than a decade later, the problem persists, exacerbated not only by workforce remodelling but also by the proliferation of school-based routes into teaching. Although teaching is nominally an all-graduate profession, 'achieving QTS requires only compliance with a series of state-defined competencies', not mastery of a specific body of formal knowledge acquired through higher education (Wilkinson 2005: 430). This is highly problematic, because,

> [w]ithout an explicit articulation of teacher knowledge, stipulations about the proper roles of teachers and HLTAs are unreasoned and arbitrary. In such circumstances even teachers' newly proposed jurisdiction will not be able to withstand the professional ambitions of the subordinate profession indefinitely.
>
> (ibid.: 430)

This lack of consensus over formal knowledge is compounded by a lack of consensus over pedagogy (Alexander 2004). This makes it very difficult to specify which aspects of the educative process are so crucial and demanding as to be non-transferable to support staff, and which are not. Even the list of so-called *administrative and clerical tasks* is contested, with some teachers claiming it takes real skill to create eye-catching and thought-provoking displays that enable all children to feel equally proud of their work (Dixon 2003). How much more difficult, then, is it to decide which (if any) elements of *pastoral support* and/or *teaching* can be delegated without compromising a student's education?

The logic of workforce remodelling suggests that planning, preparation and assessment demand a teacher's expertise in a way that interacting with students in class does not (Wilkinson 2005): the former activity is something for which only teachers get guaranteed non-contact time, whereas the latter is something both teachers and TAs do. Such a line of argument opens up 'the potential for a new division of labour to emerge between those who "coordinate" and "evaluate" and those who "deliver"' (Stevenson 2007a: 237). The former group will be small in number and enjoy well-paid, secure jobs, with titles like *advanced skills teacher* and *excellent teacher*. The latter group will be much larger, with the demarcation between teacher and TA all but removed. They will compete for low-paid, insecure work that ebbs and flows according to a particular school's roll and the latest fashion in group size. Undoubtedly, such a division of labour would be decried by all qualified teachers initially. However, as we saw in Chapter 2, union opposition to government policy has become more muted and less effective. The NUT's refusal to sign *The National Agreement* was a brave, unilateral decision, but it had little impact on the ensuing process. Unless the profession undergoes the sort of transformation described at the end of Chapter 3, it will not be well placed to resist the more radical workforce reform envisaged by Stevenson (ibid.).

The empirical evidence concerning what teaching assistants do

While some authors have debated the normative question of what TAs should and should not be allowed to do, others have carried out empirical studies to discover what they actually do. The largest of these is the five-year *Deployment and Impact of Support Staff in Schools* (*DISSS*) study mentioned on p. 125. In Strand 1, Wave 1 of the study (covering summer and autumn 2004, i.e. prior to the introduction of 10 per cent PPA time), three questionnaires were sent to 10,000 schools in England and Wales, one for school leaders, one for teachers and one for all support staff (not just TAs). A total of 2,318 questionnaires were returned from school leaders, 2,127 from support staff and 1,824 from teachers (Blatchford *et al.* 2006). Approximately two years later (in spring and summer 2006, i.e. after the introduction of 10 per cent PPA time), the data collection process was repeated in Strand 1, Wave 2 of the study. This time, 2,017 questionnaires were returned from school leaders, 2,693 from support staff and 1,297 from teachers (Blatchford *et al.* 2007a). In addition to these questionnaires, 1,670 support staff completed a 12-hour timelog indicating, in 20-minute segments, which of 91 tasks they performed that day (Blatchford *et al.* 2008). A third wave of data collection took place in 2008, but the results have not yet been published.

As well as the three waves of Strand 1 described above, the *DISSS* team undertook a second piece of research, focusing on children in Years 1, 3, 7 and 10 during the 2005/6 academic year. Strand 2 involved surveying pupils in 76 schools to see whether receiving additional support (from either a TA or an LSA) had any impact on their attitudes to learning. The *DISSS* researchers also observed 686 pupils in 49 schools and conducted 496 semi-structured interviews with headteachers, teachers, support staff and pupils in 47 schools (Blatchford *et al.* 2008). Such extensive data collection makes the *DISSS* study by far the most authoritative of its kind to date, and, accordingly, the following sections draw extensively upon it.

Who are support staff?

The *DISSS* study highlights the huge variation in support staff biographies, qualifications, experiences, duties, pay, working conditions and future aspirations. According to Blatchford *et al.* (2007a), 89 per cent of support staff are female, but site staff are predominantly male. Ninety per cent are aged 36 or over, and 97 per cent describe themselves as ethnically white. Ten per cent have no qualifications at all, while 14 per cent have a degree and 5 per cent have a postgraduate qualification. Thirty-eight per cent have qualifications above GCSE level. A fifth work full-time (35 hours or more), while a third work 15 hours per week or less. Forty-five per cent are paid for 52 weeks of the year (with holiday entitlement), but the rest have shorter annual contracts.

With regard to pay, the average hourly rate for all support staff was £9.37 in 2007 (UNISON 2007: 32). However, this figure masks quite significant extremes. In 2006, for example, 39 per cent of support staff were paid less than £7.50 an hour, but 3 per cent (almost all administrative staff) were paid more than £15.00 per hour (Blatchford *et al.* 2007a: 53). Even within the same job category, there were large differences, depending upon the school location, the percentage of pupils eligible for FSMs, and the employee's gender. TAs, for example, were paid anything from £5.05 to £17.95, but, on average, male TAs were paid £1.52 per hour more than females. For administrative staff, the disparity was even greater, with males being paid an average of £3.44 per hour more than females. Such anomalies strengthen the argument for a national pay scale for support staff, similar to that already enjoyed by teaching staff in UK schools, and by both academic and support staff in UK higher education.

Who are teaching assistants?

According to Dixon (2003: 28):

> The unspoken assumption seems to be that these teacher assistants, a-k-a 'Mums', are in their forties, probably middle-class, educated at least to Further Education level if not beyond, and will do any job for the love of it. In practice, quite a number are between sixteen and twenty-five and amongst those who leave secondary school without qualifications.

In fact, only a third of TAs possess qualifications above GCSE level, but, equally, only 2 per cent have no qualifications whatsoever (Blatchford *et al.* 2007a: 106).

There are also huge variations in the number of TAs schools employ. Outer London schools have, on average, five TAs each, whereas inner London schools have 13 (Bach *et al.* 2006). Obviously, this is partly determined by the school budget, and reflects the number of SEN children on roll. However, other contextual factors play a part. For example, if unemployment in the surrounding area is high or the school finds it hard to attract teachers, more TAs are likely to be recruited (ibid.).

TAs also vary in their aspirations (Wilson and Bedford 2008; Butt and Lance 2009), meaning that the government's desire to see more TAs become fully qualified teachers (DfES 2004: 41) may be wishful thinking. In Bach *et al.*'s (2006: 12) sample, only 'a very small minority' saw it as a stepping stone to becoming a teacher (a group labelled 'the ambitious'). Far more prevalent were the 'steady starters' and the 'developers' (ibid.: 12). The 'steady starters' had often begun as volunteers. They enjoyed the job but needed to fit it around other obligations, and lacked confidence. By contrast, the 'developers' had made a conscious decision to go into education. Not surprisingly, the 'developers' tended to have higher expectations than the 'steady starters' in terms of what the job should offer them and the training they should be given. Even so, the 'developers' had no intention of becoming teachers because they thought qualifying would take too long, and the job could not be fitted around their childcare obligations. They also did not want to deal with the poor behaviour and excessive paperwork they saw weighing teachers down.

What do support staff actually do?

In a survey of over a thousand support staff in more than 700 schools (UNISON 2007), two-thirds said workforce remodelling had altered their job content, and just under half said it had changed their job title. Staff were being expected to perform existing work to a higher standard, and new duties were being added to their remit. They worked with students (some with SEN, some not) individually, in small groups and in whole classes. They managed nursery and early years classes as well as supervising lunchbreaks and clubs. They liaised with parents and were involved with *extended schools* provision. They mentored colleagues, led teams and line-managed subordinates. In terms of administration, they took the register, input data, kept records, wrote reports, invigilated exams and arranged cover for teachers and other staff. Most said their pay rises were insufficient, given their increased responsibilities. Some also complained that their duties had become too hard or too time-consuming. However, job satisfaction remained high, despite slipping from 'overwhelmingly positive' (Blatchford *et al.* 2006: 80) in 2004 to 'generally positive' (Blatchford *et al.* 2008: 100) in 2006.

What do teaching assistants actually do?

Drawing on his own experience, Kerry (2005) describes 11 different roles for TAs, including dogsbody (or 'pig-ignorant peasant'), teacher's PA, behaviour manager and mobile paraprofessional. The more systematic observations of the *DISSS* study reveal that TAs spend two-thirds of their time interacting with pupils directly, and only one-third supporting the teacher or the school (by preparing materials, making displays, correcting work, etc.). The team therefore conclude that 'classroom-based support staff now have a distinct pedagogical role, supporting and interacting with pupils' (Blatchford *et al.* 2008: 10). In primary schools, TAs most often sit or work with a small group of students, whereas in secondary schools they either work exclusively with one student or move around the classroom helping different students, as necessary. The *DISSS* team rarely observed a TA taking a whole class, but, of course, school staff may have deliberately engineered this.

Most often, TAs work with students who have SEN, lower ability or behavioural issues, and they concentrate on improving numeracy and literacy (Blatchford *et al.* 2004, 2008). When a TA is present, both students and teachers spend more time on-task, and students get more individual attention (Blatchford *et al.* 2007a). Whereas teachers normally address groups or the whole class, and keep any individual exchanges very short, TAs have more frequent and longer one-to-one conversations. On the other hand, the presence of a TA reduces the amount of teacher–student interaction for all students, but especially for those working with the TA. This means TAs provide *alternative* rather than *additional* support, and, paradoxically, students most in need of the teacher's attention receive it least (Blatchford *et al.* 2004, 2007a and b, 2008, 2009).

What impact do teaching assistants have?

Between 1999 and 2002, the government allocated £350 million to recruit and train TAs, with a further £200 million being given each year between 2001 and 2004 (Butt and Lance 2009). Despite this considerable investment of public money, it remains unclear whether students have actually benefited. Heads and teachers speak very positively of TAs, believing they reduce teacher workload, facilitate better classroom management, increase teaching effectiveness and enhance learning (Wilson *et al.* 2003; Blatchford *et al.* 2004; Butt and Lance 2009). However, their impact on student attainment appears negligible. Blatchford *et al.* (2004, 2007b) used multilevel regression models to analyse Key Stage 1 and Key Stage 2 SATs scores, together with the results of similar standardized tests taken by Year 4 and 5 students. Despite a data set comprising over 20,000 participants, the research team found 'no evidence that the presence of TAs, or any characteristic of TAs, such as training or experience, had a measurable impact on pupil attainment' (Blatchford *et al.* 2007b: 21). This finding reflects previous research in England (Muijs 2003), Scotland (Schlapp *et al.* 2001) and the US (Finn *et al.* 2000), all indicating that having extra adults in classrooms does not improve attainment.

The evidence that workforce remodelling reduces teacher workload is equivocal, as we shall see, and it has undoubtedly increased senior staff workload quite considerably (MacBeath and Galton 2007). This makes the government's continuing commitment to TAs rather curious. When the DCSF asked Richard Handover to investigate how it might save money during the global recession, he suggested that 40,000 TA posts could be cut (BBC 2009). The very next day, the Schools Secretary, Ed Balls, issued a statement saying he would not be following this recommendation (DCSF 2009). Even so, as the recession bites, it will surely become increasingly difficult for the government and individual school governing bodies to justify the amount of money spent on TAs unless clearer evidence of their direct contribution to school improvement is forthcoming.

Barriers to the effective deployment of teaching assistants

Notwithstanding the ideological debate about whether or not TAs should *teach*, several studies have identified a range of issues hampering their effectiveness. Workload data are notoriously slippery, and so it is hard to judge how far the increase in support staff has reduced teachers' hours. In one study (Butt and Lance 2005), 80 per cent of teachers said it had, but in another (Blatchford *et al.* 2006) the figure was only 46 per cent. Meanwhile, a different study (MacBeath and Galton 2007) indicates that teachers are still working longer hours than in 2002. PPA time may make them feel valued, but it does not reduce their workload because more is being demanded of them, and liaising with TAs takes time. Even more worryingly, the workloads of heads and senior staff have continued to increase, not least because they now coordinate more support staff. As a result, they are simply not finding time within the school day for their strategic responsibilities, even though it is stipulated in *The National Agreement* that they should be able to.

Another issue concerns role clarity. Almost all schools give their support staff written job descriptions (UNISON 2007), but in a quarter of cases this does not match what staff are asked to do (Mistry *et al.* 2004). Butt and Lance (2009: 226) write of 'a miscellany of roles' that 'is supported neither by appropriate training, nor by the provision of unambiguous job descriptions, clear line management or any means of reviewing the tasks that TAs are expected to undertake in schools'.

It is also worrying that TAs usually work with those children in greatest need, because, as was noted earlier, TA-supported students generally receive less attention from their qualified teachers. Furthermore, studies in Cyprus and the US suggest that when SEN children are allocated a TA, teachers feel less responsibility for their progress (Marks *et al.* 1999; Angelides *et al.* 2009). Moreover, TAs receive little, if any, relevant training for this demanding role (MacBeath and Galton 2007). Consequently, some experience considerable stress, and inadvertently encourage students to become overly dependent (Rose 2000; Quirke 2003; Angelides *et al.* 2009).

There is also evidence that the pace and style of primary teaching imposed by the National Literacy and Numeracy Strategies left 25 per cent of pupils floundering and that the government-imposed targets were achieved only because of the intense remedial work TAs did with these children (Hancock and Eyres 2004). Using TAs to prop up ill-advised government prescription in this way is doubly insulting to teacher professionalism.

The low pay and lack of a national pay structure have already been mentioned. TAs have one of the ten lowest-paid jobs in Britain (Toynbee

2003), with some being paid less than the school cleaners (Blatchford *et al.* 2004). At best, this hampers the establishment of genuine teacher–TA partnerships because one salary is three times higher than the other (Wilson and Bedford 2008), and at worst it encourages a 'second-class performance' (Hammersley-Fletcher 2008: 501). Even those awarded HLTA status are not necessarily paid more money. In 2007, only 36 per cent of staff with HLTA status were being paid exclusively at the higher level (Wilson *et al.* 2007). Sixteen per cent had split contracts, despite strong union opposition to this. Disturbingly, 17 per cent did some HLTA work without being paid more for it, and 29 per cent did no HLTA work. Schools, it seems, are choosing not to appoint HLTAs because of fears over funding (Wilson and Bedford 2008), despite the government's rhetoric highlighting their worth (Morris 2001; Miliband 2003; DCSF 2009).

Another problem is not being paid for the time they spend planning work or liaising with teachers (Blatchford *et al.* 2004, 2006, 2007a; Butt and Lance 2005, 2009; Wilson and Bedford 2008). Blatchford *et al.* (2008: 14) summarize the issue well:

> Class-based support staff were found to have to work in excess of their paid time, as they became more drawn into lesson planning, preparation and feedback, in direct and indirect support of the teachers with whom they worked. This expanded role, whilst welcomed by many individuals, was not often matched with higher rates of pay, increased hours of paid work, inclusion in meetings and decision-making, or opportunities for training in preparation for their new roles. In practice, the goodwill of support staff was indispensable in making the policy work.

Any policy that relies on unpaid overtime ought to be challenged, but this is especially exploitative when the staff are on such low salaries to begin with.

Making workforce remodelling work

Clearly, some issues need tackling at a national level, beginning with a nationally agreed pay scale for all support staff. There also needs to be more, and better training available (Blatchford *et al.* 2004; Butt and Lance 2005; Kerry 2005; Bach *et al.* 2006). Although 90 per cent of support staff had had some form of training in the previous 12 months, from either their school or the LA (UNISON 2009), two-thirds were ambivalent about its quality and relevance (UNISON 2007). Training needs to be less fragmented, and, for TAs, to focus on child development as well as technical competencies (Dixon 2003). Crucially, it should be scheduled at convenient times – not after school or during INSET days for those with childcare commitments – and attendees should be paid for their time. For some topics, such as behaviour management, it would be beneficial for teachers and TAs to attend together (Wilson and Bedford 2008).

In addition, it is vital that all support staff have a clear job description accurately reflecting what they do. There also needs to be a mechanism for regularly monitoring both the job description and the employee's performance. A third of support staff do not have a line manager (Blatchford *et al.* 2007a) and only around half have an annual review (UNISON 2007). It is hard to see how these employees can be adequately supported, let alone developed. Equally, however, those who line-manage support staff need appropriate training. This is especially important for those teachers who have not managed other adults before (Mistry *et al.* 2004; Burgess 2008; Butt and Lance 2005; Wilson and Bedford 2008).

Although the greatest barrier to the effective deployment of TAs is the lack of paid liaison time (Wilson and Bedford 2008), there are other ways schools can improve communication without spending a fortune. These include making support staff welcome in the staffroom, providing them with pigeon-holes, giving them their own space on notice-boards and scheduling meetings at convenient times (Mistry *et al.* 2004).

Conclusion

Given that the NUT stood outside *The National Agreement*, it is no surprise that a report it commissioned (MacBeath and Galton 2007) finds little evidence to suggest the original aims have been achieved. Nonetheless, the study's methodology is suitably robust, so there is no reason to doubt the findings. Teachers still do a range of administrative tasks because they enjoy doing them, think them too important to relinquish or find delegating them too tiresome. The benefits of PPA time, particularly at secondary level, are being negated by an increase in disruptive behaviour and by the fallout from inclusion policies. Heads and the SLT are under more pressure, not less, as they struggle to manage an ever-increasing number of support staff and cope with new initiatives such as Every Child Matters (ECM) and *extended schools*. Although 'the argument for a more differentiated profession is a compelling one, allowing people with differing responsibilities to play to their strengths' (MacBeath and Galton 2007: 31), workforce remodelling 'has proved to be something of a palliative for a system on the verge of implosion'. It may have reduced the hours of some teachers, but it has certainly not improved the work–life balance of heads or TAs. Much more importantly, though, it has studiously avoided any engagement with pedagogy, and any discussion of such fundamental questions as:

- What is the purpose of education?
- What does teaching mean?
- From whom, and under what circumstances, can students learn best?

Unless these wider issues are openly debated and a provisional consensus reached, the full benefits of any structural reorganization of the workforce will not be realized.

10 Appraisal and performance

Introduction

As we saw in Chapter 1, the past 20 years have witnessed a global rise in public sector managerialism and the emergence of sophisticated systems of performance management. Debate is hindered by a lack of consensus over terminology, and by a tendency to gloss over contextual differences. Nonetheless, there is now a widespread (though not uncontested) belief that educational institutions function better if the performance of employees is systematically managed.

This chapter starts by examining the history of appraisal in England and Wales. It then considers the inherent tension between evaluative and developmental appraisal, and between the needs of the individual and the demands of the institution. It argues that the power dynamics underlying any form of appraisal need to be acknowledged and addressed, because the potential for abuse exists at both ends of the spectrum: in certain contexts, underperforming staff may be able to avoid censure indefinitely, short-changing colleagues and students alike, whereas in other contexts, Machiavellian leaders may be able to remove subordinates for no other reason than personal spite. This latter situation is explored through two case studies from the United Arab Emirates (UAE), where sponsorship laws provide expatriate employees with virtually no protection against instant dismissal. What then becomes clear is that the success or failure of any appraisal system depends far less on the particular policies and procedures adopted than on the internal ethos of the institution and the external conditions of employment within which the appraisal system operates.

A note on terminology

The literature uses a wide range of terms, including *teacher appraisal*, *teacher evaluation*, *performance management* and *performance review*, with little consensus regarding what each term means. In this chapter, therefore, the word *appraisal* will be used in the broadest possible sense to indicate any systematic examination of an employee's performance, for whatever purpose.

Appraisal and public sector managerialism

The emergence of appraisal has been linked to global policy agendas that call for more efficient and accountable public services (Walsh 1988; Simons and Elliott 1989; Rutherford 1992; Wilson and Beaton 1993; Huisman and Currie 2004; Bush and Middlewood 2005). The US has a tradition of quality assurance in education stretching back to the late nineteenth century (Huisman and Currie 2004), but schools and colleges elsewhere have caught up only in the past 20 years. What we are now witnessing is,

> [a]n unstable, uneven but apparently unstoppable flood of closely interrelated reform ideas [that] is permeating and reorienting education systems in diverse social and political locations which have very different histories. . . . The key elements of the education reform 'package' . . . are embedded in three interrelated *policy technologies*: the market, managerialism and performativity.
>
> (Ball 2003: 215, italics in original)

These policy technologies achieve what Marginson (1997) calls 'steering from a distance'. Educational institutions are seemingly given greater autonomy and decision-making powers, but are simultaneously constrained by the policy context. The UK's 1988 Education Reform Act is a classic example of this. On the one hand, state schools are allowed to control a much greater percentage of their own budgets, and employ their own staff directly rather than relying on a local authority. Yet on the other, central control is exercised covertly through a system of checks and balances to which all state schools must submit. In England, these now include a National Curriculum (specifying content) and National Strategies (specifying pedagogy); an Ofsted inspection regime, whose reports and judgements are instantly downloadable; and performance tables that rank every school according to its examination results. Schools and colleges can choose how to act, but this freedom is severely restricted by government policies that create a quasi-market for education, and mould public expectations in particular directions (Pollitt 1993; Clarke and Newman 1997). In this way, 'Direct central regulation is reduced, but the centre determines the rules of the game, the forms and limits of what can be achieved, so that the system/institution is steered by remote control' (Marginson 1997: 65).

Although this trend is evident all over the world, appraisal is not the same everywhere. Its precise aims, processes and instruments differ from institution to institution, depending on the organizational culture and the national context (Townley 1993; Aycan 2005; Bush and Middlewood 2005; Gerhart and Fang 2005). Although Rihab and Al Fanar (the two UAE case study institutions) explicitly modelled their appraisal systems on those of Western universities, the nature of employee sponsorship meant that appraisal in the UAE was nothing like that experienced by Western expatriates in their home countries.

The introduction of appraisal in England and Wales

During the past two hundred years, the teaching profession in England and Wales has experienced a series of pendulum swings with regard to external regulation. The 1833 Althorpe Act introduced the first school inspections (Brighouse 1995, cited in Shaw *et al.* 2003). These were 'not intended as a means of exercising control, but of affording assistance' (Shuttleworth 1839, quoted in Shaw *et al.* 2003). For political reasons, the 1862 Revised Code introduced a far more draconian system in which elementary teachers were paid according to the attendance rates and test scores of their pupils. In 1926, such *payment by results* was abolished, again for political reasons, and teachers were once more observed by inspectors whose function was to disseminate good practice. At this point, state schooling moved from 'an essentially visible, prescriptive and centralized system to an essentially invisible and diffuse mode' (Grace 1985: 11). By the 1950s, teachers had become trusted, autonomous professionals (Tropp 1957, cited in Bartlett 2000), and full inspection by HMI had 'virtually ceased' (DES/Welsh Office 1982, cited in Shaw *et al.* 2003).

Two decades later, the pendulum swung again, when four factors prompted the public to lose confidence in the teaching profession. First, right-wing educationalists published a series of damning pamphlets between 1969 and 1977. These so-called *Black Papers* criticized progressive education and persuaded the public that teachers were responsible for declining academic standards and rising illiteracy, violence and indiscipline. Second, the economic crisis of 1973–5 raised questions about how well schools prepared students for the workplace. Third, the controversy at William Tyndale Junior School over the use of progressive teaching methods triggered demands for more centralized control (Davis 2002). Fourth, a speech by James Callaghan, the then prime minister, at Ruskin College, Oxford, in 1976 called for 'a national debate' (among both educationalists and non-educationalists) about how best to prepare students for the workforce (Callaghan 1976).

When a new Conservative Government, under Margaret Thatcher, was elected in 1979, the pace of disillusionment quickened (Bartlett 2000). Two government White Papers (DES 1983, 1985) claimed that standards would rise if teacher performance were formally assessed. A pilot appraisal scheme, commissioned by the Department of Education and Science (DES), was introduced in Suffolk Local Education Authority. The results, presented in *Those Having Torches* (Suffolk County Council Education Department 1985), suggested that teachers would welcome appraisal, just so long as it focused on development.

Ironically, just as this favourable pilot evaluation was published, teachers began industrial action, and so many voluntary appraisal schemes were abandoned. Appraisal was then made compulsory by the 1986 Education Act, although arrangements remained localized and ad hoc until 1991, when the Education (School Teacher Appraisal) Regulation came into force. This required all state-school teachers to be appraised every two years, using a cycle of classroom observation, an appraisal interview, a written statement with targets, and a review meeting. The next five years saw sporadic implementation and conflicting evaluation reports – one (Barber *et al.* 1995) concluding that appraisal was improving classroom performance, and another (Ofsted 1996) concluding that it was not.

The TTA and Ofsted investigated further, producing a joint report (TTA and Ofsted 1996) which suggested that appraisal should be integrated into other management functions to reduce costs and increase coherence, should adopt an annual cycle and should focus more sharply on classroom performance. However, with a general election looming, 'appraisal looked set to disappear altogether as a meaningless, potentially expensive process' (Bartlett 2000: 32).

Against expectations, however, the incoming Labour Government made appraisal a key component of the *standards agenda*. Another White Paper, *Excellence in Schools*, argued that '[a] fair and robust performance appraisal regime which recognises success but also acts on failure is the hallmark of a profession which truly sets a premium on standards' (DfEE 1997: 49). A year later, a Green Paper (DfEE 1998) claimed that teacher recruitment, retention and motivation were low because good teaching was not properly recognized or financially rewarded. Accordingly, one of the most ambitious and extensive performance related pay schemes in the UK public sector (Farrell and Morris 2004) was introduced into English schools in 2000 and Welsh schools in 2001 (DfEE 1998, 1999). Teachers would still receive annual increments during their first six years. Thereafter, however, they would have to apply to cross a pay threshold, and provide their head with a portfolio of evidence. Successful teachers would get a £2,000 pay rise (a 10 per cent increase). Once over the threshold, teachers would not receive any automatic annual increments, but could still move up the points scale by taking on extra responsibilities.

Heads and teachers were vehemently opposed to PRP because they thought it was divisive, and believed that the problems with recruitment, retention and motivation were caused by poor working conditions, not pay (Storey 2000; Farrell and Morris 2004). The introduction of PRP went ahead regardless. A University of Exeter study of 1,000 English schools found that 86 per cent of eligible teachers applied to cross the threshold in the first round, and of those, 97 per cent were successful (Wragg *et al.* 2004). Thus, 'the exercise seemed more of a general pay rise than a sieving of the most competent, barely worth the time and effort involved' (ibid.: 53). Moreover, the team noted that, during three years of research, 'few teachers made significant changes to well-established classroom routines as a result of performance management' (ibid.: 147). Many other studies have reached a similar conclusion, and appraisal's apparent lack of impact on teaching is a point to which we will return.

The introduction of appraisal into tertiary education was similarly sporadic, though compared with schools there were fewer permutations and less government intervention. The Jarratt Report (1985) into higher education called for greater efficiency and accountability, underpinned by 'a more stratified and hierarchical system of line management' (Hutchinson 1995: 48). Two years later, staff appraisal was introduced as one condition of the Association of University Teachers salary settlement (CVCP 1987, cited in Haslam *et al.* 1993). Likewise, in further education the 1991 salary settlement agreed by the National Joint Council for Further Education introduced a framework for lecturer appraisal (Betts 1996). Interestingly, this framework insisted that appraisal should not just focus on the individual, but also form part of departmental and institutional reviews.

Unlike teacher appraisal in schools, the precise details of each scheme were left up to individual institutions, featuring only occasionally in government publications. According to the Office of Public Sector Information website, the word *appraisal* appears only once in the *1992 Further and Higher Education Act*, and again just once in the 1998 Teaching and Higher Education Act. It does not appear at all in the 2003 White Paper *The Future of Higher Education*, or in the 2004 Higher Education Act. Moreover, compared with the school sector there has been far less empirical research into tertiary-level appraisal, and nothing on the same scale as the three-year University of Exeter study mentioned earlier. It remains to be seen whether, given time, appraisal in tertiary education will become as tightly regulated as it is in state schools. More likely, other performance management technologies, such as the Research Excellence Framework, will continue to overshadow its importance.

Although formal appraisal has been mandatory for over 15 years in the UK education sector, its precise focus, purposes and outcomes remain contested. Enduring tensions persist, encapsulated in two questions:

1 Should the purpose of appraisal be teacher evaluation, professional development or some finely balanced combination of the two?
2 Should the focus of appraisal be the individual, the organization or some meso-level group in between (such as the department)?

As always, the messy reality depicted in empirical studies does not match the sleek rhetoric espoused by some government officials, or the neat conceptual frameworks penned by some authors. The appraisal system an institution adopts both reflects and shapes not just 'the value system and existing internal structures of the organization' (Hutchinson 1997: 46) but also the 'wider structural, economic and political frameworks' (Grace 1985: 3). Whether or not appraisal achieves its intended aims depends partly upon how it addresses the specific tensions outlined above, and partly upon how staff perceive the organization and its leaders more generally. As we shall see from the two UAE case studies, context is highly significant and deeply determining.

The purpose of appraisal: development or evaluation?

Different authors use different pairs of words, but two distinct purposes of appraisal are consistently highlighted. One focuses on 'accountability' (Peaker 1986; Goddard and Emerson 1992; Middlewood and Cardno 2001), 'efficiency-driven performance assessment' (Pollitt 1987), 'managerial, control-oriented appraisal (Walsh 1988) or 'managerialist appraisal' (Hutchinson 1997). The other focuses on 'improvement' (Peaker 1986), 'participative appraisal' (Walsh 1988) or 'professional development' (Pollitt 1987; Goddard and Emerson 1992; Hutchinson 1997; Middlewood and Cardno 2001).

Most authors advocate the use of both approaches, but not within the same time period (Pollitt 1987; Fidler and Cooper 1992; Goddard and Emerson 1992; Casey *et al.* 1997; Walker and Dimmock 2000). Their argument is that people are unlikely to be honest about their weaknesses and future aspirations if this information can then be used to determine their chances of promotion or their next pay rise.

To overcome this difficulty, Fidler and Cooper (1992) advocate using two cycles of appraisal at least six months apart. House and Lapan (1989) go further by recommending the use of different data collection tools at different times with different people. In order to maintain minimum standards of competence, all teachers should be subjected to occasional summative assessment using a 'craft model' of teaching, with its emphasis on 'a repertoire of specialized techniques and knowledge'. More often, however, formative assessment using 'professional' and 'art' models of teaching should prevail, so that teachers can enhance their ability to provide creative, individualized learning experiences for all (ibid.: 56–60).

A minority of authors are less adamant about keeping the developmental and evaluative elements entirely separate (Peaker 1986; Turner and Clift 1988; Wilson and Beaton 1993; Poster and Poster 1997; Hughes 1998; Miles and Hyle 1999; Isherwood *et al.* 2007). For some, the reasons are pragmatic. Appraisal is extremely time-consuming, particularly for the appraiser, and the outcomes rarely justify the amount of time involved. Operating two cycles six months apart may be desirable in theory, but in practice it is unworkable. Miles and Hyle (1999: 355), for instance, contend that 'it is, in part, the efficiency of including both forms of assessment in one review that makes evaluation acceptable and practical to conduct'.

Others believe appraisal can never be entirely non-evaluative because appraisers inevitably make judgements about what they see. Even if these are never voiced, they will still exert an influence over subsequent events. Consequently, attempts to separate the two functions are doomed to failure, and such pretences should be abandoned (Hughes 1998: 22). Several empirical studies support this. Teachers, principals and administrators in two southern US states all saw appraisal as having two functions ('improvement' and 'accountability') that were 'entirely compatible, even interdependent'

(Peaker 1986: 78). Similarly, 99 per cent of the New Zealand schoolteachers in Fitzgerald's (2001) survey suggested appraisal should include elements of both professional development and accountability. For Middlewood (2001), the figure among schoolteachers in the English Midlands was 90 per cent.

The focus of appraisal: the individual or the institution

The twin purposes of appraisal (development and/or evaluation) are mirrored by twin foci – the individual and/or the institution – with similar debates about the extent to which the two are complementary. Much of the literature suggests that the desires of individual teachers and the demands of their educational institutions can and should be integrated (Rutherford 1992; Hughes 1998). In other words, 'Appraisal must be for the benefit of *both* the individual *and* the organisation' (Poster and Poster 1997: 152, italics in original). Such a smooth synthesis is not often seen in practice, however. Empirical studies frequently reveal appraisal schemes that focus on individual professional development, without reference to institutional goals. The secondary heads in Cullen's (1997: 181) study, for example, 'clearly viewed appraisal as serving to promote their personal, professional development' without any mention of 'the larger aim of improving the quality of educational provision in schools'. Likewise, in higher education Hughes (1998) found that appraisal in most of the 75 universities and colleges in his survey focused on the individual, thereby ignoring its strategic potential to improve whole departments.

Not linking individual professional development to institutional goals is clearly wasteful of resources, but not linking individual performance to institutional constraints is simply unjust. A fair appraisal cannot ignore the conditions under which an individual works. Yet all too often, the appraiser is also the appraisee's line manager and, as such, partly responsible for the appraisee's working environment. This being so, it is easier for the appraiser to blame the teacher's incompetence than admit to providing poor leadership or insufficient resources.

Poster and Poster (1997: 154) draw a four-part matrix to illustrate how the purpose and focus of appraisal might interact, depending on the priorities and climate of a particular institution, so as to produce appraisal that is managerial, judgemental, developmental or laissez-faire.

The managerial and judgemental approaches focus on organizational goals, whereas the developmental and laissez-faire approaches focus on individual goals. The managerial approach is based on hierarchical authority and aims to maximize organizational efficiency and effectiveness through the setting of short-term performance targets and the use of incentives, praise and reproach. The judgemental approach has a similar aim but seeks to achieve this in a more authoritarian or controlling way by rating individuals against each other and by using systematic PRP to increase extrinsic motivation.

By contrast, the developmental approach is based on collegiality and collective authority. It aims to uphold moral, ethical and professional values through peer appraisal and self-appraisal. It tries to promote trust, openness and cooperation, with an emphasis on self-directed, intrinsically motivated, longer-term personal and professional development. The laissez-faire approach is similar to the developmental approach, but more emphasis is placed on the individual and less on the professional community. Neither the management nor one's peers drive the process; everything is left up to the individual, with a resulting lack of systematic focus, direction and purpose.

Whichever approach is adopted, empirical studies show that most appraisal schemes produce two paradoxes. First, although appraisal is intended to improve teaching quality by facilitating continuous professional development, in reality few teachers actually alter their classroom practice as a result. Second, although appraisal is intended to ensure minimum standards of competence by facilitating the removal of persistently under-performing staff, in reality few teachers are ever dismissed as a result. Each of these apparent failings will now be explored in more detail, using the two UAE case studies.

The impact of appraisal on teaching quality

Much of the literature says that the primary purpose of appraisal must be to improve learning outcomes (Fidler and Cooper 1992), or at least teaching quality (Magennis 1993). This is an ambitious aim, given how difficult it is to measure learning outcomes, let alone demonstrate causality between improved achievement and particular forms of classroom practice. It is also at odds with much empirical research. Studies by Turner and Clift (1988) and Winstanley and Stuart-Smith (1996) both found no evidence that appraisal results in improved performance. Likewise, the three-year study of 1,000 English schools previously mentioned found that few teachers changed their classroom practice as a result of appraisal (Wragg *et al.* 2004).

Case studies: appraisal and teaching quality at Rihab and Al Fanar

This was also the case with the two institutions in the UAE. Only 3 of the 14 teachers at Rihab reported trying to improve their teaching as a consequence of appraisal. One used a very constructive and detailed post-lesson debrief; the other two used feedback from the Student Evaluation of Teaching (SET) online questionnaire. Another teacher mentioned changing her behaviour as a result of ongoing informal student feedback (rather than the SET questionnaire). A further seven said appraisal had no effect on their classroom behaviour, including one teacher who said, 'I've learnt nothing about my teaching from the whole process . . . so, in itself, it's useless for me.' Worryingly, the remaining three teachers said the SET questionnaire had actually had a negative effect on their teaching, because now they concentrated on keeping the students happy rather than helping them learn. One, for instance, confessed she was 'more focused on trying to please the students rather than trying to teach them English', which meant doing more computer work, more library visits, more videos and fewer grammar exercises, even though this was not what the students really needed. These three teachers also admitted inflating student grades in an effort to boost their SET scores.

The results were equally discouraging from the 15 Al Fanar teachers. Only two said appraisal had had a positive impact. One had changed her teaching as a result of formal student evaluations. The other had been allowed to take a training course requested on her self-evaluation form. Ten other teachers said the appraisal system had had no impact, and again, a further three said the effect had been negative. One of these had not passed probation and was understandably scathing about the whole process. Another mentioned how all the non-teaching commitments she felt pressurized to undertake left her with less time and energy for her students. The third said she had stopped challenging students to work harder because she feared what would happen if they complained.

Thus, despite the different context, appraisal at Rihab and Al Fanar had the same insignificant impact upon classroom behaviour as other studies conducted in the UK, the US and Australia.

The impact of appraisal on dismissal

Despite the government rhetoric advocating a 'fair and robust performance appraisal regime which recognizes success but also acts on failure' (DfEE 1997: 49), very few UK schoolteachers are dismissed for incompetence, and, as we have seen, 97 per cent of teachers who applied to pass the pay scale threshold were successful (Wragg *et al.* 2004). The situation is the same in the US, despite its longer tradition of quality assurance. Menuey, for example, cites a long list of American authors in support of her contention that, on average, 5 per cent of classroom teachers are incompetent. She then compares this with a dismissal rate of less than 1 per cent and concludes that 'this gross disparity between the prevalence of incompetent teachers and their dismissal is truly staggering' (2007: 310).

With regard to higher education, Currie and Vidovich (2000) mention Australian academics being threatened with the non-renewal of their temporary contracts if they do not comply with aspects of managerialism, but Deem (2000) suggests that UK academic managers are more committed to persuasion or reassignment than coercion or removal. Likewise, Huisman and Currie (2004: 50) report French, Swedish, American and Dutch academic managers all favouring 'the rather weak implementation of accountability measures' and 'soft monitoring'. Ryan (2005: 94) writes of the 'anti-dismissal ethos' of UK universities, while Hellawell and Hancock (2001: 193) claim that it is still 'notoriously difficult' to sack UK academics 'for anything other than serious breaches of the disciplinary code'. Similarly, Hughes (1998: 16) notes how some HEIs 'have developed a convention that poor performance should not be referred to at all'. US universities are also reluctant to tackle underperformance (Miles and Hyle 1999). Indeed, Poskanzer (2002) estimates that every year, out of the many thousands of HE academics, only around 50 are terminated 'for cause', a category that includes intellectual dishonesty and moral turpitude as well as simple incompetence.

Case studies: the impact of appraisal on dismissal at Rihab and Al Fanar

The situation in the UAE was very different. As was noted in Chapter 7, expatriate employees could have their sponsorship revoked at any point, for any reason. In addition, at the time of the research, trade unions for expatriates were banned and the labour courts rarely found in their favour. Teachers and managers at both Rihab and Al Fanar frequently mentioned how easily expatriate staff could be dismissed (see pp. 102–3 for specific quotations). This perception meant that the potential benefits of appraisal were subverted in three ways.

First, lesson observations were seen as a chance to show off, rather than engage in collaborative experimentation or critical reflection. One Al Fanar teacher, after giving a 'performance lesson' for her first observation, had given a 'regular lesson' for her second. The manager observing her had requested a more detailed lesson plan, and other faculty had told her, 'You're not supposed to do regular lessons. You're supposed to do performances . . . when you are being observed you do a special observation lesson. It's not what you normally teach.' This view was endorsed by two other Al Fanar managers. The first said she told her faculty, 'It'll go in your evaluations, so yes, do an all-singing, all-dancing [lesson].' This seems like sound advice, because the manager went on to say, 'The minute anything, any problem, is mentioned at appraisal, it's bye-bye.' Similarly, the second Al Fanar manager likened lesson observation to hosting a dinner party where 'I'm not going to bring out my broken crockery and cups – I'm going to get the best stuff'. She, too, suggested that identifying anyone as being at risk would be their 'death knell'.

One of the Rihab managers clearly shared the same worry, although she tackled the issue differently. Once or twice in her lifetime she had observed 'a total disaster', but, for all other observations, she had given top marks for everything, and written only positive comments. Occasionally she discussed points for development orally, but these were never put on paper. She justified this by saying, 'People seem to become very paranoid of what is in a file; understandably so, because people come and go, and if information in a file is not absolutely crystal clear, it could so easily be misinterpreted.'

The potential benefits of appraisal were also subverted by teachers believing that students had the power to get them sacked. A typical interviewee spoke of seeing two colleagues she thought were competent teachers forced to leave, because, 'Students have basically been like a lynch mob. As a class, or as a group, or the majority of them just decided they had it in for that person, and those people lost their jobs.' This fear made several teachers pander to the students' whims, letting them watch videos instead of doing grammar exercises, for example, and not pushing them to work harder because 'the students don't like being pressured . . . [and] I have to think about the fact that if a student complains, they could sack me'. Even more worryingly, four teachers (three at Rihab and one at Al Fanar) admitted inflating grades to keep students happy, a practice they said they had also observed in colleagues. One said:

> It's extremely important. You want to get good grades from your students because it has a major impact on whether you stay or go . . . so . . . you go out of your way to please the students. And you give the students what they want, and you give students inflated grades. . . . You don't want students to fail and give you a bad evaluation. . . . I've been partnered with other teachers who have said, 'Right . . . they are all going to pass'. We decide that beforehand, and let's give them all As and Bs. So a failing girl would get a B.

Finally, because teachers believed dissidents were just as likely to be dismissed as people with poor teaching skills or dissatisfied students, they avoided criticism of the institution or its management. One teacher claimed, 'Appraisal operates on the basis of reactions to your opinions and your ideas, and not simply to how well you do your job.' Another highlighted how appraisal could be developmental or evaluative in terms of data collection, but then humanitarian or political in terms of data use. In other words, 'there are political purposes; there are manipulative purposes; there are organizational systemic things that don't fit on this [developmental/evaluative] line'. So, in a heavily political setting, exactly the same data could be interpreted either positively or negatively, depending upon whether management – for entirely different reasons – wanted to retain or reject someone. A third teacher believed she 'could just be sacked tomorrow for some spurious reason', which silenced debate. At her previous institutions, whenever change was mooted, 'there were massive debates and discussions, and teachers all arguing because everyone's got opinions', whereas at Al Fanar, teachers were 'passive . . . disengaged . . . everyone will just nod in agreement – it's so bizarre'.

Although one of the senior managers claimed that appropriately phrased criticism was welcomed in private, she then described how an excellent teacher had been dismissed a few months earlier for complaining to the chancellor about the head of the college: 'The reason she's not here is because of public criticism of [the head of the college]. He won't say that, and no paperwork will ever say that but there is no other reason for her to go.'

Thus, although interviewees disagreed about precisely how prevalent it was, almost all agreed that the UAE context made it extremely easy for Western senior managers to sack expatriate staff, even for reasons that would be challenged in their home countries. Two interviewees explicitly contrasted the UAE situation with that in North America, where, they said, it was impossible to remove anyone, even if they persistently underperformed. One told an anecdote about her spouse, a senior American academic, trying to dismiss an 'out-of-control' lecturer and then being sued for sexual discrimination in a suit that 'dragged on for years'. She claimed, 'It is literally impossible to dismiss anybody in the universities now in the States – now that is going too far.' Likewise, the other interviewee described her experience in Canada, where, 'In a union environment, appraisal becomes fairly meaningless because it's almost impossible to get rid of anybody . . . [even] horrible, completely lazy, horrible, horrible, useless workers.' Both contended that it was a good thing to be able to dismiss people whose work continued to be inadequate, despite repeated opportunities for professional development. The crucial point, however, was that such freedom had to be exercised with extreme caution and complete fairness. In other words:

> The system here [in the UAE] of being able to get rid of people is good, but being able to get rid of people for no reason without criteria, not explaining, not knowing, the people themselves don't even know why they are fired, that's not OK, that's going too far . . . the system they've got here could be great . . . because they've got the power to do a great job, but they have to take that power and turn it into an altruistic humanitarian way, and not just for the purpose of amassing their own power and maintaining that hierarchy.

Conclusion

The primary purpose of appraisal is to enhance communication about work performance so that appraisers and appraisees have a shared understanding of the aims, purposes and goals of the organization. Appraisees should receive valuable feedback about their contribution through the year; appraisers should come to understand the issues and concerns hindering full effectiveness. Appraisal conversations should be positive and developmental, and should celebrate and affirm the appraisee's role in the organization. Current progress should be reviewed and future goals formulated. Steps to ameliorate any concerns identified through the appraisal process should be considered and planned. It is important that the individual's role and work is reviewed in the context of the wider organization and their own professional development.

Poor performance should not be ignored, but it is best dealt with through separate conduct and capability procedures. Should a conduct or capability issue emerge from the appraisal process, the appraisee should be informed immediately. Managers should initiate appropriate steps, including target-setting and monitoring, within the institution's relevant procedures. Where this is not done, and appraisal includes the risk of dismissal, as in the UAE case studies described above, trust is lost and the process becomes much less effective. Healthy organizations do not muddle discipline and development.

11 Conclusion

From micro-politics to sustained improvement

This chapter critiques the claim that effective HRM policies can help educational institutions transcend the tensions and paradoxes of the global reform agenda. Using the arguments and case-study evidence presented in earlier chapters, it identifies those features of schools and colleges that, in contemporary contexts around the world, seem either to facilitate or to obstruct the emergence and growth of *intelligent* or learning organizations. It also recommends ways that the challenges posed by new managerialism might be overcome, the potential for exploitation restrained and the transformative power of employees tapped.

In Part I, comprising the first three chapters, we set out the current *context* of HRM in education by critically examining worldwide trends in education policy, government legislation, societal values and teacher cultures.

In Chapter 1, we argued that current educational reform, as embodied in the discourse of school effectiveness, is underpinned by an unshakeable commitment to neo-liberalism and human capital theory. The primary purpose of education, according to government rhetoric, is to maximize a country's potential for economic growth by ensuring that every individual is optimally equipped with whatever knowledge and skills are demanded by the labour market. There is scope for social justice, but only as long as it does not undermine a country's global competitiveness. This is a limiting and, sometimes, self-defeating view of education, in which individuals and their economic skills are overemphasized. Schools and colleges have huge potential to contribute to the strength and cohesion of families, communities and the wider society. Never has the need for this been greater, given the growing fragmentation of society, the rising intolerance of difference and the increasing marginalization of the disadvantaged. However, current education policies do not appear to value this kind of contribution, and schools are frequently frustrated in this endeavour by a government-imposed culture of performativity.

In Chapter 2, we looked at how elaborate national and supra-national legal frameworks, at least within Europe, now provide comprehensive protection against workplace discrimination and exploitation. We also looked at the changing role of education unions, and the 'historic' social partnership formed in England and Wales by five education unions, central government and local authorities in January 2003. We argued that although at certain times, in certain places, education unions have increased democracy and social justice, they have not been able to overcome 'the self-interested conspiracy of silence amongst the relatively affluent majority of votes in many of the world's most advanced countries' (Beck 1999: 234). To do so, teachers would need to revitalize their sense of vocation, regain confidence in their own professional judgement and speak with a more united voice.

In Chapter 3, we outlined some contradictions within the discourse of teacher professionalism, investigating the controversial claim that government policies have made teachers into an educational proletariat and demoralized the profession. We suggested that teachers need to reiterate the moral imperative of teaching at every opportunity. Their job is not just to ensure students score highly on standardized tests; it is also to help learners develop as moral human beings, capable of living worthwhile and fulfilled lives within vibrant, tolerant communities. We endorsed Sachs's (2001, 2003) notion of *democratic professionalism*, in which teachers work alongside other stakeholders, particularly marginalized students and communities, to eliminate injustice, exploitation and oppression both within and beyond the school gates. We also endorsed three specific recommendations made by Dainton (2005), calling for education representatives to draft a common statement of professionalism, challenge workforce remodelling and reform teacher education so that the moral dimension of teaching is given far greater prominence.

In Part II (Chapters 4–7), we explored two pairs of contemporary *themes* in HRM. On the one hand, we compared individual leaders and their followers. On the other, we contrasted learning and so-called *greedy* organizations.

In Chapter 4, we analysed transformational and distributed leadership. Since 1997, the Labour Government in England has invested heavily in leadership, and policy-makers are perturbed by the growing evidence that educational leaders cannot replicate the productivity gains reported for business and commerce (Bell *et al.* 2003; Hallinger 2003; Harris 2004). The case studies of Norcross and Felix Holt schools indicate that even when outstanding heads exercise transformational leadership, student outcomes are only slightly better than one would have predicted, given the school's intake. Deprivation continues to exert a powerful influence upon student achievement, while leadership effects are small, mediated and difficult to detect (Hallinger and Heck 1998). The quality of teaching is the single most important variable over which the school has control, and focusing on leadership, even transformational and distributed leadership, is probably to the detriment of high-quality pedagogy.

In Chapter 5, we considered the strengths and weaknesses of teamwork. The Felix Holt case study demonstrated how departmental performance can be improved by distributing authority and trust to middle leaders. However, it was also acknowledged that the Felix Holt faculty teams were operating within limits defined by hyper-accountability. Goals and targets were set and driven from the top, so the teams were self-directed only in relation to means, not ends. Innovation, creativity and learning were valued only in so far as they generated very specific changes in the results profile, i.e. more GCSE C grades. This form of empowerment, constrained by an externally imposed definition of quality and progress, cannot realize the full potential of teamwork. To achieve this, schools must embrace the principles of the learning organization.

In Chapter 6, we critiqued the learning organization, and in Chapter 7 we described its nemesis, the *greedy* organization. From The Shire School case study, we concluded that the learning organization is a relevant and useful concept for educational leaders. Again, however, we had to acknowledge that a pervasive culture of performativity can all too easily turn educational institutions into debilitating hothouses for all within them (including students). Rather than accommodating differences and allowing people to develop at their own pace, *greedy* organizations use cutting-edge technologies to extract ever more effort and commitment from staff in pursuit of a vision generated elsewhere. The two UAE case studies, presented in Chapter 7, graphically highlight how wealthy, ambitious countries can – intentionally or otherwise – develop legal frameworks and employer mindsets that encourage the development of *greedy* organizations in which staff are systematically exploited and the moral purpose of teaching is subverted. The lesson here seems to be that learning organizations require ample space and time in which to develop organically, in directions that are not predetermined. As such, they are incompatible with a culture of performativity. This makes calls for educational institutions to become learning organizations premature. First, teacher professionalism has to be restored, and genuine collegiality reclaimed.

In Part III, comprising Chapters 8–10, three contemporary HRM *practices* were discussed, namely the selection and development of professionals, the remodelling of school teams and the management of performance.

In Chapter 8, we looked at how leaders and teachers in various countries around the world are selected and developed. We noted how, in this area more than in any other dealt with by the book, context shapes attitude and behaviour. Transformational leadership may be completely meaningless in parts of the developing world, where heads are appointed because of their political affiliations without ever having set foot inside a classroom (Oplatka 2004). Similarly, it may be entirely inappropriate to expect teachers to engage in professional development when their most basic human needs (such as access to safe housing and clean water) are not being met. We also noted how aligning professional development to the achievement of particular standards or competencies, such as those laid down by the TDA (2007) for teachers, and the DfES (2004) for heads, can be unduly restricting. Of course, a balance needs to be struck between the priorities of the organization and the desires of the individual, because resources are always finite. Nonetheless, if we genuinely believe that teaching is a moral *art*, and not simply painting by numbers, staff have to be allowed to pursue areas of interest, for their own sake. Schools cannot engender creativity, risk-taking and a passion for learning in their students if they do not afford staff similar opportunities to grow in self-directed, unpredictable ways.

In Chapter 9, we evaluated the impact of *workforce remodelling* and the national agreement on *Raising Standards and Tackling Workload* (DfES 2003a). We argued that the pay, working conditions and training of support staff are all woefully inadequate, given what is now expected of them. We also noted that even though the Labour Government has spent millions of tax pounds recruiting and retaining thousands of support staff, their worth remains an article of faith rather than a demonstrable fact. There is no evidence, for example, that the exponential rise in teaching assistants has resulted in higher student attainment (Blatchford *et al.* 2007b). By contrast, there is evidence that *workforce remodelling* has reduced teacher workload only slightly, and increased senior staff workload quite considerably (MacBeath and Galton 2007). We concluded that there is an urgent need to debate three fundamental questions so studiously avoided by *The National Agreement*, namely:

1. What is the purpose of education?
2. What does teaching mean?
3. From whom, and under what circumstances, can students learn best?

Unless and until a provisional consensus is reached regarding these questions, decisions about who can do what within English and Welsh state schools remain arbitrary (Wilkinson 2005).

In Chapter 10, we discussed appraisal and performance, exploring how any system of performance management both reflects and shapes the wider organizational ethos as well as societal culture. We discussed the tension between evaluative and developmental appraisal, and between the needs of the institution and the desires of the individual. We noted how most appraisal schemes combine evaluative and developmental features, despite the frequent warnings against this in the literature. We also noted how rarely, in practice, the needs of the institution and the desires of the individual are synthesized, and how often the potential of appraisal to facilitate departmental or group (rather than individual) professional development is overlooked. Using the two UAE case studies, we argued that appraisal is equally unjust if it fails either to tackle underperformance or to curb abuses of power.

Education policy in the twenty-first century is full of contractions, some of which we described in Chapter 1. A robust and viable alternative exists, however, and is exemplified by the Australian school described by Smyth (2005) and the Norwegian and German schools described by Wrigley

(2005). In these examples, schools have become genuine learning communities by:

- really listening to students and involving them in decision-making;
- developing inclusive, compassionate cultures;
- promoting respectful relationships between older and younger learners, and (especially) between teachers and students;
- offering a meaningful curriculum that has sufficient scope and flexibility to excite and inspire every learner;
- using authentic assessments that celebrate growth and point out areas for improvement, without ranking or comparing individuals;
- restructuring secondary schools on a smaller, more 'human' scale, so that learners do not rotate, every hour, around 15 different teachers.

These strategies have enabled schools to resist the 'terrors of performativity' (Ball 2003) and to provide, instead, genuinely life-changing educational experiences, particularly for disadvantaged students. In our judgement, very similar strategies underpin effective HRM. This means that educational leaders hoping to harness the enormous potential of their staff should:

- provide genuine opportunities for all staff to say what they think, and allow collective decision-making at every opportunity;
- develop inclusive, compassionate cultures;
- promote respectful relationships, between all staff, irrespective of their roles or positional power;
- offer meaningful professional development opportunities, with sufficient scope and flexibility to excite and inspire every staff member;
- use authentic schemes of performance management that celebrate growth and point out areas for improvement, without ranking or comparing individuals.

We are not suggesting for a moment that it is easy for individual teachers and leaders to make sense of the profound contradictions in the current policy context. What we are suggesting is that the two lists above provide challenging yet realistic advice about how teacher and leaders, individually and collectively, might enhance the learning opportunities their students experience, decrease the inequities their communities suffer, and manage human resources better.

References

Addison, R. and Brundrett, M. (2008) 'Motivation and demotivation of teachers in primary schools: the challenge of change', *Education 3–13*, 36(1): 79–94.

Aldridge, M. (2008) *School Business Managers: Their Role in Distributed Leadership. How Can SBMs/Bursars Compliment and Support Distributed Leadership*, Nottingham: NCSL.

Alexander, R. (2000) *Culture and Pedagogy: International Comparisons in Primary Education*, Oxford: Blackwell.

Alexander, R. (2004) 'Still no pedagogy? Principle, pragmatism and compliance in primary education', *Cambridge Journal of Education*, 34(1): 7–33.

Allix, N. (2000) 'Transformational leadership', *Educational Management and Administration*, 28(1): 7–20.

Allman, D. (2007) 'Strategy and style: how middle leaders perceive their role in school improvement', dissertation submitted in part-fulfilment of the Degree of MA in Leadership for Learning, University of Leicester.

Angelides, P., Constantinou, C. and Leigh, J. (2009) 'The role of paraprofessionals in developing inclusive education in Cyprus', *European Journal of Special Needs Education*, 24(1): 75–89.

Angle, H., Gilby, N., Fearn, A., Bassett, C., Elston, D. and McGingal, S. (2008) *Teachers' Workloads: Diary Survey*, March, School Teachers' Review Body.

Antonacopoulou, E. (2006) 'The relationship between individual and organizational learning: new evidence from managerial learning practices', *Management Learning*, 37(4): 455–73.

Antonacopoulou, E. and Chiva, R. (2007) 'The social complexity of organizational learning: the dynamics of learning and organizing', *Management Learning*, 38(3): 277–95.

Apple, M. W. (2004) 'Creating difference: neo-liberalism, neo-conservatism and the politics of educational reform', *Educational Policy*, 18: 12–44.

Apprenticeships, Skills, Children and Learning Bill 2008–09 (2008–9) London: The Stationery Office. Online, available at: http://services.parliament.uk/bills/2008-09/apprenticeshipsskillschildrenandlearning.html (accessed 14 May 2009).

Argyris, C. (1993) *Knowledge for Action: A Guide to Overcoming Barriers to Organizational Change*, San Francisco, CA: Jossey-Bass.

Argyris, C. (1999) *On Organizational Learning*, Oxford: Blackwell.

Argyris, C. and Schön, D. (1978) *Organizational Learning: A Theory of Action Perspective*, London: Addison-Wesley.

Armstrong, A. and Foley, P. (2003) 'Foundations for a learning organization: organization learning mechanisms', *The Learning Organization*, 10(2): 74–82.
ATL (2005) *Position Statement on New Professionalism*, London: ATL.
Avis, J. (2005) 'Beyond performativity: reflections on activist professionalism and the labour process in further education', *Journal of Education Policy*, 20(2): 209–22.
Aycan, Z. (2005) 'The interplay between cultural and institutional/structural contingencies in human resource management practices', *International Journal of Human Resource Management*, 16(7), 1083–119.
Bach, S., Kessler, I. and Heron, P. (2006) 'Changing job boundaries and workforce reform: the case of teaching assistants', *Industrial Relations Journal*, 37(1): 2–21.
Ball, S. (1981) *Beachside Comprehensive*, Cambridge: Cambridge University Press.
Ball, S. (1987) *The Micro-politics of the School*, London: Methuen.
Ball, S. (1988) 'Staff relations during the teachers' industrial action: context, conflict and proletarianisation', *British Journal of Sociology of Education*, 9(3): 289–306.
Ball, S. (1990) *Politics and Policymaking in Education*, London: Routledge.
Ball, S. (1994) *Education Reform: A Critical and Post-structural Approach*, Buckingham, UK: Open University Press.
Ball, S. (2003) 'The teacher's soul and the terrors of performativity', *Journal of Education Policy*, 18(2): 215–28.
Balter, D. and Duncombe, W. (2005) 'Teacher hiring practices in New York State School Districts', Educational Finance and Accountability Program, Center for Policy Research, The Maxwell School, Syracuse University.
Bangs, J. (2006) 'The social partnership: the wider context', *Forum*, 48(2): 201–8.
Barber, M. (2001) 'Large-scale education reform in England: a work in progress', a paper for the Managing Education Reform Conference, Moscow, 29–30 October. The paper was also presented, with small modifications, to the Federal Reserve Bank of Boston 47th Economic Conference, 19–21 June 2002, and the Technology Colleges Trust Vision 2020 Second International Conference, October/November/December.
Barber, M. (2005) 'Informed professionalism: realising the potential', presentation to a conference of the Association of Teachers and Lecturers, London, 11 June.
Barber, M., Evans, A. and Johnson, M. (1995) *An Evaluation of the National Scheme of School Teacher Appraisal*, a report for the Department for Education, London: Department for Education.
Barker, B. (1999) 'Double vision: 40 years on', in H. Tomlinson, H. Gunter and P. Smith (eds) *Living Headship: Voices, Values and Vision*, London: Paul Chapman.
Barker, B. (2001) *Leading Improvement*, Cambridge: Pearson.
Barker, B. (2005) *Transforming Schools: Illusion or Reality*, Stoke-on-Trent: Trentham Books.
Barker, B. (2006) 'Rethinking leadership and change: a case study in leadership succession and its impact on school transformation', *Cambridge Journal of Education*, 36(2): 277–92.
Barker, B. (2007) 'The leadership paradox: can school leaders transform student outcomes?', *School Effectiveness and School Improvement*, 18(1): 21–43.
Barker, B. (2008) 'School reform policy in England since 1988: relentless pursuit of the unattainable', *Journal of Education Policy*, 23(6): 669–83.
Barker, B. (2009) 'Public service reform in education: why is progress so slow?', *Journal of Educational Administration and History*, 41(1): 57–72.
Barth, R. (1990) *Improving Schools from Within*, San Francisco, CA: Jossey-Bass.

Bartlett, S. (2000) 'The development of teacher appraisal: a recent history', *British Journal of Educational Studies*, 48(1): 29–47.

Bass, B. and Avolio, B. (eds) (1994) *Improving Organizational Effectiveness Through Transformational Leadership*, Thousand Oaks, CA: Sage.

Bassey, M. (2007) Case studies in A. Briggs and M. Coleman (eds) *Research Methods in Educational Leadership and Management*, London: Sage.

BBC (2002) 'Teachers split over workload offer', 22 October. Online, available at: http://news.bbc.co.uk/1/hi/education/2347697.stm (accessed 5 October 2009).

BBC (2005) Performance tables. Online, available at: http://news.bbc.co.uk/1/shared/bsp/hi/education/04/school_tables/secondary_schools/html/916_va_lea.stm (accessed 8 March 2006).

BBC (2008a) 'Teachers throng Paris over cuts', 18 May. Online, available at: http://news.bbc.co.uk/1/hi/world/europe/7407571.stm (accessed 15 May 2008).

BBC (2008b) 'French pension strike sparks numbers battle', 22 May. Online, available at: http://news.bbc.co.uk/1/hi/world/europe/7415789.stm (accessed 15 May 2009).

BBC (2009) 'Schools waste millions – report', 27 September. Online, available at: http://news.bbc.co.uk/1/hi/uk_politics/8276991.stm (accessed 5 October 2009).

Beach, D. (2008) 'The changing relations between education professionals, the state and citizen consumers in Europe: rethinking restructuring as capitalisation', *European Educational Research Journal*, 7(2): 195–207.

Becher, T. (1999) *Professional Practices: Commitment and Capability in a Changing Environment*, New Brunswick, NJ: Transaction.

Beck, J. (1999) 'Makeover or takeover? The strange death of educational autonomy in neo-liberal England', *British Journal of Sociology of Education*, 20(2): 223–38.

Beck, J. and Young, M. F. D. (2005) 'The assault on the professions and the restructuring of academic and professional identities: a Bernsteinian analysis', *British Journal of Sociology of Education*, 26(2): 183–97.

Belbin, M. (1981) *Management Teams: Why They Succeed or Fail*, Oxford: Butterworth-Heinemann.

Bell, L. (1992) *Managing Teams in Secondary Schools*, London: Routledge.

Bell, L. and Stevenson, H. (2006) *Education Policy: Process, Themes and Impact*, London: Routledge.

Bell, L., Bolam, R. and Cubillo, L. (2003) *A Systematic Review of the Impact of School Headteachers and Principals on Student Outcomes*, London: EPPI-Centre, Social Science Research Unit, Institute of Education, University of London.

Bennett, N., Wise, C., Woods, P. and Harvey, J. (2003) *Distributed Leadership: Full Report*, Nottingham: NCSL.

Bernstein, B. (1970) 'Education cannot compensate for society', *New Society*, 389: 344–7.

Betts, D. (1996) 'Staff appraisal and staff development in the corporate college', in J. Robson (ed.) *The Professional FE Teacher*, Aldershot, UK: Avebury.

Blackmore, J. (1999) *Troubling Women: Feminism, Leadership and Educational Change*, Buckingham, UK: Open University Press.

Blatchford, P., Russell, A., Bassett, P., Browne, P. and Martin, C. (2004) *The Effects and Role of Teaching Assistants in English Primary Schools (Years 4–6) 2002–2003: Results from the Class Size and Pupil–Adult Ratios (CSPAR) KS2 Project*, Research Report 605, London: DfES.

Blatchford, P., Bassett, P., Brown, P., Martin, C., Russell, A., Webster, R. and

Heywood, N. (2006) *The Deployment and Impact of Support Staff in Schools: Report on Findings from a National Questionnaire Survey of Schools, Support Staff and Teachers (Strand 1, Wave 1, 2004)*, DCSF Research Report 776, London: DCSF.

Blatchford, P., Bassett, P., Brown, P., Martin, C., Russell, A., Webster, R. and Heywood, N. (2007a) *The Deployment and Impact of Support Staff in Schools: Report on Findings from a National Questionnaire Survey of Schools, Support Staff and Teachers (Strand 1, Wave 2, 2006)*, DCSF Research Report 005, London: DCSF.

Blatchford, P., Russell, A., Bassett, P., Brown, P. and Martin, C. (2007b) 'The role and effects of teaching assistants in English primary schools (Years 4 to 6) 2000–2003, *British Educational Research Journal*, 33(1): 5–26.

Blatchford, P., Bassett, P., Brown, P., Martin, C., Russell, A., Webster, R. with Babayigit, S. and Heywood, N. (2008) *The Deployment and Impact of Support Staff in Schools and the Impact of the National Agreement (Strand 2, Wave 1, 2005/06)*, DCSF Research Report 027, London: DCSF.

Blatchford, P., Bassett, P., Brown, P. and Webster, R. (2009) 'The effect of support staff on pupil engagement and individual attention', *British Educational Research Journal*, 45(5): 661–86.

Blohowiak, D. (2007) 'Leadership hit by generation gap', *Daily Telegraph*, 14 August. Online, available at: www.telegraph.co.uk/finance/2953175/Leadership-hit-by-generation-gap.html (accessed 15 May 2009).

Blumer, H. (1969) *Symbolic Interactionism: Perspective and Method*, Berkeley, CA: University of California Press.

Bolam, R. (2004) 'Reflections on the NCSL from a historical perspective', *Educational Management Administration and Leadership*, 32: 251–67.

Bolam, R. and Weindling, D. (2006) *Synthesis of Research and Evaluation Projects Concerned with Capacity-Building Through Teachers' Professional Development*, London: General Teaching Council for England.

Borman, G. D. and Dowling, N. M. (2008) 'Teacher attrition and retention: a meta-analytic and narrative review of the research', *Review of Educational Research*, 78: 367–409.

Bottery, M. (1996) 'The challenge to professionals from the new public management; implications for the teaching profession', *Oxford Review of Education*, 22(2): 179–97.

Boyd, S. (2002) *Partnership Working: European Social Partnership Models*, Scottish Trades Union Congress. Online, available at: www.scotland.gov.uk/publications/2004/05/19376/37359 (accessed 15 May 2009).

Brighouse, T. (1995) 'The history of inspection', in T. Brighouse and B. Moon (eds) *School Inspection*, London: Pitman.

Brimelow, P. (2003) *The Worm in the Apple: How the Teacher Unions Are Destroying American Education*, New York: HarperCollins.

Brower, M. (1995) 'Empowering teams: what, why, and how', *Empowerment in Organizations*, 3(1): 13–25.

Brundrett, M., Fitzgerald, T. and Sommefeldt, D. (2007) *The Creation of National Programmes of School Leadership Development in England and New Zealand: A Comparative Study*, Auckland, NZ: Unitec New Zealand School of Education Journal Articles.

Burchell, B., Day, D., Hudson, M., Ladipo, D., Mankelow, R., Nolan, J. P., Reed, H.,

Wichert, I. C. and Wilkinson, F. (1999) *Job Insecurity and Work Intensification: Flexibility and the Changing Boundaries of Work*, York: Joseph Rowntree Foundation. Summary of findings online, available at: www.jrf.org.uk/KNOWLEDGE/findings/socialpolicy/849.asp (accessed 4 April 2009).

Burgess, H. (2008) *Primary Workforce Management and Reform*, Interim Report, Cambridge: University of Cambridge.

Burns, J. (1978) *Leadership*, New York: Harper & Row.

Bush, T. (2005) *School Management Training Country Report: England: HEAD Country Report*, Oslo, Norway: Centre for Education Management Research.

Bush, T. (2008) 'From management to leadership: semantic or meaningful change?', *Educational Management Administration and Leadership*, 36(2): 271–88.

Bush, T. and Middlewood, D. (2005) *Leading and Managing People in Education*, London: Sage.

Bush, T. and Moloi, K. (2008) 'Race and racism in leadership development', in J. Lumby, G. Crow and P. Pashiardis (eds) *International Handbook on the Preparation and Development of School Leaders*, New York: Routledge.

Bush, T. and Oduro, G. K. T. (2006) 'New principals in Africa: preparation, induction and practice', *Journal of Educational Administration*, 44(4): 359–75.

Butt, G. and Lance, A. (2005) 'Modernizing the roles of support staff in primary schools: changing focus, changing function', *Educational Review*, 57(2): 139–49.

Butt, G. and Lance, A. (2009) '"I am not the teacher!" Some effects of remodelling the roles of teaching assistants in English primary schools', *Education 3–13*, 37(3): 219–31.

Caldwell, B. (2006) *Re-imagining Educational Leadership*, London: Sage.

Callaghan, J. (1976) 'Towards a national debate'. Online, available at: http://education.guardian.co.uk/thegreatdebate/story/0,9860,574645,00.html (accessed 9 November 2009).

Calveley, M. and Healy, G. (2003) 'Political activism and workplace industrial relations in a UK "failing" school', *British Journal of Industrial Relations*, 41(1): 97–113.

Campbell, R. J., Kyriakides, L., Muijs, R. D. and Robinson, W. (2004) 'Effective teaching and values: some implications for research and teacher appraisal', *Oxford Review of Education*, 30(4): 451–65.

Carter, B. (1997) 'The restructuring of teaching and the restructuring of class', *British Journal of Sociology of Education*, 18(2): 201–15.

Casey, R. J., Gentile, P. and Bigger, S. W. (1997) 'Teaching appraisal in higher education: an Australian perspective', *Higher Education*, 34(4): 459–82.

Castka, P., Bamber, C., Sharp, J. and Belohoubeck, P. (2001) 'Factors affecting successful implementation of high performance teams', *Team Performance Management: An International Journal*, 7(7/8): 123–34.

Clarke, J. and Newman, J. (1997) *The Managerial State*, London: Sage.

Clarke, J., Gewirtz, S. and McLaughlin, E. (2000) *New Managerialism: New Welfare?*, London: Sage.

Clegg, S. (2008) 'Academic identities under threat?', *British Educational Research Journal*, 34(3): 329–45.

Codd, J. (2005) 'Teachers as "managed professionals" in the global education industry: the New Zealand experience', *Educational Review*, 57(2): 193–206.

Coleman, M. (2007) 'Gender and educational leadership in England: a comparison

of secondary headteachers' views over time', *School Leadership and Management*, 27(4): 383–99.
Collins, J. (2001) *Good to Great: Why Some Companies Make the Leap . . . and Others Don't*, New York: HarperCollins.
Cooper, B. S. (2000) 'An international perspective on trade unions', in T. Loveless (ed.) *Conflicting Missions? Teachers Unions and Educational Reform*, Washington, DC: Brookings Institution.
Coopey, J. (1995) 'The learning organization, power, politics and ideology', *Management Learning*, 26(2): 193–213.
Coppieters, P. (2005) 'Turning schools into learning organizations', *European Journal of Teacher Education*, 28(2): 129–39.
Covey, S. R. (1992) *Principle-Centered Leadership*, London: Simon & Schuster.
CPD Review Group (2005a) 'The impact of collaborative CPD on classroom teaching and learning: how do collaborative and sustained CPD and sustained but not collaborative CPD affect teaching and learning?', London: EPPI-Centre, Social Science Research Unit, Institute of Education, University of London.
CPD Review Group (2005b) 'The impact of collaborative CPD on classroom teaching and learning: what do teacher impact data tell us about collaborative CPD?', London: EPPI-Centre, Social Science Research Unit, Institute of Education, University of London.
Cullen, K. (1997) 'Headteacher appraisal: a view from the inside', *Research Papers in Education*, 12(2): 177–204.
Curral, L., Forrester, R., Dawson, J. and West, M. (2001) 'It's what you do and the way that you do it: team task, team size, and innovation-related group processes', *European Journal of Work and Organizational Psychology*, 10(2): 187–204.
Currie, J. and Vidovich, L. (2000) 'Privatization and competition policies for Australian universities', *International Journal of Educational Development*, 20(2): 135–51.
Curtis, P., Hencke, D. and Glendinning, L. (2008) 'Teacher strike shuts out 1m children', *Guardian*, 24 April. Online, available at: www.guardian.co.uk/education/2008/apr/24/schools.uk1 (accessed 15 May 2009).
Dainton, S. (2005) 'Reclaiming teachers' voices', *Forum*, 47(2/3): 159–67.
Darling, J. and McNutt, A. (1996) 'Incorporating social style into administrative team-building in the community college', *Community College Journal of Research and Practice*, 20(5): 455–73.
David, M. (2000) 'New Labour's post-Thatcherite modernisation project: a Third Way?', *Journal of Social Policy*, 29(1): 143–6.
Davis, J. (2002) 'The Inner London Education Authority and the William Tyndale Junior School Affair, 1974–1976', *Oxford Review of Education*, 28(2): 275–98.
Day, C. (1999) *Developing Teachers: The Challenges of Lifelong Learning*, London: Falmer Press.
Day, C. and Bakioğlu, A. (1996) 'Development and disenchantment in the professional lives of headteachers', in I. Goodson and A. Hargreaves (eds) *Teachers' Professional Lives*, London: Falmer Press.
Day, C. and Gu, Q. (2007) 'Variations in the conditions for teachers' professional learning and development: sustaining commitment and effectiveness over a career', *Oxford Review of Education*, 33(4): 423–43.
DCSF (2007) *The Children's Plan: Building Brighter Futures*. Online, available

at: www.dcsf.gov.uk/childrensplan/downloads/The_Childrens_Plan.pdf (accessed 1 April 2009).

DCSF (2008) 'School workforce in England (including Local Authority level figures)', January (revised). Online, available at www.dcsf.gov.uk/rsgateway/DB/SFR/s000813/SFR26_2008.pdf (accessed 28 September 2009).

DCSF (2009) Response to the story on the Handover report, 28 September. Online, available at: www.dcsf.gov.uk/news/content.cfm?landing=response_to_the_story_on_the_handover_report&type=1 (accessed 29 September 2009).

De Villiers, R. and Degazon-Johnson (2007) 'Editorial: the political dichotomy of teacher migration', *Perspectives in Education*, 25(2): vii–xii.

Deem, R. (1998) '"New managerialism" and higher education: the management of performance and cultures in universities in the United Kingdom', *International Studies in Sociology of Education*, 8(2): 47–70.

Deem, R. (2000) '"New managerialism" and the management of UK universities', End of Award Report of the Findings of an ESRC Funded Project, Department of Education Research and the Management School, Lancaster University.

Deem, R. and Brehony, K. J. (2005) 'Management as ideology: the case of "new managerialism" in higher education', *Oxford Review of Education*, 31(2): 217–35.

Deem, R. and Lucas, L. (2007) 'Research and teaching cultures in two contrasting UK policy contexts: academic life in Education Departments in five English and Scottish universities', *Higher Education*, 54(1): 115–33.

Delli, D. A. and Vera, E. M. (2003) 'Psychological and textual influences on teacher selection interview: a model for future research', *Journal of Personnel Evaluation in Education*, 17(2): 137–55.

Demeulemeester, J.-L. and Diebolt, C. (2005) 'The economics of education: unkept promises?', Association Française de Cliométrie, Working Papers 8. Online, available at: http://cdiebolt.free.fr/pdf/wp/AFC_WP_08-2005.pdf (accessed 21 August 2009).

DES (1983) *Teaching Quality*, London: DES.

DES (1985) *Better Schools*, London: DES.

DES Welsh Office (1982) *Study of HM Inspectorate in England and Wales* (Rayner Report), London: DES/WO.

DfEE (1997) *Excellence in Schools*, Cm 3681, London: DfEE.

DfEE (1998) *Teachers Meeting the Challenge of Change*, London: DfEE.

DfEE (1999) *Teachers Meeting the Challenge of Change*, Technical Consultation Document on Pay and Performance Management, London: DfEE.

DfES (2001) *Patterns of Educational Attainment in the British Coalfields*, Research Report 314, London: DfES.

DfES (2003a) 'Raising standards and tackling workload: a national agreement'. Online, available at: www.teachernet.gov.uk/docbank/index.cfm?id=3479 (accessed 21 November 2008).

DfES (2003b) *Raising Attainment in Schools in Former Coalfield Areas*, Research Report 423, Nottingham: DfES.

DfES (2004) 'National standards for headteachers'. Online, available at: http://publications.teachernet.gov.uk/eOrderingDownload/NS4HFinalpdf.pdf (accessed 1 April 2009).

DfES (2005) Secondary school performance tables. Online, available at: www.dfes.gov.uk/performancetables/schools_05.shtml (accessed 16 March 2006).

Dermott, E. (2001) 'New fatherhood in practice? Parental leave in the UK', *International Journal of Sociology and Social Policy*, 21(4/5/6): 145–64.

Dew, J. (2000) 'The middle manager in a team environment', Quality Congress, ASQC Annual Quality Congress Proceedings, Milwaukee.

Dimmock, C. (2000) *Designing the Learning-Centred School: A Cross-cultural Perspective*, London: Falmer Press.

Dinham, S. and Scott, C. (1998) 'A three domain model of teacher and school executive career satisfaction', *Journal of Educational Administration*, 36(4): 362–78.

Dixon, A. (2003) 'Teaching assistants: whose definition?', *Forum*, 45(1): 26–9.

Dixon, N. (1998) 'The responsibilities of members in an organization that is learning', *The Learning Organization*, 5(4): 1–8.

Drever, E. (1995) *Using Semi-structured Interviews in Small-Scale Research*, Edinburgh: Scottish Council for Research in Education.

Driver, M. (2002) 'The learning organization: Foucauldian gloom or Utopian sunshine?', *Human Relations*, 55(1): 33–53.

Dymoke, S. and Harrison, J. K. (2006) 'Professional development and the beginning teacher: issues of teacher autonomy and institutional conformity in the performance review process', *Journal of Education for Teaching*, 32(1): 71–92.

Earley, P. and Weindling, D. (2007) 'Do school leaders have a shelf life? Career stages and headteacher performance', *Educational Management Administration and Leadership*, 35(1): 73–88.

Easterby-Smith, M. (2004) 'Constructing contributions to organizational learning: Argyris and the next generation', *Management Learning*, 35(4): 371–80.

Eironline (n.d.) 'ECJ rules that pension entitlement may be backdated'. Online, available at: www.eurofound.europa.eu/eiro/2000/05/feature/eu0005251f.htm (accessed 14 May 2009).

Elliott, J. (2001) 'Characteristics of performative cultures', in D. Gleeson and C. Husbands (eds) *The Performing School: Managing Teaching and Learning in a Performance Culture*, London: RoutledgeFalmer.

Elmuti, D. (1997) 'Self-managed work teams approach: creative management tool or a fad?', *Management Decision*, 35(3): 233–9.

Enteman, W. (1993) *Managerialism*, Madison, WI: University of Wisconsin Press.

EOC (2007) *Working outside the Box: Changing Work to Meet the Future*, Interim report of the EOC's investigation into the Transformation of Work, Manchester: Equal Opportunities Commission. Online, available at: www.equalityhumanrights.com/uploaded_files/Employers/working_outside_box_summary.pdf (accessed 4 April 2009).

Equality and Human Rights Commission (n.d.) 'Part-time workers'. Online, available at: www.equalityhumanrights.com/en/foradvisers/EocLaw/eoclawenglandwales/Equalpay/Isthereadefence/Pages/Part-timeworkers.aspx (accessed 15 May 2009).

Equality Bill (2009) Online, available at: www.publications.parliament.uk/pa/cm200809/cmbills/085/voli/09085i.i-ii.html (accessed 14 May 2009).

Eraut, M. (2000) 'Teacher education designed or framed?', *International Journal of Educational Research*, 33: 557–74.

Eurofound (2008) 'Industrial relations context'. Online, available at: www.eurofound.europa.eu/areas/industrialrelations/dictionary/dictionary0.htm (accessed 14 May 2009).

Europa (n.d.) 'Burden of proof in cases of discrimination based on sex'. Online, available at: http://europa.eu/legislation_summaries/employment_and_social_policy/equality_between_men_and_women/c10913_en.htm (accessed 14 May 2009).

European Union (2000) Working Time Directive. Online, available at: <http://eur-lex.europa.eu/smartapi/cgi/sga_doc?smartapi!celexapi!prod!CELEXnumdoc&lg=en&numdoc=32000L0034&model=guichett (accessed 2 July 2009).

Exworthy, M. and Halford, S. (eds) (1999) *Professionals and the New Managerialism in the Public Sector*, Buckingham: Open University Press.

Farrell, C. and Morris, J. (2004) 'Resigned compliance: teacher attitudes towards performance related pay in schools', *Education Management, Administration and Leadership*, 32(1): 81–104.

Fenwick, T. (2007) 'Limits of the learning organization: a critical look'. Online, available at: www.ualberta.ca/-tfenwick/ext/pubs/print/lngorgeric.htm (accessed 6 August 2007).

Fidler, B. (2001) 'A structural critique of school effectiveness and school improvement', in A. Harris and N. Bennett (eds) *School Effectiveness and School Improvement*, London: Continuum.

Fidler, B. and Cooper, R. (eds) (1992) *Staff Appraisal and Staff Management in Schools and Colleges: A Guide to Implementation*, Harlow, UK: Longman.

Fielding, M. (1999) 'Communities of learners: myth: schools are communities', in B. O'Hagan (ed.) *Modern Educational Myths: The Future of Democratic Comprehensive Education*, London: Kogan Page.

Fielding, M. (2001) 'Learning organisation or learning community? A critique of Senge', *Reason in Practice*, 1(2): 17–29.

Fielding, M. (2006) 'Leadership, personalization and high performance schooling: naming the new totalitarianism', *School Leadership and Management*, 26(4): 347–69.

Findlay, K. (2006) 'Context and learning factors in the development of teacher identity: a case study of newly qualified teachers during their induction year', *Journal of In-Service Education*, 32(4): 511–32.

Finger, M. and Brand, S. (1999) 'The concept of the "learning organization" applied to the transformation of the public sector', in M. Easterby-Smith, L. Araujo and J. Burgoyne (eds) *Organizational Learning and the Learning Organization*, London: Sage.

Fink, D. and Brayman, C. (2006) 'School leadership succession and the challenges of change', *Educational Administration Quarterly*, 42(62): 62–89.

Finn, J. D., Gerber, S. B., Farber, S. L. and Achilles, C. M. (2000) 'Teacher aides: an alternative to small classes?', in M. C. Wang and J. D. Finn (eds) *How Small Classes Help Teachers Do Their Best,* Philadelphia, PA: Temple University Center for Research in Human Development.

Fisher, K. (2000) *Leading Self-Directed Teams: A Guide to Developing New Team Leadership Skills*, New York: McGraw-Hill Professional.

Fisher, S., Hunter, T. and MacRosson, W. (2001) 'A validation study of Belbin's team roles', *European Journal of Work and Organizational Psychology*, 10(2): 121–44.

Fitzgerald, T. (2001) 'Potential paradoxes in performance appraisal: emerging issues for New Zealand schools', in D. Middlewood and C. Cardno (eds) *Managing Teacher Appraisal and Performance*, London: RoutledgeFalmer.

Flynn, R. (1999) 'Managerialism, professionalism and quasi-markets', in M. Exworthy and S. Halford (eds) *Professionals and the New Managerialism in the Public Sector*, Buckingham, UK: Open University Press.

Fullan, M. (1982) *The Meaning of Educational Change*, New York: Teachers' College Press.

Fullan, M. (2003) *The Moral Imperative of School Leadership*, Thousand Oaks, CA: Corwin Press.

Furlong, J. (2005) 'New Labour and teacher education: the end of an era', *Oxford Review of Education*, 31(1): 119–34.

Furlong, J., Barton, L., Miles, S., Whiting, C. and Whitty, G. (2000) *Teacher Education in Transition: Re-forming Professionalism?*, Buckingham, UK: Open University Press.

Garavan, T. (1997) 'The learning organization: a review and evaluation', *The Learning Organization*, 4(1): 18–29.

Garvin, D. (1993) 'Building a learning organization', *Harvard Business Review*, 71(4): 78–91.

GEO (2009) 'Harman: Equality Bill will build a fairer and stronger Britain', 27 April. Online, available at: www.equalities.gov.uk/media/press_releases/equality_bill.aspx (accessed 15 May 2009).

Gerhart, B. and Fang, M. (2005) 'National culture and human resource management: assumptions and evidence', *International Journal of Human Resource Management*, 16(6): 971–86.

Giddens, A. (1990) *The Consequences of Modernity*, Cambridge: Polity Press.

Gillard, D. (2005) 'Rescuing teacher professionalism', *Forum*, 47(2/3): 175–80.

Glaser, B. G. and Strauss, A. (1967) *The Discovery of Grounded Theory*, Chicago, IL: Aldine.

Gleeson, D., Davies, J. and Wheeler, E. (2009) 'On the making and taking of professionalism in the further education workplace', in S. Gewirtz, P. Mahony, I. Hextall and A. Cribb (eds) *Changing Teacher Professionalism: International Trends, Challenges and Ways Forward*, London: Routledge.

Goddard, I. and Emerson, C. (1992) *Appraisal and Your School*, Oxford: Heinemann.

Gold, A., Evans, J., Earley, P., Halpin, D. and Collarbone, P. (2003) 'Principled principals? Values-driven leadership: evidence from ten case studies of "outstanding" school leaders', *Educational Management and Administration*, 31(2): 127–37.

Goleman, D., Boyatzis, R. and McKee, A. (2003) *The New Leaders: Transforming the Art of Leadership into the Science of Results*, London: Time Warner.

Gomm, R., Hammersley, M. and Foster, P. (2000) 'Case study and generalization', in R. Gomm, M. Hammersley and P. Foster (eds) *Case Study Method*, London: Sage.

Goodson, I. and Hargreaves, A. (eds) (1996) *Teachers' Professional Lives*, London: Falmer Press.

Gorard, S. and Taylor, C. (2001) 'The composition of specialist schools in England: track record and future prospect', *School Leadership and Management*, 21(4): 365–81.

Gorard, S., See, B. H., Smith, E. and White, P. (2006) *Teacher Supply*, London: Continuum.

Grace, G. (1985) 'Judging teachers: the social and political contexts of teacher evaluation', *British Journal of Sociology of Education*, 6(1): 3–16.

Grace, G. (1987) 'Teachers and the state in Britain: a changing relationship', in M. Lawn and G. Grace (eds) *Teachers: The Culture and Politics of Work*, London: Falmer Press.

Grant, C. (1995) 'Delors after power' (interview), *Prospect*, issue 1, October. Online, available at: www.prospect-magazine.co.uk/article_details.php?search_term=Delors+after+power&id=4977 (accessed 14 May 2009).

Gray, J. (2001) 'Introduction', in M. Maden (ed.) *Success against the Odds – Five Years On*, London: RoutledgeFalmer.

Gray, J., Jesson, D. and Sime, N. (1990) 'Estimating differences in the examination performances of secondary schools in six LEAs: a multi-level approach to school effectiveness', *Oxford Review of Education*, 16(2): 137–58.

Green, F. (2004) 'Why has work effort become more intense?', *Industrial Relations*, 43(4): 709–41.

Green, F. (2006) *Demanding Work: The Paradox of Job Quality in the Affluent Economy*, Princeton, NJ: Princeton University Press.

Green, F. (2008) 'Work effort and worker well-being in the age of affluence', in C. Cooper and R. Burke (eds) *The Long Work Hours Culture: Causes, Consequences and Choices*, Bingley, UK: Emerald Group Publications. Online, available at: www.kent.ac.uk/economics/documents/gfg/FG_Paper_KentDP.pdf (accessed 4 April 2009).

Greenfield, T. and Ribbins, P. (eds) (1993) *Greenfield on Educational Administration: Towards a Humane Science*, London: Routledge.

Gronn, P. (2003) *The New Work of Educational Leaders*, London: Paul Chapman.

GTCS (2003) *Classroom Assistants: A GTC Position Paper*, Edinburgh: GTCS.

Guarino, C. M., Santibañez, L. and Daley, G. A. (2006) 'Teacher recruitment and retention: a review of recent empirical literature', *Review of Educational Research*, 76(2): 173–208.

Gunter, H. (2001) *Leaders and Leadership in Education*, London: Paul Chapman.

Gunter, H. (2007) 'Remodelling the school workforce in England: a study in tyranny', *Journal for Critical Education Policy Studies*, 5(1). Online, available at: http://www.jceps.com/index.php?pageID=article&articleID=84 (accessed 10 March 2010).

Guskey, T. R. (2000) *Evaluating Professional Development*, Thousand Oaks, CA: Corwin Press.

Hackman, J. (2002) *Leading Teams: Setting the Stage for Great Performances*, Boston, MA: Harvard Business School Press.

Hallinger, P. (2003) 'Leading educational change: reflections on the practice of instructional and transformational leadership', *Cambridge Journal of Education*, 33(3): 329–51.

Hallinger, P. and Heck, R. (1998) 'Exploring the principal's contribution to school effectiveness: 1980–1995', *School Effectiveness and School Improvement*, 9(2): 157–91.

Hammersley-Fletcher, L. (2008) 'The impact of workforce remodelling on change management and working practices in English primary schools', *School Leadership and Management*, 28(5): 489–503.

Hampton, G. and Jones, J. (2000) *Transforming Northicote School: The Reality of School Improvement*, London: RoutledgeFalmer.

Hancock, R. and Eyres, I. (2004) 'Implementing a required curriculum reform: teachers at the core, teaching assistants on the periphery?', *Westminster Studies in Education*, 27(2): 223–35.

Hansford, B. and Ehrich, L. C. (2006) 'The principalship: how significant is mentoring?', *Journal of Educational Administration*, 44(1): 36–52.

Hargreaves, A. (1994) *Changing Teachers, Changing Times*, London: Cassell.

Hargreaves, A. (2003) *Teaching in the Knowledge Society: Education in the Age of Insecurity*, Maidenhead, UK: Open University Press.

Hargreaves, A. and Goodson, I. (1996) 'Teachers' professional lives: aspirations and actualities', in I. Goodson and A. Hargreaves (eds) *Teachers' Professional Lives*, London: Falmer Press.

Hargreaves, L., Cunningham, M., Hansen, A., McIntyre, D., Oliver, C. and Pell, T. (2007) *The Status of Teachers and the Teaching Profession in England: Views from Inside and Outside the Profession*, Final Report of the Teacher Status Project, University of Cambridge, Report 831A.

Harris, A. (2004) 'Distributed leadership and school improvement: leading or misleading', *Educational Management, Administration and Leadership*, 32(11): 11–22.

Harvey, D. (2007) *A Brief History of Neoliberalism*, Oxford: Oxford University Press.

Haslam, C., Bryman, A. and Webb, A. L. (1993) 'The function of performance appraisal in UK universities', *Higher Education*, 25: 473–86.

Hatcher, R. (1994) 'Market relationships and the management of teachers', *British Journal of Sociology of Education*, 15(1): 41–61.

Hellawell, D. (1990) 'Effects of the national dispute on the relationships between head teachers and school staffs in primary schools', *British Journal of Sociology of Education*, 11(4): 397–410.

Hellawell, D. and Hancock, N. (2001) 'A case study of the changing role of the academic middle manager in higher education: between hierarchical control and collegiality?', *Research Papers in Education*, 16(2): 183–97.

Higham, R., Hopkins, D. and Ahtaridou, E. (2007) *Improving School Leadership: Country Background Report for England*, London: Centre for Leadership in Learning, OECD.

Hofstede, G. (1991) *Cultures and Organizations: Software of the Mind*, New York: McGraw-Hill.

Hofstede, G. and Hofstede, G. J. (2005) *Cultures and Organizations: Software of the Mind*, 2nd edn, Maidenhead, UK: McGraw-Hill.

Holton, F. III (2002) 'Theoretical assumptions underlying the performance paradigm of human resource development', *Human Resource Development International*, 5(2): 199–215.

Hopkins, D. (1984) 'What is school improvement? Staking out the territory', in D. Hopkins and M. Wideen (eds) *Alternative Perspectives on School Improvement*, Lewes, UK: Falmer Press.

Hopkins, D. (2007) *Every School a Great School: Realizing the Potential of System Leadership*, Maidenhead, UK: Open University Press/McGraw-Hill Education.

House, E. and Lapan, S. (1989) 'Teacher appraisal', in H. Simons and J. Elliott (eds) *Rethinking Appraisal and Assessment*, Milton Keynes, UK: Open University Press.

Howe, E. R. (2006) 'Exemplary teacher induction: an international review', *Educational Philosophy and Theory*, 38(3): 287–97.

Howson, J. (2003) *9th Annual Report, The State of the Labour Market for Senior Staff in England and Wales (2002–2003)*, Oxford: Education Data Surveys.

Howson, J. (2005) *20th Annual Survey of Senior Staff Appointments in Schools in England and Wales*, Oxford: Education Data Surveys.

Howson, J. (2007) *22nd Annual Survey of Senior Staff Appointments in Schools in England and Wales*, Oxford: Education Data Surveys.

Howson, J. (2008a) *14th Annual Report, The State of the Labour Market for Senior Staff in Schools in England and Wales*, Oxford: Education Data Surveys.

Howson, J. (2008b) *23rd Annual Survey of Senior Staff Appointments in schools in England and Wales*, Oxford: Education Data Surveys.

Hoyle, E. (1986) *The Politics of School Management*, Sevenoaks, UK: Hodder & Stoughton.

Huber, S. G. and Pashiardis, P. (2008) 'The recruitment and selection of school leaders', in J. Lumby, G. Crow and P. Pashiardis (eds) *International Handbook on the Preparation and Development of School Leaders*, New York: Routledge.

Hughes, P. (1998) *Appraisal in UK Higher Education*, Sheffield: Universities' and Colleges' Staff Development Agency.

Huisman, J. and Currie, J. (2004) 'Accountability in higher education: bridge over troubled water?', *Higher Education*, 48: 529–51.

Hursh, D. (2005) 'Neo-liberalism, markets and accountability: transforming education and undermining democracy in the United States and England', *Policy Futures in Education*, 3(1): 3–15.

Hutchinson, B. (1995) 'Staff appraisal: personal, professional and organisational development?', *Educational Management and Administration*, 23(1): 47–57.

Hutchinson, B. (1997) 'Appraising appraisal: some tensions and some possibilities', in L. Kydd, M. Crawford and C. Riches (eds) *Professional Development for Educational Management*, Buckingham, UK: Open University Press.

Infed (2007) 'The learning organization'. Online, available at: www.infed.org/biblio/learning-organization.htm (accessed 6 August 2007).

Ingersoll, R. M. (2004) *Why Do High-Poverty Schools Have Difficulty Staffing Their Classrooms with Qualified Teachers?*, report prepared for Renewing Our Schools, Securing Our Future, A National Task Force on Public Education, Washington, DC: Center for American Progress and the Institute for America's Future.

Ingvarson, L., Meiers, M. and Beavis, A. (2005) 'Factors affecting the impact of professional development programs on teachers' knowledge, practice, student outcomes and efficacy', *Education Policy Analysis Archives*, 13(10): 1–28.

Ironside, M. and Seifert, R. (1995) *Industrial Relations in Schools*, London: Routledge.

Ironside, M., Seifert, R. and Sinclair, J. (1997) 'Teacher union responses to education reforms: job regulation and the enforced growth of informality', *Industrial Relations Journal*, 28(2): 120–35.

Isherwood, M., Johnson, H. and Brundrett, M. (2007) 'Performance management – motivating and developing good teachers? The experiences of teachers in a small special school', *Education 3–13*, 35(1): 71–81.

James, G. (2006) 'The Work and Families Act 2006: legislation to improve choice and flexibility?', *Industrial Law Journal*, 35(3) (September): 272–8.

Jarratt Report (1985) *Report of the Steering Committee for Efficiency Studies in Universities*, London: Committee of Vice-Chancellors and Principals.

Jeffrey, B. and Woods, P. (1998) *Testing Teachers: The Effect of School Inspections on Primary Teachers*, London: Falmer Press.

John, E. (2007) 'To what extent is distributed leadership a panacea for sustained school improvement? A case study of distributed leadership in practice at The Kingswood School', dissertation submitted in part-fulfilment of the requirements of the MA degree in Leadership for Learning, School of Education, Leicester.

Johnson, S. M. (1983) 'Teacher unions in schools: authority and accommodation', *Harvard Educational Review*, 53: 309–26.

Jones, M. (2002) 'Qualified to become good teachers: a case study of ten newly qualified teachers during their year of induction', *Professional Development in Education*, 28(3): 509–26.

Judkins, M. and Rudd, P. (2005) 'Evaluation of high-performing specialist schools', Slough: NFER. Paper presented at the British Educational Research Association Annual Conference, University of Glamorgan, Pontypridd, 15–17 September.

Keating, I. and Moorcroft, R. (eds) (2006) *Managing the Business of Schools*, London: NCSL/Paul Chapman.

Kelly, P. and Colquhoun, D. (2003) 'Governing the stressed self: teacher "health and well-being" and "effective schools"', *Discourse: Studies in the Cultural Politics of Education*, 24(2): 191–204.

Kennedy, A. (2007) 'Continuing professional development (CPD) policy and the discourse of teacher professionalism in Scotland', *Research Papers in Education*, 22(1): 95–111.

Kerry, T. (2005) 'Towards a typology for conceptualizing the roles of teaching assistants', *Educational Review*, 57(3): 373–84.

Kim, S. and Kim, E. P. (2005) 'Profile of school administrators in South Korea', *Educational Management, Administration and Leadership*, 33(3): 289–310.

Kirkman, B. and Rosen, B. (1999) 'Beyond self-management: antecedents and consequences of team empowerment', *The Academy of Management Journal*, 42(1): 58–74.

Knight, P., Tait, J. and Yorke, M. (2006) 'The professional learning of teachers in higher education', *Studies in Higher Education*, 31(3): 319–39.

Knott, A. (2004) 'Employer liabilities for consequences of teacher stress: House of Lords decision', *Australian and New Zealand Journal of Law and Education*, 9(2): 85–90.

Kotter, J. (1996) *Leading Change*, Boston, MA: Harvard Business School Press.

LaFasto, F. and Larson, C. (2001) *When Teams Work Best: 6,000 Team Members and Leaders Tell What It Takes to Succeed*, Thousand Oaks, CA: Sage.

Larsen, K., McInerney, C., Nyquist, C., Santos, A. and Silsbee, D. (1996) 'Learning organizations'. Online, available at: http://home.nycap.rr.com/klarsen/learnorg (accessed 6 August 2007).

Lawn, M. and Whitty, G. (1992) 'The re-formation of teacher unionism', *Education Review*, 6: 5–12.

Leader (2007) '"No" to business leaders becoming heads', *Leader: The Education Leader Magazine*, February. Online, available at: www.leadermagazine.co.uk/article.php?id=638 (accessed 28 September 2009).

Lefstein, A. (2005) 'Thinking about the technical and the personal in teaching', *Cambridge Journal of Education*, 35(3): 333–56.

Leithwood, K. and Levin, B. (2008) 'Understanding and assessing the impact of leadership', in J. Lumby, G. Crow and P. Pashiardis (eds) *International Handbook on the Preparation and Development of School Leaders*, New York: Routledge.

Leithwood, K. and Riehl, C. (2003) *What we know about successful school leadership*, Philadelphia, PA: Laboratory for Student Success, Temple University. Online, available at: www.cepa.gse.rutgers.edu/whatweknow.pdf (accessed 23 January 2006).

Leithwood, K., Doris, J. and Steinbach, R. (1998) 'Leadership and other conditions which foster organizational learning in schools', in K. Leithwood and K. Louis (eds) *Organizational Learning in Schools*, Lisse, Netherlands: Swets & Zeitlinger.

Levine, A. (2005) *Educating School Leaders*. Online, available at: www.edschools.org/pdf/Final313.pdf (accessed 25 August 2009).

Lewin, K. M. (2002) 'The costs of supply and demand for teacher education: dilemmas for development', *International Journal of Educational Development*, 22: 221–42.

Lipman, P. (2009) 'Paradoxes of teaching in neo-liberal times: education "reform" in Chicago', in S. Gewirtz, P. Mahony, I. Hextall and A. Cribb (eds) *Changing Teacher Professionalism: International Trends, Challenges and Ways Forward*, London: Routledge.

Litwin, G. and Stringer, R. (1968) *Motivation and Organizational Climate*, Boston, MA: Division of Research, Harvard Business School.

Lodge, C. (1998) 'What's wrong with our schools?', in L. Stoll and K. Myers (eds) *No Quick Fixes: Perspectives on Schools in Difficulty*, London: Falmer Press.

Lyotard, J.-F. (1984) *The Postmodern Condition: A Report on Knowledge*, Manchester: Manchester University Press.

Mabey, C. and Ramirez, M. (2004) *Developing Managers: A European Perspective*, London: Chartered Management Institute.

MacBeath, J. (2005) 'Leadership as distributed: a matter of practice', *School Leadership and Management*, 25(4): 349–66.

MacBeath, J. and Galton, M. with Steward, S. and Page, C. (2007) *Pressure and Professionalism: The Impact of Recent and Present Government Policies on the Working Lives of Teachers*, A Report Commissioned for the NUT, London: National Union of Teachers.

McClelland, D. C. (1987) *Human Motivation*, New York: Cambridge University Press.

McClelland, D. C. and Burnham, D. H. (1995) 'Power is the great motivator', *Harvard Business Review*, January/February, Classic Reprint 95108, originally published in March/April 1976, 100–10.

McConville, T. (2006) 'Devolved HRM responsibilities, middle-managers and role Dissonance', *Personnel Review*, 35(6): 637–53.

McCrimmon, M. (1995) 'Teams without roles: empowering teams for greater creativity', *Journal of Management Development*, 14(6): 35–41.

McNamara, D. (1993) 'Towards re-establishing the professional authority and expertise of teacher educators and teachers', in D. P. Gilroy and M. Smith (eds) *International Analyses of Teacher Education*, Abingdon, UK: Carfax Publishing.

MacRuairc, G. and Harford, J. (2008) 'Researching the contested place of reflective practice in the emerging culture of performativity in schools: views from the Republic of Ireland', *European Educational Research Journal*, 7(4): 501–11.

Maden, M. (ed.) (2001) *Success against the Odds – Five Years On*, London: RoutledgeFalmer.

Magennis, S. (1993) 'Appraisal systems and their contribution to quality in teaching', in R. Ellis (ed.) *Quality Assurance in University Teaching*, Buckingham, UK: Open University Press.

Majrowski v. Guys and St Thomas' NHS Trust (2006) Online, available at: www.bailii.org/uk/cases/UKHL/2006/34.html (accessed 15 May 2009).

Mansell, W. (2007) *Education by Numbers: The Tyranny of Testing*, London: Politico's Publishing.

Marginson, S. (1997) 'Steering from a distance: power relations in Australian higher education', *Higher Education*, 34(1): 63–80.

Marks, S. U., Schrader, C. and Levine, M. (1999) 'Paraeducator experiences in inclusive settings: helping, hovering, or holding their own?', *Exceptional Children*, 65(3), 315(1). Online, available from Expanded Academic ASAP via Gale: http://find.galegroup.com/itx/start.do?prodId=EAIM (accessed 3 September 2009).

Marley, D. (2009a) 'Non-teacher head quits after just five months', *TES Connect*, 20 January. Online, available at: www.tes.co.uk/article.aspx?storycode=6007884 (accessed 5 October 2009).

Marley, D. (2009b) 'Non-teaching head not given enough time', *TES Connect*, 27 March. Online, available at: www.tes.co.uk/article.aspx?storycode=6010842 (accessed 5 October 2009).

Meikle v. Nottinghamshire County Council (2003) Online, available at: www.bailii.org/uk/cases/UKEAT/2003/0033_03_2609.html (accessed 14 May 2009).

Menuey, B. P. (2007) 'Teachers' perceptions of incompetence and barriers to the dismissal process', *Journal of Personnel Evaluation in Education*, 18(4): 309–24.

Mercer, J. (2007) 'Challenging appraisal orthodoxies: teacher evaluation and professional development in the United Arab Emirates', *Journal of Personnel Evaluation in Education*, 18: 273–87.

Meyer, C. (1998) 'How the right measures help teams excel', in J. R. Katzenbach (ed.) *The Work of Teams*, Cambridge, MA: Harvard Business Review Books.

Middlewood, D. (2001) 'Appraisal and performance in the UK', in D. Middlewood and C. Cardno (eds) *Managing Teacher Appraisal and Performance*, London: RoutledgeFalmer.

Middlewood, D. and Cardno, C. (eds) (2001) *Managing Teacher Appraisal and Performance*, London: RoutledgeFalmer.

Middlewood, D. and Lumby, J. (1998) *Human Resource Management in Schools and Colleges*, London: Paul Chapman.

Miles, M. and Hyle, A. E. (1999) 'Faculty appraisal: a prickly pair', *Higher Education*, 38: 351–71.

Miliband, D. (2003) '21st century teaching: leading modern professionalism', speech by the Minister of State for School Standards at the launch of the TTA corporate plan, London, 7 April.

Milne, J. (2007) 'Headteachers' union votes to rejoin social partnership', *The Times Educational Supplement*, 26 January. Online, available at: www.tes.co.uk/article.aspx?storycode=2335881 (accessed 15 May 2009).

Mistry, M., Burton, N. and Brundrett, M. (2004) 'Managing LSAs: an evaluation of the use of learning support assistants in an urban primary school', *School Leadership and Management*, 24(2): 125–37.

Monteils, M. (2004) 'The analysis of the relation between education and economic growth', *Compare: A Journal of Comparative and International Education*, 34(1): 103–15.

Moon, B. (2007) 'Research analysis: attracting, developing and retaining effective teachers: a global overview of current policies and practices', UNESCO Working Paper, Geneva: UNESCO.

Moorcroft, R. and Summerson, T. (2006) 'Leaders backing leaders: a programme of school business management', *Professional Development in Education*, 32(2): 255–74.

Moreau, M.-P., Osgood, J. and Halsall, A. (2005) *The Career Progression of Women Teachers in England: A Study of Barriers to Promotion and Career Development*,

Institute for Policy Studies in Education, London: London Metropolitan University.

Moreau, M.-P., Osgood, J. and Halsall, A. (2007) 'Making sense of the glass ceiling in schools: an exploration of women teachers' discourses', *Gender and Education*, 19(2): 237–53.

Morgan, C., Hall, V. and Mackay, H. (1983) *The Selection of Secondary School Headteachers*, Milton Keynes: Open University Press.

Morgan, P., Allington, N. and Heery, E. (2000) 'Employment insecurity in the public services', in E. Heery and J. Salmon (eds) *The Insecure Workforce*, London: Routledge.

MORI (2006) *Opinions of Professions*. Online, available at: www.mori.com/polls/trends/truth.shtml (accessed 25 October 2006).

MORI/Audit Commission (2003) *Trust in Public Institutions*, London. Online, available at: www.ipsos-mori.com/DownloadPublication/1180_sri_trust_in_public_institutions_2003.PDF (accessed 3 June 2009).

Morris, E. (2001) 'Professionalism and trust', A speech by the Rt Hon. Estelle Morris MP, Secretary of State for Education and Skills, to the Social Market Foundation. London: Department for Education and Skills.

Morris, T. and Dennison, W. (1982) 'The role of the comprehensive school HoD analysed', *Research Education*, 28 November.

Morrison, K. (1998) *Management Theories for Educational Change*, London: Paul Chapman.

Mortimore, P. and Whitty, G. (2000) *Can School Improvement Overcome the Effects of Disadvantage?*, London: Institute of Education, University of London.

Muijs, D. (2003) 'The effectiveness in the use of learning support assistants in improving the mathematics achievement of low achieving pupils in a primary school', *Educational Research*, 45(3): 219–30.

Muijs, D. and Lindsay, G. (2006) *Evaluating Continuing Professional Development: Testing Guskey's Model in the UK*. Online, available at: www.leadership.fau.edu/icsei2006/Papers/Muijis%20and%20Lindsay.pdf (accessed 1 April 2009).

Munt, V. (2004) 'The awful truth: a microhistory of teacher stress at Westwood High', *British Journal of Sociology of Education*, 25(5): 577–91.

Murray, A. (2003) *Waking Up to the Pensions Timebomb*, London: Centre for European Reform.

Murray, H. (1938) *Explorations in Personality*, New York: Oxford University Press.

NASBM (2008) 'History of the Association'. Online, available at: www.nasbm.co.uk/Home/About-NASBM/History-and-Aims.aspx (accessed 24 September 2009).

NCEA (1994) 'Social justice unionism: a call to education activists', *Rethinking Schools*, 9(1). Online, available at: www.rethinkingschools.org/special_reports/union/sjun.shtml (accessed 15 May 2009).

NCSL (2001) *Leadership Development Framework*, Nottingham: NCSL.

NCSL (2002) 'NCSL pledges to widen professional development opportunities for school leaders', Nottingham: NCSL. Online, available at: www.ncsl.org.uk/about us-index/pressreleases-index/pressreleases-2002.htm?id=13920 (accessed 1 April 2009).

NCSL (2003a) *Co-coaching guide*, RL/CC/01. Nottingham: NCSL.

NCSL (2003b) *Leadership Programme for Serving Headteachers: Facilitator Guide*, Nottingham: NCSL.

NCSL (2004) *Distributed Leadership*, Nottingham: NCSL.

NCSL (2006a) *Leadership Development Framework*, Nottingham: NCSL. Online, available at: www.nationalcollege.org.uk/docinfo?id=17113&filename=career-moves.pdf (accessed 4 October 2006).

NCSL (2006b) *Succession Planning: Formal Advice to the Secretary of State*, Nottingham: NCSL. Online, available at: www.nationalcollege.org.uk/succession-planning-national-college-advice-2.pdf (accessed 1 April 2009).

NCSL (2007) *Leading from the Middle*, Nottingham: NCSL. Online, available at: www.nationalcollege.org.uk/index/professional-development/lftm (accessed 8 September 2007).

NCSL (n.d.a) *Learning to Lead: NCSL's Strategy for Leadership Learning*, Nottingham: NCSL. Online, available at: www.nationalcollege.org.uk/docinfo?id=17400&filename=strategy-for-leadership-learning.pdf (accessed 1 April 2009).

NCSL (n.d.b) *Recruiting Headteachers and Senior Leaders: Overview of Research Findings*, Nottingham: NCSL. Online, available at: www.ncsl.org.uk/media-536–22-recruiting-headteachers-overview-findings.pdf (accessed 1 April 2009).

NCSL (n.d.c) *National Professional Qualification for Headship*, Nottingham: NCSL. Online, available at: www.nationalcollege.org.uk/index/professional-development/npqh.htm (accessed 5 October 2009).

NUT (2003) 'A price too high'. Online, available at: www.suffolknut.org.uk/Workload%20(2966).pdf (accessed 14 May 2009).

O. v. The Governing Body of Park View Academy and Others (2007) Online, available at: www.bailii.org/ew/cases/EWCA/Civ/2007/592.html (accessed 14 May 2009).

O'Connor, J. S. (2005) 'Policy coordination, social indicators and the social-policy agenda in the European Union', *Journal of European Social Policy*, 15(4): 345–61.

OECD (2003) *Attracting, Developing and Retaining Effective Teachers: Country Background Report for Italy*, Paris: Organisation for Economic Co-operation and Development.

OECD (2004) *Attracting, Developing and Retaining Effective Teachers: Country Note for Germany*, Paris: Organisation for Economic Co-operation and Development.

OECD (2005) 'Ageing populations: high time for action' (background paper prepared by the OECD Secretariat), from Meeting of G8 Employment and Labour Ministers, London, 10–11 March. Online, available at: www.oecd.org/data oecd/61/50/34600619.pdf (accessed 15 May 2009).

OECD (2007) Society at a Glance: OECD Social Indicators – 2006 Edition: 'Age-dependency ratios'. Online, available at: www.oecd.org/dataoecd/4/24/38148 786.pdf (accessed 15 May 2009).

Ofsted (1996) *The Appraisal of Teachers 1991–1996*, London: Ofsted.

Ofsted (2000) 'Inspection report', The Shire School.

Ofsted (2002) *Leadership and Management Training for Headteachers*, London: Ofsted.

O'Neill, J. (1997) 'Managing through teams', in T. Bush and D. Middlewood (eds) *Managing People in Education*, London: Paul Chapman.

Oplatka, I. (2004) 'The principalship in developing countries: context, characteristics and reality', *Comparative Education*, 40(3): 427–48.

Örtenblad, A. (2001) 'On differences between organizational learning and learning organization', *The Learning Organization*, 8(3): 125–33.

O'Sullivan, F., Thody, A. and Wood, E. (2000) *From Bursar to School Business Manager: Re-engineering Leadership for Resource Management*, London: Prentice Hall.

Ozga, J. (2002) 'Education governance in the United Kingdom: the modernisation project', *European Educational Research Journal*, 1(2): 331–41.

Ozga, J. (2005) 'Modernizing the education workforce: a perspective from Scotland', *Educational Review*, 57(2): 207–19.

P. (FC) [2003] UKHL 8. Online, available at: www.bailii.org/uk/cases/UKHL/2003/8.html (accessed 14 May 2009).

Peaker, G. (1986) 'Teacher management and appraisal in two school systems in the southern USA', *Journal of Education for Teaching*, 12(1): 77–83.

Penuel, W. R., Fishman, B. J., Yamaguchi, R. and Gallagher, L. P. (2007) 'What makes professional development effective? Strategies that foster curriculum implementation', *American Educational Research Journal*, 44(4): 921–58.

Perryman, J. (2006) 'Panoptic performativity and school inspection regimes: disciplinary mechanisms and life under special measures', *Journal of Education Policy*, 21(2): 147–61.

Peters, M., Marshall, J. and Fitzsimons, P. (2000) 'Managerialism and educational policy in a global context: Foucault, neoliberalism and the doctrine of self-management', in N. C. Burbules and C. A. Torres (eds) *Globalization and Education: Critical Perspectives*, New York: Routledge.

Peters, T. (1989) *Thriving on Chaos*, London: Pan Books.

Phillips, D. (1993) 'Subjectivity and objectivity: an objective inquiry', in M. Hammersley (ed.) *Educational Research: Current Issues*, London: Paul Chapman.

Pollitt, C. (1987) 'The politics of performance assessment: lessons for higher education', *Studies in Higher Education*, 12(1): 87–98.

Pollitt, C. (1993) *Managerialism and the Public Services*, 2nd edn, Oxford: Blackwell.

Popkewitz, T. S. (2000) 'The denial of change in educational change: systems of ideas in the construction of national policy and evaluation', *Educational Researcher*, 29: 17–29.

Poskanzer, S. G. (2002) *Higher Education, Law: The Faculty*, Baltimore, MD: Johns Hopkins University Press.

Poster, C. and Poster, D. (1997) 'The nature of appraisal', in L. Kydd, M. Crawford and C. Riches (eds) *Professional Development for Educational Management*, Buckingham, UK: Open University Press.

PricewaterhouseCoopers (2001) *Teacher Workload Study*, London: Department for Education and Skills.

PricewaterhouseCoopers (2007) *Independent Study into School Leadership: Main Report*, London: Department for Education and Skills.

Pring, R. (1999) 'Universities and teacher education', *Higher Education Quarterly*, 53(4): 290–311.

Pring, R. (2001) 'Managing the professions: the case of the teachers', *Political Quarterly*, 72 (3): 278–312.

Purdon, A. (2003) 'A national framework of CPD: continuing professional development or continuing policy dominance?', *Journal of Education Policy*, 18(4): 423–37.

Quirke, J. (2003) 'Teaching assistants: students or servants?', *Forum*, 45(2): 71–4.

Radford, M. (2006) 'Researching classrooms: complexity and chaos', *British Educational Research Journal*, 32(2): 177–90.

Reina, D. and Reina, M. (1999) *Trust and Betrayal in the Workplace*, San Francisco, CA: Berrett-Koehler.

Reynolds, D., Stringfield, S. and Schaffer, E. C. (2006) 'The High Reliability Schools project: some preliminary results and analyses', in A. Harris and J. H. Chrispeels (eds) *Improving Schools and Educational Systems: International Perspectives*, London: Routledge.

Reynolds, R. and Ablett, A. (1998) 'Transforming the rhetoric of organizational learning to the reality of the learning organisation', *The Learning Organization*, 5(1): 24–35.

Robson, C. (1993) *Real World Research: A Resource for Social Scientists and Practitioner-Researchers*, Oxford: Blackwell.

Robson, J. (1998) 'A profession in crisis: status, culture and identity in the further education college', *Journal of Vocational Education and Training*, 50(4): 585–607.

Rose, R. (2000) 'Using classroom support in a primary school: single school case study', *British Journal of Special Education*, 27(4): 191–6.

Rottmann, C. (2008) 'Organized agents: Canadian teacher unions as alternative sites for social justice activism', *Canadian Journal of Education*, 31(4): 975–1014.

Rutherford, D. (1992) 'Appraisal in action: a case study of innovation and leadership', *Studies in Higher Education*, 17(2): 201–10.

Ryan, A. (2005) 'New Labour and higher education', *Oxford Review of Education*, 31(1): 87–100.

Sachs, J. (2001) 'Teacher professional identity: competing discourses, competing outcomes', *Journal of Education Policy*, 16(2): 149–61.

Sachs, J. (2003) *The Activist Teaching Profession*, Maidenhead, UK: Open University Press.

Sammons, P., Nuttall, D., Cuttance, P. and Thomas, S. (1995) 'Continuity of school effects: a longitudinal analysis of primary and secondary school effects on GCSE performance', *School Effectiveness and School Improvement: An International Journal of Research, Policy and Practice*, 6(4): 285–307.

Sarason, S. (1996) *Revisiting 'The Culture of the School and the Problem of Change'*, New York: Teachers College Press. (Original: *The Culture of the School and the Problem of Change*, Boston, MA: Allyn & Bacon, 1st edn, 1971.)

Scheerens, J. (1989) *Effective Schooling: Research, Theory and Practice*, London: Cassell.

Schein, E. (1999) 'Empowerment, coercive persuasion and organizational learning: do they connect?', *The Learning Organization*, 6(4): 163–72.

Schein, E. (2004) *Organizational Culture and Leadership*, San Francisco, CA: Jossey-Bass.

Schlapp, U., Wilson, V. and Davidson, J. (2001) *An Extra Pair of Hands? Evaluation of the Classroom Assistants Initiative*. Interim Report. Report 104, Edinburgh: Scottish Council for Educational Research.

Schön, D. (1973) *Beyond the Stable State: Public and Private Learning in a Changing Society*, Harmondsworth, UK: Penguin.

School Financial Management (n.d.) 'School heads as bursars?' Online, available at: www.teachingexpertise.com/articles/school-bursars-heads-3507 (accessed 5 October 2009).

School Standards and Framework Act (1998) Chapter 31, London: The Stationery Office. Online, available at: www.opsi.gov.uk/Acts/acts1998/ukpga_19980031_en_1 (accessed 15 May 2009).

Scofield, J. (1993) 'Increasing the generalizability of qualitative research', in M. Hammersley (ed.) *Educational Research*, vol. 1: *Current Issues*, London: Paul Chapman/The Open University.

Scott, C., Cox, S. and Dinham, S. (1999) 'The occupational motivation, satisfaction and health of English school teachers', *Educational Psychology*, 19(3): 287–308.

Scott, C., Stone, B. and Dinham, S. (2001) 'International patterns of teacher discontent', *Education Policy Analysis Archives*, 9(28). Online, available at: http://epaa.asu.edu/epaa/v9n28.html (accessed 3 June 2009).

Senge, P. (1990) *The Fifth Discipline: The Art and Practice of the Learning Organization*, London: Random House.

Senge, P. (1999) *The Fifth Discipline: The Art and Practice of the Learning Organization*, 2nd edn, London: Random House.

Senge, P., Kleiner, A., Roberts, C., Ross, R. and Smith, B. (1997) *The Fifth Discipline Fieldbook: Strategies and Tools for Building a Learning Organization*, London: Nicholas Brealey.

Shaw, I., Newton, D. P., Aitkin, M. and Darnell, R. (2003) 'Do Ofsted inspections of secondary schools make a difference to GCSE results?', *British Educational Research Journal*, 29(1): 63–75.

Sikes, P. (2001) 'Teachers' lives and teaching performance', in D. Gleeson and C. Husbands (eds) *The Performing School: Managing Teaching and Learning in a Performance Culture*, London: RoutledgeFalmer.

Sikes, P. (2006) 'Working in a "new" university: in the shadow of the Research Assessment Exercise?', *Studies in Higher Education*, 31(5): 555–68.

Simkins, T. (2000) 'Education reform and managerialism: comparing the experience of schools and colleges', *Journal of Education Policy*, 15(2): 317–32.

Simons, H. and Elliott, J. (eds) (1989) *Rethinking Appraisal and Assessment*, Milton Keynes, UK: Open University Press.

Sinyolo, D. (2007) *Teacher Supply, Recruitment and Retention in Six Anglophone Sub-Saharan African Countries*, Brussels, Belgium: Education International.

Smethem, L. (2007) 'Retention and intention in teaching careers: will the new generation stay?', *Teachers and Teaching: Theory and Practice*, 13(5), 465–80.

Smithers, A. and Robinson, P. (2001) *Teachers Leaving*, Buckingham, UK: University of Buckingham, Centre for Education and Employment Research.

Smithers, A. and Robinson, P. (n.d.) *School Headship: Present and Future*, Buckingham, UK: University of Buckingham, Centre for Education and Employment Research. Online, available at: www.nut.org.uk/resources/pdf/Headsfin.pdf (accessed 1 April 2009).

Smyth, J. (2005) 'Modernizing the Australian education workplace: a case of failure to deliver for teachers of young disadvantaged adolescents', *Educational Review*, 57(2): 221–33.

Smyth, J., Dow, A., Hattam, R., Reid, A. and Shacklock, G. (2000) *Teachers' Work in a Globalizing Economy*, London: Falmer Press.

Southworth, G. (2000) 'How primary schools learn', *Research Papers in Education*, 15(3): 275–91.

Spillane, J., Halverson, R. and Diamond, J. (2004) 'Towards a theory of leadership practice: a distributed perspective', *Journal of Curriculum Studies*, 36(1): 3–34.

Stake, R. E. (1995) *The Art of Case Study Research*, London: Sage.

Stevenson, H. (2005) 'From "school correspondent" to "workplace bargainer"? The changing role of the school union representative', *British Journal of Sociology of Education*, 26(2) (April): 219–33.

Stevenson, H. (2006) 'Moving towards, into and through principalship: developing a framework for researching the career trajectories of school leaders', *Journal of Educational Administration*, 44(4): 408–20.

Stevenson, H. (2007a) 'Restructuring teachers' work and trade union responses in England: bargaining for change?', *American Educational Research Journal*, 44 (2): 224–51.

Stevenson, H. (2007b) 'Guest editorial: Changes in teachers' work and the challenges facing teacher unions', *International Electronic Journal for Leadership in Learning*, 11(13), 21 December.

Stevenson, H., Carter, B. and Passy, R. (2007) '"New professionalism," workforce remodelling and the restructuring of teachers' work', *International Electronic Journal for Leadership in Learning*, 11(15): 21 December.

Stewart, D. (2001) 'Reinterpreting the learning organization', *The Learning Organization*, 8(4): 141–52.

Stewart, W. (2008) 'Meet the man running two schools who has never been trained to teach', *TES Connect*, 6 June. Online, available at: www.tes.co.uk/article.aspx?storycode=2631665 (accessed 5 October 2009).

Storey, A. (2000) 'A leap of faith? Performance pay for teachers', *Journal of Education Policy*, 15: 509–23.

Storey, J. (1995) 'Human resource management: still marching on or marching out?', in J. Storey (ed.) *Human Resource Management: A Critical Text*, London: Routledge.

Strauss, A. and Corbin, J. (1990) *Basics of Qualitative Research: Techniques and Procedures for Developing Grounded Theory*, Thousand Oaks, CA: Sage.

Stringfield, S., Reynolds, D. and Schaffer, E. C. (2008) 'Improving secondary students' academic achievement through a focus on reform reliability: 4- and 9-year findings from the High Reliability Schools project', *School Effectiveness and School Improvement*, 19(4): 409–28.

Stronach, I., Corbin, B., McNamara, O., Stark, S. and Warne, T. (2002) 'Towards an uncertain politics of professionalism: teacher and nurse identities in flux', *Journal of Education Policy*, 17(1): 109–38.

Su, Z., Adam, J. P. and Mininberg, E. (2000) 'Profiles and preparation of urban school principals: a comparative study in the United States and China', *Education and Urban Society*, 32: 455–80.

Suffolk County Council Education Department (1985) *Those Having Torches. Teacher Appraisal: A Study*, Ipswich: County Hall.

Swann, W. and Loxley, A. (1998) 'The impact of school-based training on classroom assistants in primary schools', *Research Papers in Education*, 13(2): 141–60.

Symon, G. (2002) 'The "reality" of rhetoric and the learning organization in the UK', *Human Resource Development International*, 5(2): 155–74.

Synott, J. (2007) 'The Korean Teachers and Educational Workers Union: collective rights as the agency of social change', *International Electronic Journal for Leadership in Learning*, 11(23), 21 December.

Taylor, A. (2007) 'Developing understanding about learning to teach in a university–schools partnership in England', *British Educational Research Journal*, 34(1): 63–90.

Taylor, W. (2008) 'Professional freedom: a personal perspective', in D. Johnson and

R. Maclean (eds) *Teaching: Professionalization, Development and Leadership*, Dordrecht: Springer.

TDA (2007) 'Professional standards for teachers: Qualified Teacher Status'. Online, available at: www.tda.gov.uk/upload/resources/pdf/s/standards_qts.pdf (accessed 5 October 2009).

TDA (n.d.a) 'HLTA professional standards'. Online, available at: www.tda.gov.uk/support/support_staff_roles/learningsupportstaff/hlta/professstandards.aspx (accessed 5 October 2009).

TDA (n.d.b) 'Preparing for HLTA assessment'. Online, available at: www.tda.gov.uk/support/support_staff_roles/learningsupportstaff/hlta/becomingahlta/preparing_assessment.aspx (accessed 5 October 2009).

TDA (n.d.c) 'HTLA assessment process'. Online, available at: www.tda.gov.uk/support/support_staff_roles/learningsupportstaff/hlta/becomingahlta/assessment_process.aspx (accessed 5 October 2009).

Teddlie, C. and Reynolds, D. (2001) 'Countering the critics: responses to recent criticisms of school effectiveness research', *School Effectiveness and School Improvement*, 12: 41–82.

Thompson, M. (2006) 'Re-modelling as de-professionalisation', *Forum*, 48(2): 189–200.

Thomson, S. (2006) 'Improving the Shire School', paper presented at a research seminar held at the Centre for Educational Leadership and Management, School of Education, University of Leicester, February.

Thornbury, R. (ed.) (1973) *Teachers' Centers*, New York: Agathon Press.

Tickle, L. (2001) 'Professional qualities and teacher induction', *Journal of In-Service Education*, 27(1): 51–64.

Torres, C. A., Cho, S., Kachur, J., Loyo, A., Mollis, M., Nagao, A. and Thompson, J. (2000) 'Political capital, teachers' unions and the state: value conflicts and collaborative strategies in educational reform in the United States, Canada, Japan, Korea, Mexico, and Argentina'. Online, available at: www.international.ucla.edu/lac/cat/montim.pdf (accessed 15 May 2009).

Tosey, P. (2005) 'The hunting of the learning organization: a paradoxical journey', *Management Learning*, 36(3): 335–52.

Townley, B. (1993) 'Performance appraisal and the emergence of management', *Journal of Management Studies*, 30(2): 222–39.

Toynbee, P. (2003) *Hard Work: Life in Low-Pay Britain*, London: Bloomsbury.

Troman, G. (2000) 'Teacher stress in the low-trust society', *British Journal of Sociology of Education*, 21(3): 331–53.

Troman, G. and Woods, P. (2000) 'Careers under stress: teacher adaptations at a time of intense reform', *Journal of Educational Change*, 1: 253–75.

Tropp, A. (1957) *The School Teachers: The Growth of the Teaching Profession in England and Wales*, London: Heinemann.

Trowler, P. (1998) 'What managerialists forget: higher education credit frameworks and managerialist ideology', *International Studies in Sociology of Education*, 8(1): 91–109.

Tsang, E. (1997) 'Organizational learning and the learning organization: a dichotomy between descriptive and prescriptive research', *Human Relations*, 50(1): 73–89.

TTA and Ofsted (1996) *Review of Headteacher and Teacher Appraisal*, London: TTA.

Tuckman, B. (1965) 'Development sequences in small groups', *Psychological Bulletin*, 63: 384–99.

Tuckman, B. and Jensen, M. (1977) 'Stages of small-group development revisited', *Group Organization and Management*, 2(4): 419–27.

Turner, G. and Clift, P. (1988) *Studies in Teacher Appraisal*, Lewes, UK: Falmer Press.

UNISON (2007) *School Support Staff Survey 2004: A Report on the Role, Training, Salaries and Employment Conditions of School Support Staff*, London: UNISON.

UNISON (2009) *Time to Train: A Report about School Support Staff Training*, London: UNISON.

Van Velzen, W. (1987) 'The international school improvement project', in D. Hopkins (ed.) *Improving the Quality of Schooling: Lessons from the OECD International School Improvement Project*, Lewes, UK: Falmer Press.

Van Vianen, A. and De Dreu, C. (2001) 'Personality in teams: its relationship to social cohesion, task cohesion, and team performance', *European Journal of Work and Organizational Psychology*, 10(2): 97–120.

Vogt, F. (2003) 'Managerialism, collegiality and teamwork', in L. Kydd, L. Anderson, and W. Newton (eds) *Leading People and Teams in Education*, London: Paul Chapman.

Voulalas, Z. and Sharpe, F. (2005) 'Creating schools as learning communities: obstacles and processes', *Journal of Educational Administration*, 43(2): 187–208.

Walker, A. and Dimmock, C. (2000) 'One size fits all? Teacher appraisal in a Chinese culture', *Journal of Personnel Evaluation in Education*, 14(2): 155–78.

Wallace, M. (2001) 'Sharing leadership of schools through teamwork: A justifiable risk?', *Educational Management and Administration*, 29(2): 153–67.

Wallace, M. (2002) 'Modelling distributed leadership and management effectiveness: primary school senior management teams in England and Wales', *School Effectiveness and School Improvement*, 13(2): 163–86.

Wallace, M. and Huckman, L. (2003) 'Senior management teams: creating a team in their own image?', in L. Kydd, L. Anderson and W. Newton (eds) *Leading People and Teams in Education*, London: Paul Chapman.

Walsh, K. (1988) 'Appraising the teachers: professionalism and control', in R. Dale, R. Fergusson and A. Robinson (eds) *Frameworks for Teaching: Readings for the Intending Secondary Teacher*, Milton Keynes, UK: Open University Press.

Wang, J., Odell, S. J. and Schwille, S. A. (2008) 'Effects of teacher induction on beginning teachers' teaching: a critical review of the literature', *Journal of Teacher Education*, 59: 132–52.

Watson, L. J. (1969) 'Office and expertise in the secondary school', *Educational Research*, 11(2): 104–12.

Weick, K. (1988) 'Educational organizations as loosely coupled systems', in A. Westoby (ed.) *Culture and Power in Educational Organizations*, Milton Keynes, UK: Open University Press.

Weindling, D. and Earley, P. (1987) *Secondary Headship: The First Years*, Windsor, UK: NFER-Nelson.

Whitty, G. (2006) 'Teacher professionalism in a new era', paper presented at the first General Teaching Council for Northern Ireland Annual Lecture, Belfast, March.

Wilkinson, G. (2005) 'Workforce remodelling and formal knowledge: the erosion of teachers' professional jurisdiction in English schools', *School Leadership and Management*, 25(5): 421–39.

Williams, A. and Soares, A. (2000) 'The role of higher education in the initial training of secondary school teachers: the views of the key participants', *Journal of Education for Teaching*, 26(3): 225–44.

Williams, S. (2004) 'Accounting for change in public sector industrial relations: the erosion of national bargaining in further education in England and Wales', *Industrial Relations Journal*, 35(3): 233–48.

Wilson, E. and Bedford, D. (2008) '"New Partnerships for Learning": teachers and teaching assistants working together in schools – the way forward', *Journal of Education for Teaching*, 34(2): 137–50.

Wilson, F. and Beaton, D. (1993) 'The theory and practice of appraisal: progress review in a Scottish university', *Higher Education Quarterly*, 46(2): 163–89.

Wilson, R., Sharp, C., Shuayb, M., Kendall, L., Wade, P. and Easton, C. (2007) *Research into the Deployment and Impact of Support Staff Who Have Achieved HLTA Status*, Final Report, Slough, UK: National Foundation for Educational Research.

Wilson, V., Schlapp, U. and Davidson, J. (2002) *More than an 'Extra Pair of Hands?'*, Research Report, Edinburgh: Scottish Council for Research in Education.

Wilson, V., Schlapp, U. and Davidson, J. (2003) 'An "extra pair of hands"? Managing classroom assistants in Scottish primary schools', *Educational Management and Administration*, 31(2): 189–205.

Winstanley, D. and Stuart-Smith, K. (1996) 'Policing performance: the ethics of performance management', *Personnel Review*, 25(6): 66–84.

Wise, C. and Busher, H. (2001) 'The subject leader', in D. Middlewood and N. Burton (eds) *Managing the Curriculum*, London: Paul Chapman.

Woods, P., Jeffrey, B., Troman, G. and Boyle, M. (1997) *Restructuring Schools; Reconstructing Teachers: Responding to Change in the Primary School*, Buckingham, UK: Open University Press.

Wragg, E. C., Haynes, G. S., Wragg, C. M. and Chamberlin, R. P. (2004) *Performance Pay for Teachers*, London: Routledge.

Wright, N. (2001) 'Leadership, "bastard leadership" and managerialism: confronting twin paradoxes in the Blair education project', *Educational Management Administration Leadership*, 29(3): 275–90.

Wrigley, T. (2005) 'Another school is possible: learning from Europe', *Forum*, 47(2–3): 223–32.

Yarker, P. (2005) 'On not being a teacher: the professional and personal cost of workforce remodelling', *Forum*, 47(2–3): 169–74.

Young, I. P. and Delli, D. A. (2003) 'The validity of the Teacher Perceiver Interview for predicting performance of classroom teachers', *Educational Administration Quarterly*, 38(5): 586–612.

Yun, S., Cox, J. and Sims, H. (2006) 'The forgotten follower: a contingency model of leadership and follower self-leadership', *Journal of Managerial Psychology*, 21(4): 374–88.

Zembylas, M. and Papanastasiou, E. (2006) 'Sources of teacher job satisfaction and dissatisfaction in Cyprus', *Compare: A Journal of Comparative and International Education*, 36(2): 229–47.

Index

Page numbers in *italics* denotes a diagram/table